ASPECTS of READING EDUCATION

THE NATIONAL SOCIETY
FOR THE STUDY OF EDUCATION

Series on Contemporary Educational Issues
Kenneth J. Rehage, Series Editor

The 1978 Titles

History, Education, and Public Policy: Recovering the American Educational Past, Donald R. Warren, Editor
Aspects of Reading Education, Susanna Pflaum-Connor, Editor
From Youth to Constructive Adult Life: The Role of the Public School, Ralph W. Tyler, Editor

The National Society for the Study of Education also publishes Yearbooks which are distributed by the University of Chicago Press. Inquiries regarding all publications of the Society, as well as inquiries about membership in the Society, may be addressed to the Secretary-Treasurer, 5835 Kimbark Avenue, Chicago, IL 60637. Membership in the Society is open to any who are interested in promoting the investigation and discussion of educational questions.

ASPECTS of READING EDUCATION

Edited by

Susanna Pflaum-Connor

University of Illinois at Chicago Circle

𝔐𝔠𝔠𝔲𝔱𝔠𝔥𝔞𝔫 𝔓𝔲𝔟𝔩𝔦𝔰𝔥𝔦𝔫𝔤 𝔠𝔬𝔯𝔭𝔬𝔯𝔞𝔱𝔦𝔬𝔫
2526 Grove Street
Berkeley, California 94704

ISBN 0-8211-1517-0
Library of Congress Catalog Card Number 77-95250

Cover design and illustration by Catherine Conner, Griffin Graphics

Series Foreword

Few if any areas in the field of education have had the consistent attention over the years that has been given to reading. And yet what has been achieved in schools in reading instruction, as well as what has *not* been achieved, continues to make headlines. New issues relating to that part of the school curriculum seem to be emerging constantly. It is precisely because the committee responsible for the Series on Contemporary Educational Issues felt that discussion of these emerging problems needs to be well informed that it was attracted to the proposal submitted by Professor Susanna Pflaum-Connor for this volume on *Aspects of Reading Education.*

The volume does not deal with all issues related to reading instruction. Professor Pflaum-Connor and her collaborators, however, have produced a book that explores in some depth the developments in reading that have been matters of great interest in the past few years, among them the relationship of psycholinguistics to the study and teaching of reading, controversies over the nature of beginning reading instruction, the assessment of achievement in reading, the teaching of reading at the secondary level, the impact of nonstandard dialects and of second-language learning on the acquisition of literacy, and the contributions of the field of learning disabilities to principles and practices in remedial reading.

The National Society for the Study of Education is most appreciative of the work of Professor Pflaum-Connor as editor as well as contributor to the volume and to all the authors who have prepared the original essays included here.

Kenneth J. Rehage

for the Committee on an Expanded
Publication Program of the
National Society for the Study
of Education

Contributors

John B. Carroll, William R. Kenan, Jr., Professor of Psychology, and Director, L. L. Thurstone Psychometric Laboratory, University of North Carolina at Chapel Hill

Jeanne Chall, Professor of Education, and Director, Reading Laboratory, Harvard University

Eugene H. Cramer, Assistant Professor, University of Illinois at Chicago Circle

Ken L. Dulin, Associate Professor, Curriculum and Instruction, Reading Education, University of Wisconsin at Madison

Michael L. Kamil, Director, Reading Clinic, and Assistant Professor, Purdue University

Susanna Pflaum-Connor, Associate Professor, University of Illinois at Chicago Circle

Margaret Ann Richek, Assistant Professor, University of Illinois at Chicago Circle

S. Jay Samuels, Director, Minnesota Reading Research Project, and Professor, University of Minnesota

Sumner W. Schachter, Doctoral Candidate, University of Minnesota, and Elementary Coordinator, Roaring Fork School District RE-1, Glenwood Springs, Colorado

María Elena de Valdés, Coordinator, Bilingual-Bicultural Education Program, and Assistant Professor, University of Illinois at Chicago Circle

Richard L. Venezky, Unidel Professor of Educational Foundations, University of Delaware

Contents

Introduction

Jeanne Chall

This volume may well take its place next to earlier publications of the National Society for the Study of Education on the subject of reading. Like those justly praised volumes, this one also may be widely recognized as a landmark of its time, for it shares many of the qualities of its predecessors. It has a sense of timeliness, a concern for the future, and a rich respect for the past. It provides an analysis of most of the issues related to the study and teaching of reading that are of current and major concern.

The timeliness of this book is demonstrated by the inclusion of such topics as the contributions of psycholinguistics to reading, controversial issues in beginning reading instruction, general theory and models of the reading process (with particular reference to reading comprehension), the effects of dialect differences and bilingualism on learning to read, and issues in the assessment of reading achievement.

Central to these concerns is a multidisciplinary approach that can be seen in the backgrounds of the authors (most of whom are specialists in reading), in the content of the chapters, and in the general viewpoints expressed. From this volume a reader can gain an understanding of some of the contributions that such disciplines as psychology, linguistics, psycholinguistics, computer sciences, and anthropology have made to the study and teaching of reading.

In 1969 Lee J. Cronbach and Patrick Suppes edited a volume *(Research for Tomorrow's Schools* [New York: Macmillan, 1969]), in

1

which it was recommended that an applied field such as reading can advance in scholarship and research best when it is securely grounded in the basic scientific disciplines. Specialization in reading, it was said, should begin only with a thorough knowledge of a supportive basic discipline. This recommendation was made when there was a great cry for more and better research in reading. Judging by the content of the present volume, it appears that the recommendation has been taken seriously, at least by some people in the field of reading. The authors generally reveal a mastery of one of the basic disciplines as well as a mastery of reading.

John B. Carroll's review of the contributions of psycholinguistics to the study and teaching of reading explicitly illustrates a multidisciplinary approach. Other chapters firmly based on interdisciplinary studies and viewpoints include Margaret Ann Richek's essay on reading and learning disability, María Elena de Valdés's analysis of difficulties encountered by bilingual students in learning to read, Richard L. Venezky's discussion of testing, and Susanna Pflaum-Connor's treatment of the effects of dialect differences upon learning to read.

The volume includes discussions of many key controversial issues related to reading, some of them with an already long history. Thus S. Jay Samuels and Sumner W. Schachter present an analysis of what is perhaps the oldest controversy in the field, namely, whether a meaning or a skills-oriented approach is the most effective for beginning reading. These authors point to some of the other labels and categories under which the issue has been studied and debated. Carroll's chapter ties this controversy to the current psycholinguistic theories of Kenneth Goodman and Frank Smith.

A more recent controversy concerns the role of dialect differences in reading and in learning to read. When this issue was first introduced in the 1960s there was a strong belief, particularly among some linguists, that dialect played a key role in the reading difficulties of children who spoke nonstandard English, although there was little firm evidence at the time to support the belief. As Pflaum-Connor notes, the evidence now seems to be weighted against the central importance of the influence of dialect on reading achievement. Indeed there seems to be a growing consensus that dialect differences have limited effect on general reading achievement, although some aspects of learning to read may be made easier for nonstandard dialect speakers by special teaching methods.

A third area of controversy during the past decade has related to the testing of reading achievement. Among the issues that have been discussed is the question of whether there is a bias in the tests that adversely affects the scores of children outside the dominant culture. Attention has also been centered on the question of whether norm-referenced or criterion-referenced tests are most helpful for assessment and particularly for guiding instruction. Venezky's analysis of the current issues in testing provides a broader context for the discussion. He suggests that currently used tests, precisely standardized and made more valid and reliable through an improved technology of test construction, may perhaps tell us less than the more simple, more direct, and commonsensical tests and observations used in the past. He notes the effectiveness with which educational reformers like Joseph M. Rice used the simpler, more direct tests and observations in 1893, as well as the increasing use in recent years of such tests and observations in case study reports.

The chapter by Richek presents a picture of dichotomous and controversial positions with respect to reading disability. Although the fields of reading disability and learning disability share considerable common ground, professionals in these fields have had different conceptions of reading and reading disability and different theories of causation, treatment, and remediation of disability. The differences between the viewpoints are still considerable, but there are recent signs of a greater rapprochement, according to Richek.

Still another continuing controversy occurs over whether the focus of research and development should be on beginning reading or on advanced reading, on decoding or on comprehension. During the 1960s and early 1970s, research emphasized beginning reading and the early prediction and prevention of disability. During more recent years, however, many scholars have called for more research on reading comprehension and on reading in the intermediate and higher grades. The National Institute of Education, for example, gave a firm commitment to the study of advanced reading by supporting the establishment in 1976 of the Center for the Study of Reading at the University of Illinois. In the present volume, such a shift in focus is represented by Eugene H. Cramer's chapter on high school reading, by Michael L. Kamil's chapter on reading models and comprehension, and by Ken L. Dulin's chapter on the affective aspects of reading, while there is no chapter, for example, on reading readiness or on early prediction.

Finally, the tension between the scholar and the practitioner, between theory and practice, is implicit in each chapter even though not directly considered in any of them. One gains the impression that while the theories, models, and experimental research have become more and more complex, the resulting recommendations retain a familiar ring. Many of the suggestions for practice were well known and widely used before the current theoretical models were developed. Some of the suggestions for application (for example, comparing listening comprehension to reading comprehension as a way of "diagnosing" whether a pupil has a reading or a language problem) have been used for quite some time by reading teachers and clinicians. The Durrell Listening and Reading Comprehension tests, which attempt to make such comparisons formally, have been widely used for at least thirty years. The need for developing the vocabularies of pupils, another practice now recommended as arising from current theory, was recognized as far back as the early 1900s by Edward L. Thorndike, William S. Gray, and Eleanor Holmes and more recently by Edgar Dale and Joseph O'Rourke.

All this is not to say that theory has little to say to the teacher of reading. Every discipline that has some relevance to the understanding of the reading process, the processes of learning and teaching to read, particularly to those children who do not achieve well, must be attended to and studied carefully.

But has the growth in sophistication of theories, models, and experimental research perhaps contributed to the lessening of confidence among practitioners? That might be the case. It would seem to be so when some researchers and scholars present as their own discoveries some proposals for applications of their theories that are already in wide use by teachers. On the other hand, teachers and practitioners may gain stature by learning that some practices familiar to them, and which they have long used successfully, have recently been confirmed by research.

And is there as little place for the practitioner in the improvement of reading instruction as some of the very enthusiastic reading researchers and theorists seem to imply? I think not. The interest in the history of reading instruction found in this volume should help excite researchers and scholars about the variety of richness of practices in reading, practices that seek ever more effective ways of teaching children and young people to read. Such knowledge can enrich the scholar in his own inquiries and also bring him into closer collaboration with practitioners — teacher, clinicians, administrators. In the past, teachers and clinicians have developed and they continue to develop effective and valid practices based on their accumulated experiences as well as on research. It is to be hoped that their clinical and practical experience can also lead to more comprehensive theory and to further research.

Previous publications on reading in the NSSE Yearbooks have been used as historical documents to portray the practices, issues, and trends of their times. How will some of the developments and trends described in this volume in the "Series on Contemporary Educational Issues" be viewed ten years from now? Predictions are always hazardous, particularly when made with respect to controversial issues. I take the risk, nevertheless, and use as a disclaimer that my predictions present only my own view. Others may have a different view.

A decade hence, readers of this volume will agree that our main source for theory and research in the 1970s came from the discipline of psycholinguistics. They will not be as certain about the influence of psycholinguistics upon practices in the teaching of reading. Some may view that influence with a degree of skepticism, claiming that most applications from psycholinguistic theory were already in use before the theory was developed. And yet in 1988 all will agree that psycholinguistics had excited and captured the imagination of the young researchers who in the late 1960s and early 1970s had diligently researched the relationships between reading and language.

Readers in 1988 will also conclude that the issue of the impact of dialect differences and bilingualism on learning to read were of great interest during the late 1960s and early 1970s. But there was a slackening in the intensity of those views by the late 1970s, when statements about the influence of dialect and bilingualism on reading achievement became more cautious and more qualified.

Readers in 1988 will probably wonder why there was so much concern with general theoretical models in the 1970s. Their preference will be for partial models, particularly that of reading comprehension, a preference that is apparent in this volume. That preference will no doubt reflect the continuing concern of 1988 about reading comprehension and about reading in the upper grades and high schools.

Venezky's chapter will probably strike readers in 1988 as still timely, and perhaps prophetic. They will be sympathetic to Venezky's eschewing of the purely theoretical and technological, to his turning to the history of reading instruction and to political and administrative realities, and to his calling for a greater simplicity in testing. Some readers in 1988 will concur with Venezky's conclusion that "The choice seems to be between a well-tried testing procedure that produces reliable, but not totally useful results, and a somewhat unsure and perhaps even suspicious procedure that, if it is successfully implemented, could produce extremely important data for reading achievement, but, if it fails, would leave us no worse off than we are now."

Where will testing in reading be in 1988? My guess is that it will have moved somewhat in the direction of simplicity, with greater use of case studies and observations. But the use of the complex standardized tests will not have disappeared or even lessened. Both methods of collecting data for purposes of evaluation will continue to be used side by side, each offering information not provided by the other.

Ten years from now readers will find even stronger the trend toward collaboration between specialists in reading disability and in learning disability, trends to which Richek alludes in this volume.

Dulin's chapter on the affective domain will be of even greater importance to the reader in 1988 than it is today. The topic is still mainly one for the future. In the 1960s and 1970s nearly everyone seemed to be occupied primarily with the cognitive and linguistic aspects of reading. The late 1970s may be a time for a change in the direction of greater concern for the affective domain.

In *Innovation and Change in Reading Instruction,* edited by Helen M. Robinson and published in 1966 as Part II of the Sixty-fifth Yearbook of the National Society for the Study of Education, the authors were pessimistic about the amount and quality of research in reading. That pessimism about research seems to have abated substantially, for less concern is expressed in this volume about the need for more and better research. In general, readers in 1988 will be aware that the 1970s saw a significant increase in the number of scholars in the field of reading, a substantial growth in doctoral programs in reading and related fields, more funded research, more training institutes, and continued growth in professional organizations concerned with reading—all of which testify to more interest in research activity than had characterized the preceding decade.

Readers in 1988 might look for and expect to find in this book greater evidence of collaboration between researchers in reading and practitioners. There is little evidence of such collaboration. Some indication is found in this volume that there may have been too much zeal in the effort to apply the results of research too early (for example, an overzealous application of linguistic theory to practice in the teaching of reading). Interest is being expressed in the late 1970s, nevertheless, in the use of research findings by teachers and administrators. It will be apparent to readers in 1988, as it is to some today, that the effective application of research results requires more than merely having practitioners use efficiently what the researchers have produced. The problem has to do with how knowledge is best created and ultimately used by all — by teachers, administrators, curriculum developers, as well as by scholars. In the research efforts of the 1960s and the early 1970s the means for meaningful collaboration among scholars, researchers, and teachers did not seem to exist. By 1988, there will be the beginnings of such efforts through collaborative research between universities and school systems and between universities and city and state departments of education. Such collaboration will be found to be productive, since knowledge and ideas can flow both ways — from theory to practice and from practice to theory.

With true collaboration we may avoid the tendency to debate the same issues again and again, under different labels. Indeed, this was one of the conclusions I drew from the fifty years of research reviewed in my *Learning to Read: The Great Debate* (New York: McGraw-Hill, 1967), and it is also the conclusion of Carroll in this volume: "The 'great debate' in reading instruction of which Chall wrote has spilled over into psycholinguistics, but in a somewhat altered form. Where previously the debate was over 'look-say' versus 'phonics' methods of teaching, the controversy is now over whether reading is a 'psycholinguistic guessing game' or a process of 'decoding' print into spoken form.'" Carroll concludes with a synthesis of these two classic positions and with the hope that there will not be yet another "great debate": "But, should that debate occur, I hope that it will not be over the same issues that have plagued the reading field for so many years, but over some other issues that will have a more refreshing and interesting character."

I have a strong suspicion that the reader in 1988 will have sympathy for those words. For, in fact, researchers even now seem to be acting on them. More refreshing and interesting problems are being researched in the late 1970s. Among them are the study of the effects of environmental factors on reading development, already mentioned in several chapters in the present volume. The concern in these studies is with those schools, classrooms, and other environmental characteristics that make for gains in reading achievement over and above the powerful influences of socioeconomic status and ethnicity. In 1988, the interest in such studies will be greater even than in 1978. Indeed, such problems as the effect of dialect differences and bilingualism on reading achievement will in all probability be studied within this broader framework. It would seem that methods and materials of instruction may also be studied in that way, for example, the question concerning the kinds of children and the kinds of classrooms for which certain methods are effective.

Another interesting and important problem will be the applications of the findings from the rapidly growing neurosciences to theory and practice in the teaching of reading and the remediation of reading and learning disabilities. With already a good beginning in 1978, such efforts should have gained momentum by 1988. By then we may have suggestions for practitioners for the prevention of reading failure and perhaps suggestions of methods that would be more effective for children with certain strengths and weaknesses, such as preference for the left or right cerebral hemispheres.

In 1988, research on the role of the family and home, including the effects of television viewing on reading, will receive much interest from researchers. The effects of "Sesame Street" and "The Electric Company" on early reading will encourage the creation of other educational shows for children. The recent suggestion of Wilbur Schramm *(Television and the Test Scores* [New York: College Entrance Examination Board, 1977]) that television viewing patterns, along with other strong variables, may have a negative effect on intellectual stimulation available to a child after the age of nine, could lead to attempts to limit television viewing. Overall, there will be greater concern with education by parents, not only with respect to their children's watching of television, but also with respect to their reading to children and encouraging them to read on their own.

By 1988, the interest in research on reading at the high school and college levels will be even greater than in 1978. With more students entering open enrollment colleges, the need to raise the reading and writing abilities of college freshmen who read only at about the eighth-grade level or lower will increase before it lessens. Indeed, to solve this problem will be not only to solve the most challenging reading problem but the most challenging problem of public education and of social mobility.

In 1988, many reading specialists will face a changing situation with regard to jobs. After a steady increase in positions for reading specialists in schools during the two previous decades, there may be a decrease. This may come from their own success. With more children and young people achieving better, the schools will need fewer reading specialists for the decreasing number of reading problems. But many reading specialists will find other professional challenges — in government, in industry, and in private practice. They may be engaged in such varied activities as readability analysis, special reading projects for the aged, training and supervising volunteer tutors, developing literacy and reading programs for the armed services, instructing parents in ways to help their children develop their reading, and much more.

1. Psycholinguistics and the Study and Teaching of Reading

John B. Carroll

What is a chapter on psycholinguistics doing in a book on reading? And why, if at all, does it deserve to be placed ahead of the remaining chapters? Psycholinguistics as an interdisciplinary science is only about a quarter of a century old. Up to the present time, probably very few children, and even fewer adults, have learned to read by virtue of any specific benefits or insights that psycholinguistics might have yielded. In fact, for the last several thousand years people have been learning to read without the help of psycholinguistics.

Yet, some children seem to have much difficulty in learning to read, and there is well-publicized evidence that substantial numbers of people leave school, even graduate from high school, without being able to read at a satisfactory level of skill and understanding. These facts comprise what is often called "the reading problem." I would be the first to deny that psycholinguistics offers any panacea for alleviating this "reading problem," for that problem has many causes, only some of which may be related to what psycholinguistics might have to say about reading. I would also be the first to deny that there is, or could be, a "psycholinguistic method" of teaching reading, because there is much more to the teaching of reading than whatever might be contributed by psycholinguistics. (To be sure, some commercial reading instruction materials have been touted as being based on psycholinguistics, but such a claim must be taken with much caution, not only for the reason just given, but also because — as we shall see — there are different brands of psycholinguistics.)

The body of knowledge that has been accumulating in the field of psycholinguistics in the last decade or so does, nevertheless, have some important implications for an understanding of the reading process and the teaching of reading. It is the purpose of this chapter to state and explain these implications.

WHAT IS PSYCHOLINGUISTICS?

Relation of Psycholinguistics to Linguistics

As the word suggests, psycholinguistics has something to do with psychology and something to do with linguistics. But the composition of the term is in a way unfortunate because it may suggest that psycholinguistics is a psychological subspecialty of linguistics, which it is not. It would be more accurate to think of it as a subspecialty of psychology. Actually, the pioneers of the field had some hesitancy in using the term, but somehow it caught on and has stuck.[1]

The best brief definition that I can offer for the term *psycholinguistics* is that it is the psychological study of the way human beings learn and use language. But the *linguistic* part of the term is important. Since psycholinguistics has to do with the learning and use of language, it must take full account of whatever is relevant from the field of linguistics, the scientific investigation of language and language systems.

The science of linguistics began in the nineteenth century or even earlier, when scholars undertook seriously to describe and compare languages.[2] In the first half of the present century, the major achievement of linguistic science was to describe and classify the enormous variety of language systems in the world and to begin to characterize the general properties of those systems. Each system, whether it was English, Latin, Chinese, Bantu, or Cherokee, was seen to have its own array of distinctive sounds (phonemes), grammatical categories and rules, and vocabulary. Some principal insights about language that came out of this period were the following.

First, the spoken form of a language is more basic and fundamental than its written form (if indeed it has any written form). All natural languages have, or have had, spoken forms; writing systems have developed for many languages, but they have functioned mainly as ways of recording and transmitting speech in a nonoral medium. Even though writing systems have tended to develop certain unique features, somewhat independent of speech, a writing system is crucially dependent upon the spoken form of the language that it represents. In fact, the most advanced writing systems, using an alphabetic principle to represent sounds, show this dependence most clearly.[3]

Second, languages differ greatly in the means they offer for expressing ideas, and yet there is a common store of underlying concepts, and of ways of relating concepts, that are available in every language for the expression of ideas.

Third, although every language has, or has had at some time in the past, a "speech community" of people among whom intelligible communication in the language could take place, there has always been a potential for variation and change in language. It has often been the case that different subgroups of a speech community speak different dialects or versions of the language, all more or less mutually intelligible, yet varying somewhat in their sounds, grammar, and vocabulary. Usually, because of geographical, political, social, or economic factors, some dialects of a language are more developed and prestigious than others, but all dialects are essentially on a par in their capability for expressing ideas.

The kind of linguistic theory that was most widely accepted among linguistic scientists up through the middle of the present century has been called "structural" or "taxonomic" linguistics, because the main goals were to describe a language in terms of identified units such as phonemes and morphemes and to ascertain the rules for the composition of linguistic forms from these units. Phonemes were seen as units of sound that, though not meaningful in themselves, are the constituents of morphemes and make for differences in meanings: for example, in English, the initial sounds in a series like *pale, bale, tale, dale, kale, gale, sale, shale* are all different phonemes because they make these words (which also happen to be morphemes) convey different meanings. Morphemes were regarded as the smallest meaningful forms in a language. Some morphemes are "free," like the words just mentioned, because they can stand alone, while others are "bound," because they can occur only in association with other morphemes. For example, in English there is a morpheme often symbolized as $\{-z\}$ that pluralizes nouns like *tale* (to form *tales*), *tack* (to form *tacks*), or *tax* (to form *taxes*), even though the actual sounds are different phonemes (phonemically, $/-z/$, $/-s/$, and $/-iz/$, respectively).

I have been writing about phonemes and morphemes in the past tense, as if these concepts are no longer used or accepted in linguistics. Actually the terms *phoneme* and *morpheme* are still widely used, although there are subtle changes in the newer theories and doctrines surrounding them. Since the mid-1950s, there have been rather radical changes in the goals and methods of linguistics. Now, linguists see that the earlier school of linguistics was primarily concerned with what is called "surface structure," that is, the structure of the actual speech (or writing) used in communication, as opposed to its "deep structure," that is, the structure of the ideas and meanings that are seen to underlie the surface structure. As Noam Chomsky pointed out in 1957,[4] one can find groups of sentences that have very similar meanings but very different surface structures. For example, the sentences in each of the following groups express the same basic idea, but with variations in the words and their arrangements.

(1) (a) The tribe gave us no fish.
     (b) The tribe didn't give us any fish.
     (c) No fish were given us by the tribe.
     (d) Fish were not given to us by the tribe.
     (e) We were given no fish by the tribe.
     (f) We weren't given any fish by the tribe.

(2) (a) Ted called up Meg.
     (b) Ted called Meg up.
     (c) It was Ted who called up Meg.
     (d) It was Meg that Ted called up.
     (e) It was Meg that was called up by Ted.

Also, there is a reverse phenomenon: some sentences can have very similar surface structures, but quite different deep structures. Consider the following sentences.

(3) (a) The cook knew the missionaries were eager to eat (because they were very hungry).
     (b) The cook knew the missionaries were ready to eat (because it was dinner time, and they were hungry).
     (c) The cannibals knew the missionaries were ready to eat (because they had been well fed and would be very tasty).

In sentences (3a) and (3b), *eager to eat* and *ready to eat* have the same surface structure and the same deep structure, because it is the missionaries who are going to do the eating. In sentence (3c), however, *ready to eat* has the same surface structure as it does in sentence (3b), but the deep structure is different, because it is the cannibals who are going to do the eating, not the missionaries.

The earlier, "taxonomic" school of linguistics gave little attention to these phenomena of syntax because it was primarily concerned with the phonemic systems of languages ("phonology") and the ways in which particular word-forms were constructed ("morphology"). The newer school of linguistics, spearheaded by Chomsky and called "transformational generative grammar," has been much concerned with variations in sentence structure and the explanation of these variations. A language system is seen as a set of rules for generating surface structures from deep structures. The goal in describing a language system is the discovery of those rules, and it is assumed that, when "ideal native speakers" of a language speak or understand sentences, their behavior is in some way governed by those rules. Speakers may not be conscious of the rules—indeed, linguists have trouble specifying the rules to their satisfaction—but speakers demonstrate their knowledge or "competence" by the fact that they do not normally utter "ungrammatical" sentences like

(4)   *The tribe us fish no gave,

and would recognize them as ungrammatical if they heard them. (The asterisk placed in front of a sentence indicates that it is regarded as ungrammatical, that is, not in accord with the language system.)

A similar line of reasoning can be employed to specify the rules whereby different linguistic forms, like *magic* and *magician,* with somewhat different sound structures, are generated from a common root form.

In this brief space, I have been able to give only an oversimplified account of the general approach and spirit of the newer linguistics. A teacher of reading hardly needs to go into the technicalities of modern linguistic theory, although there are textbooks that could make linguistic science fairly accessible to the teacher.[5]

A major outcome of contemporary linguistics is the realization that a language system, such as English, is richer and more complex than one might have thought. Linguists cannot state satisfactory rules to cover the wide range of "grammatical" sentences that even a first-grade child can utter and understand.

If psycholinguistics is concerned with how people learn and use language, what particular aspects of linguistics are of interest to psycholinguists? They basically take from linguistics the descriptions and specifications of what is learned and used, namely, the descriptions of the language system. If psycholinguists are studying how American children learn English as their native tongue, they need to take from linguistics whatever knowledge is available about the sound system, the vocabulary or lexicon, and the grammatical structure of the adult form of American English that is the general model for the child's successive approximations. If a psycholinguistic study has to do with a particular dialect form of English that is deviant from standard English, psycholinguists want to learn whatever linguists can tell them about the structural differences between that dialect and standard English with respect to phonology, morphology, syntax, semantics, and vocabulary. If it is a question of a writing system, as in the study of how children learn to read, psycholinguists need whatever knowledge is available about the relation between the language system and the way that system is represented in the writing system. In the case of English and other languages whose traditional orthographies employ an alphabetic principle, this means a particular focus on the manner in which sounds and spoken forms are represented in the writing system.

Fields of Psycholinguistics

Within psycholinguistics, or closely allied to it, a number of specializations have emerged.

Experimental psycholinguistics, an outgrowth of general experimental psychology, has had mainly to do with the processes by which mature users of a language produce and understand utterances — single words or larger utterances like sentences, in spoken or written form. To date, much of the effort in this speciality has concerned the *understanding* of language; there has been little work on how people *produce* utterances. In the study of processes of understanding, there has been an attempt to establish the "psychological reality" of grammar by seeing how variations in grammatical structure affect speed and accuracy of comprehension. For example, it appears that sentences in the active voice are understood more rapidly and accurately than passive sentences, although it is not yet clear exactly why this is so. As another example, it has been shown that people have some trouble understanding sentences like:

(5)   The dealer offered two dollars for the painting refused to sell.
Such "garden path" sentences mislead a hearer (or reader) into mak-

ing initial grammatical interpretations that prove to be wrong later on into the sentence. There are obvious implications here for the study of how people, including children, understand sentences when they read. Of late, investigators in experimental psycholinguistics have turned their attention to study of the processes in understanding stories, expository prose, and other forms of connected discourse. The hope is that this kind of investigation will lead to improved methods of teaching, and possibly to ways of composing prose so that it will be better understood.[6]

Developmental psycholinguistics is the study of how children "acquire" their native language.[7] Evidently the words "acquire" and "acquisition" are used in this connection, rather than "learn" and "learning," because researchers do not wish to prejudge the difficult issue of how children come to possess language competence. There might be a number of processes involved, only some of which would be ones that everyone could agree are instances of "learning." It is obvious that most young children do acquire most of their basic language competence before they enter the first grade, at least the mastery of the more common grammatical structures and a vocabulary that is large enough to handle most of the concepts and ideas encountered in their everyday life. The language of most primers and "basal readers" is far short of what most children can handle in lexical and grammatical complexity, and this is a fact that many believe should be reckoned with in making beginning reading materials more appropriate to children's purposes and interests.[8]

On the other hand, it has been noted that the child's mastery of grammatical constructions is by no means complete at the normal age of entry into school. For example, it is not until about the age of eight that the average child understands that in a sentence like

(6)   John promised Mary to go out.

it is John who will go out, rather than Mary.[9] Also, we should strongly emphasize that children's vocabularies, though quite large, are still severely limited at entry to first grade and that progress in reading is intimately bound up with the development of the child's vocabulary toward adult levels of competence.

Developmental psycholinguists have sought to explain exactly how children acquire language, by observing the child's use of language at various ages and developmental stages, by attempting to specify the rules of grammar that presumably underlie the child's language at a

given stage, and by studying the effects of various influences such as
the kinds of speech that are used by mothers, siblings, and others in
the child's environment. Chomsky once claimed that the models of
speech available to the child are so complicated, or "meager and de-
generate," that it was difficult to believe that the child could acquire a
system of rules from those models unless one assumed that the child
possesses some sort of innate mechanism for doing so.[10] A more moderate position seems now to be generally accepted, however. It is observed that the speech of the child's mother and peers is often much
simplified as compared with adult speech, to the extent that it should
provide sufficient opportunity for the child to induce the grammatical
patterns and characteristics of the adult language by processes of
learning and imitation—if one carefully defines imitation as a process
whereby the child mimics general patterns of sounds, in the case of individual words, and general strategies of putting words together, in
the case of complete utterances. Certainly there is a large element of
"creative" activity on the part of the child in acquiring language. The
child makes up forms like *goed* (instead of *went)* and *doed* (instead of
did) on the analogy of regular forms. It is as if the child is continually
trying out new patterns of speaking that he creates for himself, although it is perhaps too much to say that the child is "testing hypotheses." Apparently it is rare for children to learn patterns by actually im-
itating or repeating particular phrases or sentences that they hear. It is
believed that children acquire grammar by learning how to express
meanings and that meanings come first, grammar later, rather than
the other way around.[11]

Two new specialties that are related to psycholinguistics, if they are
not indeed a part of it, are *sociolinguistics* and *neurolinguistics.*

Sociolinguistics, or at least a subspecialty that is coming to be
called *pragmatics,* is concerned with social factors that surround individual speech acts. Such factors include the social relations between
speakers and hearers that, for example, cause a person to be addressed
as "Mary" by some speakers and as "Mrs. Smith" by other speakers or
that cause a person to be asked to open the window sometimes by a
polite indirect request ("Would you mind opening the window,
please?") and at other times by a blunt command ("Get that window
open in a hurry!"). Pragmatics thus deals with some of the subtle
meanings that children should be able to get out of their reading over
and above pure "literal comprehension." Other directions in sociolin-

guistics concern the social factors that are involved when teachers and
children are from different language, ethnic, or racial groups.[12]

Neurolinguistics has to do with the functioning of the brain and the
nervous system generally in producing and understanding language.
There is, currently, much research concerned with the special functions of the left and right hemispheres in language behavior. It appears that, in most people, speech processes are handled largely in the
left hemisphere, while visual perception (as in recognizing words) is
handled in the right hemisphere. As yet, the implications of these
findings for the study of reading and its teaching are not clear,
although there are indications that some difficulties in reading may be
traced to neurological factors.[13]

The various fields of psycholinguistics are interrelated in complex
ways. All are focused on much the same phenomenon, though from
different perspectives—the acquisition and use of language, in either
spoken or written form, in different kinds of learners, at different
ages, and under different conditions. The problems of explaining how
children learn to understand language reappear in experimental psycholinguistics, which asks what processes *adults* use in understanding
language. In studying adults' language reception, experimental psycholinguists often find it convenient to present language in written
form, and in so doing they are in effect studying the reading process.
Sociolinguistic and pragmatic considerations come into the picture
when we realize that, in most communication situations in real life,
people are not responding to isolated sentences, as they are often required to do in psycholinguistic experiments, but to a total social context in which the setting has a large influence in determining how sentences that might otherwise be ambiguous are to be interpreted. The
sentence "John is looking up the street" could occur either in the situation where John is gazing up the street, perhaps looking for someone
or something, or in the situation where John is using a map or direc-
tory to find the location of a street. Normally the context determines
which reading of the sentence is intended; it would, in fact, be rare
that a listener or reader would even notice the ambiguity of this
sentence.

It is perhaps unrealistic, then, to separate all these different specializations either from one another or from the broader field of cognitive
psychology. This is the field of psychology that studies the processes of
the human mind in attending to, receiving, mentally manipulating,

transforming, storing, and transmitting information, whether that information is presented in verbal form or in some other form, such as
pictures.

In the study of reading, all these fields come together—not only
psycholinguistics as it has been described above, but many other
branches of psychology and related fields. The complete description of
the act of reading involves consideration of how visual symbols (letters,
words, and so forth) are perceived and recognized as such, how these
symbols are decoded into speech (if indeed they are), how the meaning
of a message is interpreted in relation to the reader's prior knowledge
and experience, and how these meanings are put into memory for
later recall and use. Reading is one of the most complicated activities
human beings engage in, and it is no wonder that its study requires so
much from so many fields of investigation. Edmund Burke Huey, a
pioneer in the study of reading, expressed this idea well almost seventy
years ago when he wrote: "And so to completely analyze what we do
when we read would almost be the acme of a psychologist's achieve-
ments, for it would be to describe very many of the most intricate
workings of the human mind, as well as to unravel the tangled story of
the most remarkable specific performance that civilization has learned
in all its history."[14]

PSYCHOLINGUISTICS AND THE ANALYSIS OF READING BEHAVIOR

Reading Processes and Goals of Instruction

It is surprising that people, even experts, disagree on what reading
really is. One would think that the commonsense, basic interpretation
of the term—comprehending or taking in the meaning of something
written or printed—would serve most purposes. Confusion arises possibly because there are many different contexts and situations in which
reading is done.

Normally we tend to think of reading as the sort of thing that occurs
when a person sits down to read a book, newspaper, magazine, letter,
or the like. The person moves his or her eyes over the lines of print,
and, for all one can tell from immediate observation, nothing else is
happening. This is "silent reading." And yet if we question the person
later about what has been read, we may find that the person has acquired new information, attitudes, or beliefs; he may report that he
has been inspired, amused, or otherwise emotionally moved by what

has been read. But silent reading also occurs in many situations in which there is a more or less immediate response to the content of what is read, as when one is following a recipe for preparing a dish, or when a driver reads signs along the road that guide his route or warn him of danger. In all these situations, the reader is extracting some kind of meaning from printed or written language.

There are also situations in which one reads aloud, as in reading a speech, story, or poem before an audience. A driver might have occasion to announce the names of streets by reading them from the street signs as he passes them. In such situations, the printed material is converted to spoken form. A person is often judged capable of reading if he or she is able to say aloud something printed or written, even though that person may not fully attend to, or understand, the meaning of what he is "reading." Teachers are inclined to assess a child's reading ability partly by observing how well he or she can read aloud.

These different types of reading behavior — silent reading and oral reading — give rise to slightly different conceptions of reading. In silent reading, the emphasis is on the extraction of meanings from printed materials and the making of appropriate responses to those meanings, regardless of how much (if at all) the reader is engaged in converting print to some kind of inner speech. In oral reading, the emphasis is on the successful conversion of print to spoken language, regardless of the extent to which meaning is comprehended (although the oral reader must apprehend at least some aspects of meaning in order to make his vocal response intelligible at all).

It would seem, then, that reading can comprise two basic processes: the extraction of meaning from a printed message, and the conversion of print to some form of spoken language, covert or overt. The degree to which each of these processes is involved in any particular act of reading will depend on the situation, and the degree to which these two processes depend on each other is the subject of much debate and research.

If there are two basic processes involved in reading, the question arises as to which of them should be emphasized as an objective of the teaching of reading and which should be stressed at different stages of reading instruction.

One may agree that the prime goal of reading instruction is to make the reader capable of apprehending the full intended meaning of a printed or written text, efficiently and accurately, within the limits set by his experience and knowledge. (This last qualification is added because a "good reader" would not necessarily be expected to understand something out of his range of competence, like a specialized scientific article.) One can further specify reading goals to include teaching people to be able to evaluate and think critically about the meaning that is extracted and to read in appropriate ways for different purposes (for example, skimming or scanning, rather than doing careful reading, as the occasion might demand).

Nevertheless, even though the comprehension of meaning is the fundamental goal, there is much to be said for affirming the additional goal of making the reader *capable* of accurately converting print or writing into spoken language. Printed or written language is practically always convertible into spoken language. Gaining the meaning of a sentence, paragraph, or longer passage is essentially the same process, it would appear, regardless of whether the message is in spoken or written form. There always exists the possibility that the full, intended meaning of a written message can be recovered only if the reader can perceive what the corresponding spoken message would be. Suppose, for example, that a child fails to recognize the word *collie* in a text, even though the word is in his oral vocabulary, and "guesses" from the context that the word is *dog*. In so doing, the child fails to recover some of the specific meaning of *collie*. Even if the printed word were *doggie* and were read as *dog*, this would not be entirely satisfactory reading, for the diminutive connotation of *doggie* would be lost. The ability to recover the spoken form of a work is particularly critical in the case of proper names, for such words have communication value in wider contexts only when they can be more or less accurately pronounced. A person seeing a street sign, *Scarborough St.* for example, would be virtually unable to report the name of the street if he could not say it aloud in such a way that a hearer could recognize the name. The ability to work out the pronunciation of a word from its spelling is also useful to the reader in learning new words, like *reprehensible* and *obstreperous,* and adding them to his active oral vocabulary.

For these reasons it is essential to define reading ability not only in terms of the comprehension of meaning but also in terms of the capability of converting or "decoding" written messages to spoken counterparts. One can leave open the question of whether fluent readers necessarily make this conversion at any particular time they are reading. Some authorities argue that in silent reading fluent readers can and should extract meaning from print directly, that is, without going through an intermediate process of conversion to a spoken form.[15] If a child extracts meaning from print by guessing many of the words from context, without at the same time being able to convert every word to the correct spoken form, it seems unsatisfactory to regard the child as being a truly capable reader.[16]

From this perspective, reading has to be seen, not as a unitary process of extracting meaning, but as a complex set of interrelated competences involving language in both written and spoken form. Since psycholinguistics concerns the way people learn and use language, it follows that psycholinguistics must include study of the acquisition and use of the skills involved in reading. If these skills are to be studied, they must be dealt with separately, particularly if they are to be examined developmentally, for it would be absurd to suppose that all reading skills are acquired at the same time and at the same rate.

Some of the confusion among authorities on reading has stemmed from the assumption, probably false, that processes that operate in the behavior of the fluent, mature reader are precisely those that should be trained in the early stages of instruction. For example, even if one believes that adult readers extract meaning from words without attending to their letter composition, or without awareness of the sounds of the words, it would not necessarily be appropriate to teach children to respond to print in exactly this way. In the beginning reader, it is almost certain that learning to recognize words requires at least some awareness of the phonetic significance of the letter composition of words and of the sounds of the words when spoken.

Of the two basic processes that we have identified as involved in reading, only one — converting printed or written language to language in spoken form — is uniquely tied to reading behavior. The other basic process — understanding messages in linguistic form — is something that occurs even in the preliterate child, without any involvement of printed material. Thus, this latter aspect of the reading process relates more to general language development than to the development of reading competence per se. Now it is true that, in a literate society such as ours, exposure to samples of language that are grammatically and conceptually complex and that use advanced vocabulary is more likely to occur through printed texts than through orally delivered discourse. For this reason it has been mainly the re-

sponsibility of the reading teacher to help students master the complexities of the more advanced and involved kinds of discourse. It
should be borne in mind, nevertheless, that these complexities are
essentially linguistic and conceptual; they can occur in spoken discourse as well as in reading, even though perhaps not as frequently.

Perceptual and Cognitive Prerequisites to Reading Development

The acquisition of language itself depends upon a great many perceptual and cognitive learnings that take place in early life. The child
learns, among other things, to discriminate between different visual
and auditory patterns in his everyday environment and to associate
meanings with these patterns. The fact that most language development occurs during the child's first five years must mean that these
perceptual and cognitive prerequisites mature very early. Many of
these same capacities are also relevant to learning to read. Beginning
readers must be able to discriminate between letters and between
words and to associate meanings with the visual patterns exhibited in
printed words. Some children learn to read very early, by age three or
four, say, and there are instances on record of children whose acquisition of reading ability is virtually parallel to their acquisition of language.[17] It is doubtful, therefore, that there are any perceptual and
cognitive learnings required for the acquisition of reading ability that
are not already required for the development of spoken language, with
one major exception that has been largely overlooked until recently.

If a child is going to learn to read, he must have developed an
awareness that language is segmented into units. In the earliest stages,
the child must realize that language can be segmented into words, or
at least into units that are roughly comparable to the units recognized
as words in the spacing conventions of print. Next comes an awareness
that some words — the longer ones — can be divided into syllables.
Finally comes the awareness that words, or syllables, can be segmented
into individual sounds in a temporal order. Many children seem to go
through this course of development without any special instruction or
guidance; their native powers of observation, or certain kinds of
everyday encounters with language, lead them to discover linguistic
segmentation for themselves. Other children, possibly with slower
rates of development, may need special instruction or guidance in discovering the segmented character of language. The importance of this
awareness becomes obvious when we consider what a writing system is:

a way of writing down words in a visual sequence that corresponds more or less to the temporal order in which words and sounds are uttered. Some writing systems—the best modern example being that of Chinese—demand only that the reader be able to segment language into words or syllables, but any language, such as English, whose writing system uses an alphabetic principle to record the sounds of words demands in addition that the reader be able to recognize the segmentation of words into separate sounds.

The failure of many children to discover linguistic segmentation, or to be led to discover it by appropriate instruction, is probably one of the principal reasons for failure in the beginning phases of learning to read. While a child who has not progressed so far as to discover segmentation of syllables into sounds can usually be taught to recognize single "sight" words, that child is likely to have difficulty in recognizing the significance of the visual sequencing of the letters of words and in associating the letters with sounds. Instruction that attempts to teach reading with at least some reference to letter-sound correspondence will make no sense to a child who is unaware of linguistic segmentation at the level of individual sounds. It is possible that the difficulties researchers have had in demonstrating any virtues in "phonics" methods of instruction over other methods can be traced to the failure to ensure that children are adequately prepared, in terms of their awareness of linguistic segmentation, for such instruction.

It should be noted that an awareness of linguistic segmentation can be "preliterate" in the sense that it can arise before any exposure to reading instruction, or even to graphic symbols, takes place in the child's experience. Awareness of linguistic segmentation is, nevertheless, a cognitive prerequisite that is quite specific to reading because its only use is in learning to deal with written language.

Because it is only recently that the importance of linguistic segmentation has been clearly recognized by reading researchers, it has not yet been well established whether children differ inherently in their rates of maturation with respect to it, or whether the observed differences are simply due to differential amounts of exposure to relevant experiences and instruction. The limited evidence that is so far available, however, suggests that, by the age of five, most children can be quite easily led to become aware of the segmented character of language, through appropriate teaching.[18]

It may be that there are other perceptual and cognitive prerequi-

sites that are specific to learning to read, such as the ability to discriminate letters and other graphic symbols and the ability to form arbitrary associations between graphic symbols and meanings. Some
"reading readiness" tests attempt to assess the child's possession of
these prerequisites, but most evidence suggests that they are not specific to reading and that apparent failures in discriminating letters and
in learning arbitrary symbol-meaning associations are to be attributed
more to failures in selective attention and observation than to any inherent retardation in the maturation of the underlying perceptual and
cognitive capacities.[19]

The Dependence of Reading Development on
Language Development

However reading instruction is conducted, it seems obvious that one
of the behaviors that must be taught is word identification. In the early stages of learning to read, this means that the child must be able to
look at a printed word and recognize it as one that is already in his or
her oral vocabulary and one whose meaning is known. As children
progress in reading, they build up an increasingly large repertoire of
words that can be recognized in this way. The size of the repertoire
that can be built up in this way is limited in part, however, by the size
of the oral vocabulary. Normally this limitation is hardly operative in
early stages because, as is well known, by the age at which children
begin to learn to read their oral vocabularies are already quite
large—numbered in the thousands of words. Furthermore, most reading materials presented to beginning readers are very limited in their
vocabularies, probably more so than they need be.

There does come a time in reading development, however, when
words encountered in reading materials are increasingly unlikely to
exist in the oral vocabulary, particularly if the child's oral vocabulary
is limited. It is at that stage that reading development becomes much
more dependent on language development. On the other hand, it is
also at this stage that progress in reading can begin to assist materially
in general language development, in that reading provides a means of
learning many words and meanings that are not already in the oral
vocabulary, either actively or passively.

The dependence of reading on language development is not associated solely with the mismatch of the oral vocabulary with the vocabulary presented in reading materials. At every stage, even the earliest, it is also associated with other aspects of children's knowledge of the language, particularly with acquisition of the grammatical structure of the language and with their ability to use competence in language structure to read otherwise ambiguous printed words in appropriate ways, with appropriate meanings. It is particularly the case in English orthography that many words are spelled in such a way that a pure "phonetic" rendition of their sounds does not readily yield a key to recognizing these words in the oral vocabulary; also, different phonetic renderings of the same visual form are frequently demanded in different contexts (for example, *read* as /riyd/ or /red/ depending upon the tense or grammatical function; *can* as a verb or as a noun). If readers are going to be able to overcome difficulties of this sort, they must have acquired an adequate knowledge of the language so that they can utilize the overall meaning of a sentence to arrive at the proper reading.

Phenomena of this kind are the source of the famous notion of "guessing from context" that is emphasized by some authorities in the reading field. In my view, however, "guessing" is an inappropriate term to describe the process of using a context to decode a word, and this decoding process must be guided as much by the letter composition of the word to be rendered as by the context that surrounds it. One cannot think of a case where the letter composition of a word would provide no clues to the possible phonetic rendering of a word.

At even more advanced stages of reading progress, language development is relevant because of the need to apprehend the grammatical structure of long and complex sentences. The ability to segment a printed sentence into its higher-order constituents (for example, subject noun phrase versus predicate phrase, modifying clause versus noun phrase modified) should arise from development of oral language skills. Likewise, the ability to interpret anaphoric constructions (for instance, to identify properly pronoun antecedents, as in a sentence like "Tom's father thought he should get his pipe for him") depends on abilities acquired in general language development.

Insofar as psycholinguistics has been able to describe the course of general language development in vocabulary, mastery of grammatical structure, and learning of meanings, information from these studies should be of interest and value to the reading teacher. Considerable knowledge exists about the development of vocabulary, but much of this concerns reading vocabulary (words recognized in print) rather

than oral or listening vocabulary. As for the development of competence in the grammatical and syntactical aspects of language, much
more is now known about these developments in young, prereading
children than in children of elementary and high school ages. As
noted earlier, it is only recently that psycholinguists have given adequate attention to the fact that mastery of the grammatical aspects of
language is far from complete by the time the child enters school.

Problems in Teaching the Decoding Phases of Reading

Letter Identification and Knowledge of the Alphabet

Most children can be readily taught to recognize a small number of
words "at sight" without paying particular attention to the letters composing them. Such teaching can be pushed only so far, however. While
it is conceivable that a child might be taught to recognize a very large
number of words solely from their visual patterns, in the way that
Chinese children are taught to recognize the thousands of characters
in the Chinese writing system, such teaching would be inefficient for a
language that uses the alphabetic principle. Children can be brought
through the decoding barrier only if they are also taught to recognize
individual letters, in both capital and lower-case forms. Although
there has been considerable research on how children perceive letters
and letter-like forms, learning to recognize and name the letters of the
alphabet is apparently fairly rapid and easy for most children, with
appropriate instruction. Research[20] has shown, however, that knowledge of letter names is not particularly useful in learning to read,
although there is no intrinsic harm in such teaching unless the child
gets the false idea that letter names can be used in sounding out words.
It is far more important for children to learn what sounds are likely to
be represented by the letters and their various combinations. Just how
this learning should be accomplished, and indeed whether it is worthwhile at all, is the subject of one of the most heated and bitter controversies in the psychology and teaching of reading, at least in the case of
learning to read printed English.[21]

Teaching Decoding Skills Using Letter-Sound Relationships

The fundamental difficulty is the fact that, in English orthography,
the relationships between letters (graphemes) and sounds (phonemes)
are relatively complex and inconsistent. (Problems of whether and
how to teach letter-sound correspondences have arisen, however, even
in languages like German and Finnish where the correspondences are

much more regular.) Some authorities are fond of citing classic "horrible examples," such as the fact that the digraph *gh* can directly represent either no phoneme at all (as in *though, light)* or a variety of phonemes (as in *tough, hiccough, ghost).* It is also pointed out that in one systematic study of relations between letters and sounds in 6,092 common one- and two-syllable words, 211 different types of letter-sound correspondences, with 166 "rules" and 95 "exceptions" were identified.[22] The intended implication, apparently, is that teaching letter-sound correspondences is impractical and of doubtful effectiveness.

Another argument made against the teaching of letter-sound correspondences is that research has not shown convincingly that instruction in phonics or word-attack skills produces results that are decidedly superior to those of instruction that lays little or no stress on letter-sound correspondences. This argument is made despite Jeanne Chall's conclusion that, on the whole, instruction with a "decoding emphasis" (that is, some form of approach that teaches letter-sound correspondences) tends to produce better results than "look-say" or "whole-word" approaches.

Allegedly theory-based arguments against decoding approaches are also made to the effect that mature, fluent readers do not decode words into sounds in order to determine their meanings and renderings; therefore, beginning readers need not, and should not, be taught to decode words into their sounds. It is also pointed out that many words require the use of their surrounding sentence contexts as a key to their grammatical functions and meanings and, hence, to their phonetic renderings.

In my view, this line of argumentation has several flaws and must be rejected.

First, on the matter of the alleged complexity of letter-sound correspondences in English orthography, it seems to ignore the fact that there are actually a large number of regularities or spelling patterns, applying with quite high frequencies throughout the English spelling system, that can form the basis of a teaching method.[23] It also seems to underplay the fact that letters and their combinations are in almost every case useful clues to word identification, available to help the reader arrive at reasonable approximations to the rendering of a word and to choose, if necessary, among a small number of options, some of which may exist in the oral vocabulary. To be sure, children should be urged and guided to use the surrounding context of a word to "guess" the correct rendering, but this "guessing" should not ignore the letter composition of the word and the clues that it affords—clues that children can be taught to use by appropriate instruction in letter-sound correspondences.

Second, the argument that decoding approaches are not shown to be distinctly superior to other approaches now seems flawed on the basis that decoding approaches studied in past research may not have adequately taken account of the necessity of ensuring that children taught by these methods have acquired the segmentation skills that appear to be prerequisite for success. As yet, this view can be only a promising speculation, but the evidence that nearly all children can learn to read rebus and syllabary systems that do not require segmentation skills at the phonemic level[24] and that phonemic segmentation skills are relatively easy to reach[25] is sufficiently strong to allow one to recommend a more optimistic assessment of decoding approaches and renewed research to test the merits of this speculation.

One can also point to the fact that, regardless of the method of instruction, many children (even under "sight-word" approaches) work out for themselves the higher-order regularities in letter-sound correspondences[26] and employ appropriate techniques of decoding words by using the overall sentence contexts in which they are found. As far as can be determined, such children are not, contrary to the predictions made by some authorities, impeded by memory-load restrictions, and they do not necessarily get bogged down in sounding out words; instead, they are constantly seeking the meanings underlying the words and sentences. It is likely that the few children who have trouble with letter-sound correspondences and their use are those who, by reason of inadequate maturation or inadequate prior instruction, have not acquired segmentation skills.

Research has shown that it is critical also for children to be aware of the fact that letters and letter-combinations may have a variety of sound correspondences. On the one hand, children need to be exposed to an adequate sample of words and sounds from which they can induce the high-frequency regularities, but, on the other hand and at the same time, they need to be exposed to a sufficient sample of divergent and inconsistent letter-sound correspondences to establish in them what Harry Levin[27] has called a "set for diversity."

To answer the argument that children need not be taught how to sound out words because mature readers do not do so, we need to consider another phase in progress toward mature and fluent reading.

The Automatization of Word Identification

Although it may be true, as we have urged, that attention to orthographic clues and letter-sound correspondences is useful in the early stages of learning to read (say, in the first three or four years of the normal instruction sequence), it is important also, even from the beginning, to promote the child's ability to recognize words and their parts (syllables, affixes, and so on) instantly and automatically, without conscious attention to letter clues. At first, this can happen only with a few common, frequently seen words, but, as the reader encounters more and more words and adds them to his reading vocabulary, the identification of these additional words can become automatized. That is, the word as a whole is perceived nearly instantaneously and without the necessity of laboriously working out its sound rendering through phonic or word-attack approaches. Either the work of sounding out the word through letter clues would have been done before enough times to make it highly practiced or there would have been transfer from such work performed on other words with partially similar spellings.

Exactly what processes actually occur in rapid identification of well-known words in fluent readers has been the subject of much research, as yet inconclusive, in experimental studies reviewed by Dominic Massaro.[28] It is not clear what the role of phonological mediation may be, that is, the extent to which the recoding of letter information into sounds helps the reader determine the identification of the word and its meaning. Massaro is inclined to believe that phonemic recoding does not occur at what he calls the "primary recognition" stage. This stage entails the transmission of a sequence of recognized letter units to a "synthesized visual memory" that, in turn, is passed by a process of "secondary recognition" to a "generated abstract memory" where the word is actually recognized through processes of rehearsal and recall. Thus, Massaro favors the view that the meaning of a word is normally recognized directly from its visual form, not from a phonemic recoding of its letters. This view may well be correct, but nothing in the data that Massaro reviews seems inconsistent with the notion that word recognition in skilled readers does involve specific letter clues, including orthographic regularities and constraints that would have to be acquired at some time in the process of learning to read. It is these orthographic regularities and constraints and, incidentally (at least for children with normal hearing), the sounds that they represent, that would have to be the focus of instruction in "decoding" at early stages of learning to read, even though the actual phonemic encoding of words could drop out of the process of word recognition. (For many readers, however, phonemic recoding does appear to occur, either in a fairly complete form, as would be observed in extensive subvocalization, or in a very abbreviated convert form.)

It therefore seems possible, on the basis of the evidence reviewed by Massaro, to counter the argument that children need not learn to recode words phonemically because mature readers do not do so. Even though skilled readers may not recode phonemically in order to determine meanings, they are nevertheless responsive to letter clues and the orthographic regularities that they exhibit. In early stages of reading instruction, the easiest and perhaps the only way to draw children's attention to letter clues and orthographic regularities is to talk about the phonemic significance of these clues and regularities and to require students to recode the words into spoken form. Even though an actual phonemic recoding may eventually disappear from or get short-circuited out of the word identification process, the basis for word identification—the specific letter clues—must remain as a functional stimulus.

Problems in Teaching Language Comprehension

Although it is agreed that comprehending or getting meaning from printed or written materials is the basic goal of reading, it is difficult to define exactly what comprehension is or to assess whether a reader, in any particular instance, actually gets the intended meaning of a piece of writing.[29] Researchers in psycholinguistics have used various ways of defining and assessing comprehension. Sometimes they leave it up to the reader himself to assess his understanding of material, but, more often, some kind of comprehension test is employed. This could be a series of open-ended or closed-ended questions over the material read; it could be a cloze test in which the reader has to guess what words have been omitted from a text and replaced by blanks; or it could be a procedure in which the reader has to follow directions that have been included in the text. Each of these techniques has problems and pitfalls, of course. In the case of questions covering the material read, one has to make sure that the reader cannot answer the questions (better than chance) without reading the text. The cloze technique poses the problem that it may measure some aspect of general verbal ability or verbal intelligence rather than, or as well as, actual comprehension of the text. Tests of ability to follow directions may measure, for example, some aspect of motor skill or mechanical ability as much as comprehension of the text. Nevertheless, it is usually possible, with adequate research and pretesting, to develop valid tests of comprehension by any of these techniques.

The classroom teacher has the opportunity to observe and question a child over a considerable period of time and may, therefore, eventually average out the various sources of error that might be made in assessing a child's ability to comprehend what he reads. If a teacher decides that a child is characteristically having difficulty understanding reading material, the teacher has to consider what the possible source or sources of the difficulty may be. Perhaps the child is finding it hard to recognize words; this might be indicated if the child makes many errors and proceeds very slowly in oral reading. Charles Perfetti and Thomas Hogaboam[30] found that many children with poor comprehension ability are distinctly slower than good readers in recognizing words. These children may get bogged down in the process of working out the pronunciations of words and thus lose a sense of the total structure of a sentence. Some authorities cite such cases to support their view that children should not be taught methods of sounding out words that rely on letter-sound relations; rather, they recommend that children be taught to rely mainly on syntactic and semantic cues in "guessing" unfamiliar words. Such cues are often useful in reading a word accurately, of course, but, in my view, children with poor word recognition skills have not been taught these skills adequately or have not adequately automatized them. The remedy, I think, lies in giving the child additional help and practice with word recognition skills based on the alphabetic principle. The child may even need help in elementary sound segmentation skills.

Suppose, however, that the child can read orally with accuracy, but seems not to understand what he reads. Such children have sometimes been labeled "word callers," that is, children who can sound out the individual words of a sentence without comprehension of what the sentence says. There is considerable controversy as to whether such children actually exist. Ward Cromer claims that they do, but Robert

Calfee states that he has never encountered an attested case and points out that Cromer's data are flawed in various ways.[31] Unless a child puts so much effort into word recognition that he fails to "hear" the sentence he is reading, it is difficult to believe that a child who can read a sentence aloud cannot understand it *if he can understand the sentence when it is read to him aloud by another person.*

The qualification that the child understand material when it is read aloud to him is the basis for a means of evaluating his progress in reading that is proposed by Thomas Sticht and his associates.[32] When a child cannot understand a text even by listening, the comprehension problem stems not from poor decoding (word recognition) but from difficulty in understanding language. The child may not be a native speaker of the language and thus may not have progressed far enough in ability to understand the language when it is spoken. Or the child may be a member of a subcultural group speaking a nonstandard dialect of English, such that many of the words and expressions in a text are unfamiliar to him. Or the child, though a native speaker of the language, may be retarded in language development — through inadequate richness of language stimulation at home or in his environment, through some form of constitutional defect, or through some kind of emotional or cognitive disturbance.

Whatever the source of their difficulty, these children suffer from language deficiency *relative* to the language they are being taught to read, or from cognitive deficiency *relative* to the conceptual level of the material to which they are exposed in reading. (It is not implied, however, that nonnative speakers are necessarily retarded in development with respect to their own language or that speakers of nonstandard dialects thereby exhibit a deficit. Languages other than English and the various nonstandard dialects of English are valid forms of language in their own communities. I am simply pointing out that nonnative speakers and speakers of dialects may have trouble understanding reading material in "standard language" because of the differences between the standard language and the language to which they are accustomed.

The difference between a child's level of language development and the level of language development that is demanded by reading material may become critical either at early or at later stages of the process of learning to read. For some children — particularly for nonnative speakers and sometimes for those who speak dialects — it may be critical in the earliest stages, as when the child fails to understand many of the words and grammatical structures present in even the simplest types of reading material. For other children, the problem may become critical only at a much later stage. This would be true for a child who is a native speaker of English and who does well in everyday conversational situations; thus he has no difficulty understanding the material of readers in the early grades. He begins to have difficulty in comprehension in the later grades, however, when the language of his reading material becomes considerably more advanced. This category could include a great many children. It is well known that large numbers of students in the upper grades are taxed by the difficulty of the vocabulary in their reading material. According to tests and surveys conducted by one group of investigators,[33] large proportions of children in the fourth grade fail to make proper interpretations of various classes of syntactic phenomena (intrasentence, intersentence, and anaphora). In one sense, it may be said that nearly all children at some time exhibit a language deficiency relative to the reading materials they encounter. But overcoming such language deficiencies is one of the tasks of the school, and that is all the more reason for discussing the problem at this point.

Psycholinguistic analysis traces the types of difficulties that are likely to be encountered with respect to lexical, syntactic, and semantic aspects of language. This type of analysis can make the teacher more aware of what particular difficulties can arise at different stages of reading development. (Many of the difficulties stem, of course, from inadequate knowledge of the world or of specialized subject matters, but, strictly speaking, psycholinguistics does not deal with them.)

Vocabulary

When children enter first grade, their lexical repertoires are already quite large, on the average, and are usually adequate to deal with the materials in primers and in the reading materials of the early grades. They are not sufficient, however, to enable them to deal with the materials presented in the later grades in various subject matters. Estimates of the vocabularies required at different grade levels and in different subject matters are difficult to make with confidence, for various reasons. Some evidence comes from frequency lists and counts of the words in instructional materials,[34] suggesting that these vocabularies are numbered in the tens of thousands. A recent publication[35] gives information on the percentages of students at various grade levels who may be expected to know the meanings of words in different senses; data of this sort are given on more than 43,000 words and word meanings.

The problem of vocabulary is not restricted to the "big" or "rare" words. It centers also, at least for some children, in the "small" and frequently used words such as *of, in, if,* and *though,* whose meanings may not be precisely apprehended in their various contexts. Furthermore, it has been shown[36] that many children fail to understand certain common words in their more uncommon grammatical functions. It should be remembered also that a great number of words have multiple meanings that a fluent reader must be capable of recognizing.

Syntax

For some children, it appears that the very composition of words into printed sentences poses a problem. According to Bruce Denner[37] these children have no trouble in learning the meanings of graphic symbols, but when these symbols are arranged in a way analogous to printed sentences the children are unable to interpret them as they would the corresponding spoken sentences. For example, they do not understand the command implied by a sequence of arbitrary symbols whose meanings have been taught as *jump, over, block.* This betokens, apparently, a fundamental deficiency in the ability to apprehend syntactic forms in print, a deficiency that must be overcome in early stages of reading instruction. Most children, however, can interpret printed sentences in the same way that they would interpret their spoken counterparts. In fact, they use syntactic information extensively in trying to interpret the meanings of unfamiliar words, usually assigning them to the proper grammatical form-class (that is, they recognize that in the light of the grammatical structure of a sentence the unfamiliar word is a noun, a verb, or an adjective, whichever the case may be).[38]

At the same time, some evidence suggests that reading with speed and comprehension is facilitated if material is printed in "preorganized phrases," that is, in such a way that the grammatical constituents and relations are more obvious than they are in ordinary print. This indicates that some readers — even college students — have difficulty apprehending the syntactic structure of printed sentences. Thus, many students have difficulty in making an implicit "parsing" of sentences, failing to recognize certain grammatical structures and to use certain print conventions, such as punctuation, effectively. Also, many students have trouble with sentences that contain syntactic and semantic ambiguities.[39]

Discourse Structure

In well-written prose, sentences are organized into paragraphs, and paragraphs are organized into even larger units that convey major ideas and concepts. This fact has been recognized for several thousands of years, but detailed analysis of just how discourse is structured, what linguistic devices signal that structure, and how people apprehend knowledge and information from discourse has only recently been undertaken.[40] This type of analysis may yield concrete suggestions as to how teachers can help children better understand the structure of discourse and of the major ideas that are presented through discourse, but as yet work has not progressed far enough to do so in a readily usable form.

Teaching Comprehension Skills

The above review of the kinds of linguistic factors that come into play in understanding language, along with the references that have been cited, will, it is hoped, give teachers a feel for the complexity of teaching comprehension ability and, at the same time, make them more aware of the separate skills and knowledges that are involved — vocabulary, syntax, and the like — thus permitting them to focus on particular kinds of difficulties as the occasion arises.

The most general kind of recommendation is that teaching comprehension must entail a great deal of interplay between teachers and students. A teacher must always be alert to the kinds of comprehension difficulties that the student encounters. Particular word usages, syntactic expressions, and paragraph organizations must be discussed and explained to the best of the teacher's ability. The child's general language comprehension beyond the early years normally progresses relatively slowly. There are just too many facts about language to be learned: too many words to learn to recognize, too many grammatical phenomena to be absorbed and digested. Wide and extensive reading itself will help the student acquire this mass of facts, using his or her powers of inference, memory, and comparison. As recent research[41] has shown, stories and essays with meaningful, familiar contexts can facilitate the learner's acquisition of low-frequency, undefined words that are contained in them. It seems reasonable to assume that such materials would also aid the reader's competence to interpret the less common, more involved syntactic constructions.

SOME PARTING THOUGHTS

The "great debate" in reading instruction of which Chall wrote[42] has spilled over into psycholinguistics, but in a somewhat altered form. Where previously the debate was over "look-say" versus "phonics" methods of teaching, the controversy is now over whether reading is a "psycholinguistic guessing game" or a process of "decoding print into spoken form." As in all debates, each side has made some persuasive points and also some arguments that can be effectively countered by the other side. But, unlike a formal debate, this debate cannot be thought of as one that has a clear winner or a clear loser. Scientific debates should not be decided in this arbitrary way; rather, they should lead to the formulation of a higher-order synthesis of the valid ideas of each side and to the testing of further hypotheses suggested by that synthesis.

I would suggest at this time a synthesis that would contain the following major ideas, to be tested and refined by whatever laboratory or classroom research may appear appropriate.

1. Reading is a process of getting meaning, and sometimes sound, from print by converting it (recoding the visual representation) to some inner representation that is analogous to that of spoken language and that is comprehended in essentially the same way that spoken language is comprehended. (Indeed, the understanding of spoken language involves converting an auditory stimulus to an inner representation.)

2. The reader can derive meaning directly from whatever inner representation is generated by this process of conversion and does not have to make an additional conversion to a speech code, although he may do so without any great cost in time or efficiency.

3. On account of the essential and characteristic multipotentiality of linguistic symbols (whether printed or spoken), the reader must be able to use all the cues available to him — graphemic, lexical, syntactic, semantic, and situational — to derive the full intended meaning of a printed message (whether a single word or a longer statement).

4. Graphemic cues in particular words are of greatest use in reducing the reader's uncertainty as to exactly what spoken forms and meanings are intended in the message. Skilled reading involves making the best possible use of the graphemic cues in particular words, including graphemic cues that point to (even though they do not exactly indicate) what counterparts of printed words would be found in the

spoken form of the message. Use of these graphemic cues for teaching purposes should begin as soon as practicable in a reading program. In the case of a language whose orthography uses an alphabetic principle, such as English, this means organizing instruction to permit the student to learn whatever aspects of letter-sound correspondences may be found useful. Research indicates that there is enough regularity even in English orthography to be highly useful in word recognition.

5. A critical prerequisite for successfully learning to use grapheme-phoneme correspondence rules is an awareness, on the part of the learner, of the segmentation of language into words, syllables, the phonemes, and an ability to handle these language units in dealing with their graphemic representations.

6. All aspects of reading competence must be practiced and learned to the point that they become as facile and automatic as possible. In particular, this applies to the skill of recognizing words, where automatization would mean the gradual dropping out, fairly early, of conscious application of word-analysis skills that depend on grapheme-phoneme correspondence rules. But it pertains to other aspects of reading skill, such as apprehending semantic and syntactic structures, consonant with general language development.

So there you have it. My synthesis says that, yes, reading *is* a psycholinguistic guessing game, but I don't like wild guesses; I want the reader's "guesses" to be increasingly accurate, as early as possible, guided as much, if not more so, by the graphemic stimuli as by other kinds of linguistic cues. My synthesis says also that reading *is* a decoding process in which meanings and, if necessary, the sounds of printed messages are derived from an inner representation that parallels that of spoken messages, using those features of the printed message that give indications of those sounds.

Perhaps even this synthesis that I have made, based on recent work in psycholinguistics, may be found to be defective, and will give rise to still another "great debate." But, should that debate occur, I hope that it will not be over the same issues that have plagued the reading field for so many years, but over some other issues that will have a more refreshing and interesting character.

NOTES

1. The first widely publicized use of the term was in the title of a monograph, *Psycholinguistics: A Survey of Theory and Research Problems,* edited by Charles E.

Osgood and Thomas A. Sebeok and published simultaneously in 1954 in the *Journal of Abnormal and Social Psychology* 49 (October 1954): 1-203, and in the *International Review of American Linguistics* 20 (October 1954). The monograph was reprinted by Indiana University Press in 1965, with an extensive introduction by A. Richard Diebold, Jr. Current works on psycholinguistics are: J. A. Fodor, T. G. Bever, M. F. Garrett, *The Psychology of Language: An Introduction to Psycholinguistics and Generative Grammar* (New York: McGraw-Hill, 1974); and Herbert H. Clark and Eve V. Clark, *Psychology and Language: An Introduction to Psycholinguistics* (New York: Harcourt Brace Jovanovich, 1977). None of these works devotes much explicit attention to reading, however, but a chapter on phonology and reading is included in Philip S. Dale, *Language Development: Structure and Function,* 2d ed. (New York: Holt, Rinehart and Winston, 1976).

   2. See John B. Carroll, *The Study of Language* (Cambridge, Mass.: Harvard University Press, 1953).

   3. For a discussion of the evolution of writing systems in relation to problems in the teaching of reading, see Lila R. Gleitman and Paul Rozin, "The Structure and Acquisition of Reading I: Relations between Orthographies and the Structure of Language," in *Toward a Psychology of Reading,* ed. Arthur S. Reber and Don L. Scarborough (Hillsdale, N.J.: Erlbaum, 1971), 1-53.

   4. Noam Chomsky, *Syntactic Structures* (The Hague: Mouton, 1957).

   5. Dwight L. Bolinger, *Aspects of Language,* 2d ed. (New York: Harcourt Brace Jovanovich, 1975).

   6. Sam Glucksberg and Joseph H. Danks, *Experimental Psycholinguistics: An Introduction* (Hillsdale, N.J.: Erlbaum, 1975); *Language Comprehension and the Acquisition of Knowledge,* ed. Roy O. Freedle and John B. Carroll (Washington, D.C.: V. H. Winston & Sons, 1972).

   7. Dale, *Language Development.*

   8. Ruth Strickland, *The Language of Elementary School Children: Its Relationship to the Language of Reading Textbooks and the Quality of Reading of Selected Children, Bulletin of the School of Education, Indiana University,* Volume 38 (Bloomington: School of Education, Indiana University, 1962), 1-131.

   9. Carol Chomsky, *The Acquisition of Syntax in Children from 5 to 10* (Cambridge, Mass.: M.I.T. Press, 1969).

   10. Noam Chomsky, *Language and Mind* (New York: Harcourt Brace Jovanovich, 1968), 75-77.

   11. Roger Brown, *A First Language: The Early Stages* (Cambridge, Mass.: Harvard University Press, 1973); *The Ontogenesis of Grammar,* ed. Dan I. Slobin (New York: Academic Press, 1971).

   12. Recent works in sociolinguistics and pragmatics that devote attention to teaching problems are the following: *Functions of Language in the Classroom,* ed. Courtney B. Cazden, Vera P. John, and Dell Hymes (New York: Teachers College Press, 1972); Aaron V. Cicourel *et al., Language Use and School Performance* (New York: Academic Press, 1974).

   13. For cautious reviews of evidence on this point, see M. D. Vernon, *Reading and Its Difficulties: A Psychological Study* (Cambridge, Eng.: Cambridge University

Press, 1971), 149-159; Eleanor J. Gibson and Harry Levin, *The Psychology of Reading* (Cambridge, Mass.: M.I.T. Press, 1975), 485-500.

14. Edmund Burke Huey, *The Psychology and Pedagogy of Reading* (Cambridge, Mass.: M.I.T. Press, 1968; first published by Macmillan, New York, 1908), 6.

15. *Psycholinguistics and Reading,* ed. Frank Smith (New York: Holt, Rinehart and Winston, 1973).

16. The view taken here is rather different from that taken by Frank Smith or by Kenneth Goodman, who has characterized reading as a "psycholinguistic guessing game" and who writes as if he is willing to be quite tolerant of the many wrong guesses ("miscues," he calls them) made by beginning readers, as long as they seem to comprehend the meaning. See *The Psycholinguistic Nature of the Reading Process,* ed. Kenneth Goodman (Detroit, Mich.: Wayne State University Press, 1968). Goodman's approach, which involves detailed analysis of the miscues made by beginning readers, has some value, on the other hand, in laying bare the processes by which readers attain mature skills of reading, skills that, according to our view, must include those of accurate word identification and decoding.

17. Dolores Durkin, *Children Who Read Early* (New York: Teachers College Press, 1966); Ragnhild Söderbergh, *Reading in Early Childhood: A Linguistic Study of a Swedish Preschool Child's Gradual Acquisition of Reading Ability* (Stockholm: Almqvist & Wiksell, 1971).

18. Linnea C. Ehri, "Word Consciousness in Readers and Prereaders," *Journal of Educational Psychology* 67 (April 1975): 204-212; Barbara Fox and Donald K. Routh, "Analyzing Spoken Language into Words, Syllables, and Phonemes: A Development Study," *Journal of Psycholinguistic Research* 4 (October 1975): 331-342; *id.,* "Phonemic Analysis and Synthesis as Word-Attack Skills," *Journal of Educational Psychology* 68 (February 1976): 70-74; David M. Goldstein, "Cognitive-Linguistic Functioning and Learning to Read in Preschoolers," *ibid.* (December 1976): 680-688; Isabelle Y. Liberman, "Basic Research in Speech and Lateralization of Language: Some Implications for Reading Disability," *Bulletin of the Orton Society* 21 (1971): 71-87; *id. et al.,* "Phonetic Segmentation and Recoding in the Beginning Reader," in *Toward a Psychology of Reading,* ed. Reber and Scarborough, 207-225; Paul Rozin and Lila R. Gleitman, "The Structure and Acquisition of Reading II: The Reading Process and the Acquisition of the Alphabetic Principle," *ibid.,* 55-141.

19. Alan O. Ross, *Psychological Aspects of Learning Disabilities and Reading Disorders* (New York: McGraw-Hill, 1976).

20. S. Jay Samuels, "The Effect of Letter-Name Knowledge on Learning to Read," *American Educational Research Journal* 9 (Winter 1972): 65-74; Joseph R. Jenkins, R. Barker Bausell, and Linda M. Jenkins, "Comparisons of Letter Name and Letter Sound Training as Transfer Variables," *ibid.,* 75-86.

21. Jeanne S. Chall, *Learning to Read: The Great Debate* (New York: McGraw-Hill, 1967).

22. Betty Berdiansky, B. Cronnell, and J. Koehler, *Spelling-Sound Relations and Primary Form-Class Descriptions for Speech-Comprehension Vocabularies of 6-9-Year-Olds,* Technical Report No. 15 (Los Alamitos, Calif.: Southwest Regional Laboratory for Educational Research and Development, 1969), discussed by Smith in *Psycholinguistics and Reading,* 87-90.

23. Charles C. Fries, *Linguistics and Reading* (New York: Holt, Rinehart and Winston, 1962); Richard L. Venezky, "English Orthography: Its Graphical Structure and Its Relation to Sound," *Reading Research Quarterly* 2 (Spring 1967): 75-106.

24. Rozin and Gleitman, "The Structure and Acquisition of Reading II."

25. See note 18, above; see also Michael A. Wallach and Lisa Wallach, *Teaching All Children to Read* (Chicago: University of Chicago Press, 1976).

26. Gibson and Levin, *The Psychology of Reading*, 294-305.

27. *Ibid.*, 72-73.

28. *Understanding Language: An Information-Processing Analysis of Speech Perception, Reading, and Psycholinguistics*, ed. Dominic W. Massaro (New York: Academic Press, 1975).

29. John B. Carroll, "Defining Language Comprehension: Some Speculations," in *Language Comprehension and the Acquisition of Knowledge*, ed. Freedle and Carroll, 1-29.

30. Charles A. Perfetti and Thomas Hogaboam, "The Relationship between Single Word Decoding and Reading Comprehension Skill," *Journal of Educational Psychology* 67 (August 1975): 461-469.

31. Ward Cromer, "The Difference Model: A New Explanation for Some Reading Difficulties," *ibid.*, 61 (December 1970): 471-483; Robert C. Calfee, Richard Arnold, and Priscilla Drum, "Review of Gibson and Levin's *The Psychology of Reading*," *Proceedings of the National Academy of Education* 3 (1976): 26 ff.

32. Thomas G. Sticht *et al.*, *Auding and Reading: A Developmental Model* (Alexandria, Va.: Human Resources Research Organization, 1974).

33. John R. Bormuth *et al.*, "Children's Comprehension of Between and Within Sentence Syntactic Structure," *Journal of Educational Psychology* 61 (October 1970): 349-357.

34. John B. Carroll, Peter Davies, and Barry Richman, *The American Heritage Word Frequency Book* (Boston: Houghton Mifflin, 1971), xxxvii-xxxix.

35. Edgar Dale and Joseph O'Rourke, *The Living Word Vocabulary* (Elgin, Ill.: Dome, Inc., 1976).

36. John B. Carroll, *Comprehension by 3rd, 6th, and 9th Graders of Words Having Multiple Grammatical Functions*, Research Bulletin RB-71-19 (Princeton, N.J.: Educational Testing Service, 1971). ERIC: ED 048 311.

37. Bruce Denner, "Representational and Syntactic Competence of Problem Readers," *Child Development* 41 (September 1970): 881-887.

38. Rose-Marie Weber, "First Graders' Use of Grammatical Context in Reading," in *Basic Studies on Reading*, ed. Harry Levin and Joanna P. Williams (New York: Basic Books, 1970), 147-163.

39. Cromer, "The Difference Model"; Robert Oakan, Morton Wiener, and Ward Cromer, "Identification, Organization, and Reading Comprehension for Good and Poor Readers," *Journal of Educational Psychology* 62 (February 1971): 71-78; Rita S. Brause, "Developmental Aspects of the Ability to Understand Semantic Ambiguity, with Implications for Teachers," *Research in the Teaching of English* 11 (Spring 1977): 39-48.

40. For example, Teun A. Van Diyk, *Some Aspects of Text Grammars: A Study in Theoretical Linguistics and Poetics* (The Hague: Mouton, 1972); Joe E. Grimes, *The

Thread of Discourse (The Hague: Mouton, 1975); Carl H. Frederiksen, "Representing Logical and Semantic Structure of Knowledge Acquired from Discourse," *Cognitive Psychology* 7 (July 1975): 371-458; Walter Kintsch, *The Representation of Meaning in Memory* (Hillsdale, N.J.: Erlbaum, 1974).

41. Merle C. Wittrock, Carolyn Marks, and Marleen Doctorow, "Reading as a Generative Process," *Journal of Educational Psychology* 67 (August 1975): 484-489.

42. Chall, *Learning to Read.*

2. Controversial Issues in Beginning Reading Instruction: Meaning versus Subskill Emphasis

S. Jay Samuels and *Sumner W. Schachter*

There are numerous controversies concerning the psychology and pedagogy of reading. The more important controversies involve the existence of a hierarchy of reading subskills and the advisability of using either a holistic or subskill approach in teaching. Holistic and subskill approaches have shared a variety of other names, such as "look-say" and "phonic." With regard to these issues, John Downing has written:

Chall's chief contribution in *Learning to Read: The Great Debate* was to sift the rhetoric in the controversy between exponents of "look-say" versus "phonic" methods into logical categories. She reclassified teaching methods into "meaning emphasis" and "code emphasis" approaches, because she found that teachers and authors of reading textbooks placed more importance either on teaching children the meaningful communication aspects of written language or on the technical linguistic elements of the printed code for the spoken language.

My own studies of this aspect of reading education led me to a similar conclusion. In *Comparative Reading* I reviewed the controversies over methods of teaching reading in fourteen different countries with almost as many different languages. I found that a similar dichotomy of methods existed in every language. . . . Teachers everywhere discuss the relative merits of what I have termed "meaningful chunking" versus "atomistic decoding" methods. The meaningful chunking teachers use larger chunks of language in instruction because they believe that children learn to read through associating print with the meaning of language. The atomistic decoding teachers prefer to focus on the atoms of written language because they believe that the child needs to know how to work the code that signals the meaning of the message in printed texts. Meaningful chunking methods are concerned mainly with the communication functions of written language. Atomistic decoding methods try chiefly to teach the technical mechanics of the writing system. Why it is felt necessary to emphasize one aspect more than the other is not clear, yet this controversy continues to exist even though the rhetoric appears to change.[1]

The purpose of this chapter is to extract the strengths of each approach in relation to the reading acquisition process and to look for ways to improve reading instruction. In order to achieve this goal, we shall put the controversy between holistic and subskill methods of instruction in historical perspective and make a comparison between speech and reading acquisition. Arguments will be presented to the effect that learning hierarchies exist in reading. An examination of successful reading programs and the realities of classroom management suggest that subskill instruction is an important factor in teaching a complex skill such as reading.

HISTORICAL PERSPECTIVE

The debate in educational circles as to whether reading should be introduced more or less as a holistic process with an emphasis on meaning or whether it should be taught by means of a subskill approach is not new. Mitford Mathews documented the 2,500-year evolution of different approaches to reading that may be categorized as the holistic, subskill, and mixed methods.[2] Controversy over how to teach reading became dichotomized in the mid-1800s as debate in Europe and America centered on whether to teach by the Greek-originated ABC method or the "natural" word method.

In the alphabetic method the child learned to name letters before learning to read words. After mastering the names of letters, nonsense syllables such as *ab, ib,* and *ob* were introduced. The student first spelled each letter and then pronounced the syllable. He progressed to three-letter nonsense syllables, short words, and finally to sentences. With this method the child was required to name each letter prior to pronouncing the syllables or words. A major criticism of the method was that spelling the word before pronouncing it interfered with comprehension which led some educators to advocate a different approach.

In 1840 Josiah Bumstead commented that in the ABC method the practice of drilling the child month after month on letter names was tiresome to the student and the teacher. Two decades later Horace Mann, the well-known American educator, ridiculed the ABC spelling method. As an alternative, the whole-word method was proposed.

By 1870 the conflict seemed to be resolved in favor of the whole-word method. The method remained dominant until Rudolf Flesch published his influential work, *Why Johnny Can't Read.* In this book Flesch argued that children who were taught by the whole-word method had difficulty because of their failure to acquire word analysis skills.[3] This criticism led to a growing emphasis on phonics as a part of the initial reading method.

Looking back on the controversies in reading, we can see that during the mid-1800s the conflict was between the ABC and the whole-word approach, while in the mid-1900s the conflict was over the whole versus subskill methods. These differences regarding reading method were found in Europe also. For example, Friedrich Gedike (1754-1803), one of the most influential Prussian educators of his day, tried to bring the philosophical principle of "naturalness" to the act of reading. He felt that a book was the logical whole with which to begin instruction and that the synthetic method, that is, going from parts to the whole, was reserved for God. Man had to be content with going from the whole to its parts. Other reading methods based on the principle of wholeness and naturalness, where either the sentence or the word was used as the whole unit, were also developed in Europe. Instruction then proceeded from the larger to the smaller units.[4]

TWO VIEWS OF INSTRUCTION

The labels "holistic" and "subskill" are universal and are used to describe whole-to-part and part-to-whole conceptualizations of developmental aspects of reading. Researchers who favor either view would tend to agree that proficient reading represents a highly complex process in which subordinate units are integrated in the formation of higher-order skills. While researchers may share somewhat similar viewpoints concerning proficient reading, however, they differ in significant ways regarding the best way to instruct beginning readers.

The Holistic View

The most significant characteristic of the holistic view is that from the outset beginning instruction tends to focus on deriving meaning from the printed page. In this sense, reading and speaking are basically the same process of meaningful communication. From the start the child becomes aware that printed symbols represent meaning and are not a concatenation of meaningless sounds. The unit of instruction, therefore, becomes the word, phrase, sentence, or some unit that carries meaning.

According to Kenneth Goodman, reading can be considered a natural language process that has the potential for being learned with the same ease and speed at which speech is learned.[5] One of the reasons why speech is acquired with some degree of ease is that it fulfills the human needs of communication and of acquiring information. If the environment of reading instruction could be engineered to meet these basic communication needs, reading should also be acquired with relative ease. Regarding the sequencing of instruction, Goodman claims that "Sequencing of skill instruction in reading has often been strongly advocated by publishers and curriculum workers. But the reading process requires that a multitude of skills be used simultaneously. As we have indicated, many of these skills are already employed by the learner in listening. Any sequence will necessarily be arbitrary."[6]

Those who favor the holistic approach believe that the a priori assumption that children should be taught subskills is incorrect and may, in fact, be detrimental to the acquisition of fluent reading. It is believed that children learn to speak and listen without formal instruction and that reading—as a natural outgrowth of listening—could, under certain conditions, be learned with equal ease and proficiency. Kenneth and Yelta Goodman state: "We take as our principal premise in designing initial reading instruction that our goal is to create conditions which help all students to learn as naturally as some do."[7] And, with regard to sequencing of instruction, they write: "Our research has convinced us that the skills displayed by the proficient reader derive from the meaningful use of written language and that sequential instruction in these skills is as pointless and fruitless as instruction in the skills of a proficient listener would be to teach infants to comprehend speech."[8]

It should be pointed out that advocates of the holistic approach would teach subskills under certain conditions. These conditions would arise when the reader fails to get meaning because a particular skill is lacking. Then the instructor would teach the appropriate skill.

The Subskill View

Advocates of the subskill approach look upon proficient reading as the acquisition of a developmental skill. This means that the acquisition of highly complex skills such as reading may be viewed on a continuum that represents beginning, intermediate, and fluent levels of skill. Thus, beginning and fluent reading are viewed as quite different processes. For example, since so much of the beginning reader's attention is taken up with decoding printed symbols, meaning is not easily assessed. On the other hand, the skilled reader is able to decode printed symbols automatically, and, consequently, the limited attention capacity may be used for processing meaning. Frank Smith reflects this view:

I shall occasionally observe that life seems particularly hard for the beginning reader—so many necessary things are difficult for him at the outset that will be easier when his reading skills develop. For example, the mere fact that a child cannot read very fast puts a heavy burden on memory and attentional systems that are both inexperienced and overloaded with all kinds of instructions and rules. By the time the novice has built up enough speed to take some of the strain off his memory, many of the earlier rules have become unnecessary or overlearned and automatic, and the memory load is reduced in any case.[9]

One of the major premises of the subskill approach is that reading is not a natural language process and that learning to read requires specific instruction. Another assumption is that reading, as a complex skill, is comprised of subordinate units that must be mastered and integrated to form higher-order skills. Consequently, to accomplish this developmental task, a variety of subskills thought to be essential are taught routinely to students. The order of progression in these skills is from prerequisite smaller units to larger units.

READING AND SPEECH ACQUISITION COMPARED

Since some advocates of the holistic approach to reading emphasize the similarities between speech and reading, whereas advocates of the subskill approach look upon reading and speech acquisition as being quite different, it would be appropriate at this point to examine these counterclaims.

The development of the communication skills of speech and listening takes place over a relatively long period of time. Although they may be acquired in a naturalistic manner without formal instruction, these skills are not developed without considerable time, effort, and practice. Charles Fries has pointed out that the child has developed, and practiced, language skills for over ten thousand hours before formal reading instruction begins.[10]

It should be recognized that the early acquisition of a first language, with its speaking and listening components, is a unique human experience and is different in important ways from other kinds of learning, such as learning to read. A number of arguments support the belief that the child's learning a language involves innate, genetically determined mechanisms operating on information about the structure of language that a child acquires from listening to the speech of adults. The first argument is that linguistic universals such as phonetic systems and syntax are common to all languages. Second, historical investigations of languages reveal that, although spoken languages change, there is no evidence of human speech that can be described as aphonemic or ungrammatical. Third, specific language disability, characterized by the delayed onset of speech, poor articulation, and marked reading disability in which general intelligence remains unaffected, appears to be inherited. Fourth, the developmental schedule of language acquisition follows a fixed sequence so that even if the entire schedule is retarded, the order of attainment of linguistic skills remains constant. Fifth, comparisons of children learning non-Indo-European languages with children learning English indicate a high degree of concordance between the milestones of speech and motor development. Finally, the learning of a second language after cerebral lateralization, which is generally completed by the onset of puberty, occurs with difficulty, usually takes an extended period of time, and normally requires formal instruction. Whereas all children learn communication skills in their first language, not everyone masters these skills in a second language.[11]

Interesting comparisons can be made between the acquisition of speech and learning to read. Learning to speak is generally accomplished with little difficulty[12] whereas learning to read requires considerably more effort. According to Arthur and Carolyn Staats, although the acquisition of speech is gradual, beginning at infancy and extending for a considerable period of time, the introduction to reading is much more abrupt and less gradual.[13] Also, there are strong sources of reinforcement involved with the acquisition of speech, while in the typical classroom sources of reinforcement for reading appear to be much less forceful. The strong reinforcers involved in acquiring speech seem to be applied almost immediately following appropriate speech behaviors, but in learning to read the much weaker reinforcers are often delayed or may be nonexistent. The Staatses feel that perhaps the most important difference between acquiring speech and learning to read is that in the latter process intensive periods of concentration are required that may easily take on aversive characteristics.

To summarize the differences between speech and reading, it is indeed accurate to say that for nearly all people the acquisition of a first language appears to be easily mastered, but many people achieve literacy only with difficulty, if at all. Reading is not a behavior common to all humans, and its acquisition frequently requires the expenditure of considerable time and effort.

ROLE OF SUBSKILLS IN LEARNING

Critics of the subskill approach have claimed that sequential subskill instruction probably represents improper reading pedagogy. What justification is there, then, for any method of reading instruction that attempts a part-to-whole instructional sequence?

The research of William Bryan and Noble Harter in 1897 on learning Morse code has contributed knowledge regarding requirements for learning a complex task. They noted that in developing skill in Morse code there were plateaus in the learning curves during which practice did not lead to further improvement. Their interpretation of this finding was that in learning Morse code numerous lower-order skills had to be learned and integrated. These plateaus, they thought, indicated temporary periods devoted to learning the component skills or to organizing component skills into higher-order skills. Thus, before one became skilled in Morse code the subordinate skills had to be mastered and integrated.[14]

John Guthrie has provided additional support for the view that complex skill development requires the learning and integration of subordinate skills. He examined the intercorrelations among reading subskills for good and poor readers. With the good readers the intercorrelations among the skills were highly significant, suggesting that these readers had integrated the skills into higher-order units. With the poor readers, the intercorrelations were low, suggesting that these readers were still at the level of separate skills. Guthrie concluded that one source of disability among poor readers was the lack of subskill mastery and the lack of integration of these skills into higher-order units.[15]

Ernest Hilgard and Donald Marquis have written that most learning is complex and requires the simultaneous learning of several components.[16] A question remains about simple learning, such as associational learning: is the formation of simple associations influenced by subsystems?

Associational learning was traditionally believed to be a simple, single-stage process, but as psychologists continued to investigate its nature, they discovered that stimulus-response learning was anything but a simple, single-stage process. Research in associational learning over the past twenty-five years has revealed that there are stimulus-learning stages, response-learning stages, and associational stages. And these stages are influenced by other factors such as overt attention, perceptual learning, memory, and mediational strategies.

Thus, even the so-called simple learning tasks have their complex aspects, and fractionating a simple associational task into subskills can facilitate the learning process. For example, in an associational task such as learning the name of a letter, it appears that breaking the task into subskills facilitates learning. In S. Jay Samuels's experiment, an experimental group received visual discrimination training on noting distinctive features of letters. Following perceptual training, they learned the letter names. A control group was taught using a holistic approach; this group did not get perceptual pretraining. They were shown the letters and were told to learn their names. The experimental group that received subskill training learned in significantly fewer trials, and the savings were sufficient to make a practical difference as well.[17]

In what is now considered to be a classical study on instruction, Robert Gagné took a terminal behavior in mathematics, fractionated it into subskills that were ranked from lower-order to higher-order, and developed tests for each level. Following instruction on the mathematics skill, he tested the students and found that those who failed a lower-order task were unable to pass a test at the higher level. He then taught the unit again requiring the students to master each of the subordinate skills. All the students were able to complete the terminal task after having mastered the subordinate tasks.[18]

A number of examples from the psychomotor domain illustrate how a subskill approach can be used to facilitate the attainment of goals. To support the notion that one learns to read by reading meaningful material, Frank Smith mentioned that one learns to ride a bicycle by getting practice riding the bicycle.[19] It should be pointed out, however, that children often go through a graded series of experiences of increasing difficulty before they learn to ride a large-frame, two-wheel bicycle. They frequently practice first on a tricycle, graduate to a two-wheeler with a small frame, and practice getting their balance on the small-frame bicycle before they use the pedals on the large-frame two-wheeler. One might inquire into the most desirable method to use in teaching a child to ride a bicycle. Would it be preferable simply to place the child on a two-wheeler or to allow him to gain experience on a graded series of activities, each somewhat more difficult, before encountering the two-wheel bicycle?

There is evidence that perceptual learning also seems to follow a pattern from smaller to larger units. At one time, Gestalt psychology formed the basis for the belief that when a beginning reader encountered a word, the perceptual unit was the whole word. Contrary to this belief, however, research has indicated that children tend to select a single letter rather than the whole word as the cue for word recognition.[20] In fact, it is usually not until the tenth grade that a single eye fixation suffices to take in the whole word at once.[21]

One can find examples from perception and reading to illustrate the principle that smaller units are mastered prior to larger units. The model of perceptual learning developed by David LaBerge and S. Jay Samuels is hierarchical and suggests that the sequence of learning is from distinctive features, to letters, to letter clusters, and to words.[22] In the process of learning to recognize a letter, the student must first identify the features that comprise it. For the lower-case letters *b*, *d*, *p*, and *q*, the features are a vertical line and a circle in a particular relationship to each other; that is, the circle may be high or low and to the left or right side of the vertical line. Having identified the parts and after an extended series of exposure to the letters, the learner sees it as a unit; that is, the parts are perceptually unitized. We have recently gathered evidence at our laboratory that skilled readers appear to have perceptually unitized—or chunked—digraphs such as *th*, *ch*, and *sh*. These are not processed as *t* + *h*, *c* + *h*, or *s* + *h*, but as a single unit. Evidence gathered elsewhere indicates that units longer than the letter, such as affixes *ed* and *ing*, can become perceptually unitized. These findings from different laboratories suggest that perceptual learning seems to follow a pattern from smaller to larger units.

Additional evidence illustrates the point that subskill mastery may be essential for achieving reading fluency. Donald Shankweiler and Isabelle Liberman investigated whether the main source of difficulty in beginning reading is at the word level or at the level of reading connected text. In other words, how well could one predict a child's fluency in oral reading of paragraph material from his performance on selected words presented in tests? The average correlation was .70 between reading individual words on a list and reading connected discourse.[24] Thus, roughly 50 percent of the variability in oral reading of connected words is associated with how well one can read these words in isolation. The authors concluded: "These correlations suggest that the child may encounter his major difficulty at the level of the word — his reading of connected text tends to be only as good or poor as his reading of individual words."[25]

A similar conclusion was reached by a classroom teacher with perceptive insights into problems children have with reading who wrote:

—there has been great emphasis put on developing the child's comprehension ability. It is true that poor readers in the upper grades wrestle with comprehension problems. I have found this problem stems mainly from the student's lack of word-decoding skill. The comprehension cannot improve until the reading process becomes automatic, a development that takes place after the conscious analysis skills have been mastered. Therefore, though you want the child to understand the story he is learning to read, his ability will not be perfected until the child actually learns to read accurately.[26]

The importance of a subskill approach in reading was made by Mariam Goldberg who conducted a large-scale study of beginning reading of disadvantaged children. She observed that, while teachers may be stressing comprehension, the children were devising ways of breaking the sound-symbol code and trying to figure out what the printed material says rather than what it means.[27]

Still other investigators have discovered the importance of reading subskills. Harry Silberman reported on an experimental program used to teach beginning reading. He found that the brighter children acquired the necessary reading skill he wanted them to learn, but that the less bright seemed unable to transfer their knowledge to words not specifically taught. Classroom teachers brought in to evaluate the program discovered that a necessary subskill had been omitted. Only after that subskill had been included in the program were all the children able to master the transfer to untaught words. It is interesting to note that, even with an important subskill missing, the brighter children were able to surmount this obstacle.[28] Silberman's study suggests, therefore, that brighter children may be able to overcome an inadequate program, but the less bright have great difficulty.

Another example of how children were able to overcome an inadequate teaching program is reported by Dina Feitelson in her review of reading instruction in Israel. Prior to the 1950s, reading pedagogy in that country was dominated by an official viewpoint: the child's own interest was the major factor to consider in constructing a reading program, and it was assumed that as long as he was motivated, he would acquire the necessary reading skills. According to this viewpoint, in order to maintain motivation it was necessary for the child to read in units larger than the word, mostly in phrase units. This approach, which may be called the "holistic approach," indicated that beginning readers were not at all interested in analyzing words into their component parts. Teaching letter-sound correspondences was not an acceptable practice at that time. Feitelson said that, until the 1950s, this way of teaching reading was widely used, and the results, in general, were satisfactory.[29]

Subsequent to the 1950s, there was large-scale immigration from Arab countries, and schools began to report rates of failure of 50 percent at the end of first grade. It would have been easy enough to attribute the cause of failure to the influx of a foreign group into Israel. A study was made, however, to determine the possible causes of failure. One of the more startling findings emerging from this study was that failure to acquire reading was not evenly dispersed. An entire classroom would either be successful in acquiring reading skills or unsuccessful. Successful classrooms were found to have teachers who did not use a holistic approach and who devoted much time to systematic phonics drills and to the breaking of words into smaller components. A second finding of interest was that parents were very helpful in overcoming the harmful effects of the holistic approach by teaching phonics themselves. Thus, what the child was not offered in school, the parents were teaching at home. Whereas many teachers taught in holistic units, at home the parents were drilling the children on the components of words so that the children could attack new words based on letter-sound correspondences and blending.[30] In Israel, then, we find that an inadequate program was overcome by the teaching of essential decoding skills.

Before concluding this section, we wish to describe two laboratory studies that investigated a problem of some importance to reading. This problem concerned the type of initial training in reading— phonics versus the whole-word approach—that provides the best basis for transfer to reading new words. One of the studies used children who were nonreaders,[31] and the other utilized adults who had to employ an artificial alphabet in reading.[32] Both studies came to the same conclusion: that specific training on letter-sound correspondences was superior to whole-word training for transfer to recognizing new words.

This section on the role of subskills in learning has examined complex cognitive skills, such as learning telegraphy and transfer tasks in reading, and "simple" cognitive tasks, such as associational learning of letter names, perceptual learning, and psychomotor learning. Psychologists have discovered that these tasks are comprised of lower-order skills, that mastery of higher-order skills may be contingent on mastery of lower-order skills, and that successful attainment of the final task may be facilitated by helping the student to master the lower-order units.

PRAGMATIC CONCERNS

Thus far, this chapter has focused upon two views of the reading process, and, as mentioned earlier, the discussion has been theoretically oriented. We are interested, however, in finding ways to improve instruction in reading. One may raise the question as to the existence of exemplary reading programs and their characteristics. Information on successful programs was provided by the American Institutes for Research (AIR),[33] George Weber,[34] the New York State Office of Education,[35] and the CRAFT Project.[36]

The above reports, which identified outstanding reading programs, shared a common assumption: that a good reading program is more than a method; it is a system with individual elements to which there is an order and with interdependent components contributing to the whole of the system. These components, which were examined for overlap among successful programs, included needs, objectives, staff-

ing, costs and budget, management, facilities, participants' characteristics, and procedures for evaluation. It is important to keep these
components in mind as the programs are discussed and to realize that
each program does not excel in all the various components.

Seven programs selected by the AIR had as their primary concern
the initial teaching of reading in elementary school settings. Although
representing different geographical areas and school populations, the
programs appeared to share several common elements. Eight components appeared to account for the common success of a number of
programs: academic objectives that were clearly stated, that were
broken into smaller units, and that gave evidence of careful planning;
teacher training in the methods of the program; small group or individualized instruction; highly structured teaching directly relevant to
the objectives; high intensity of treatment; active parental involvement; utilization of additional reading personnel; and some sort of
continuous assessment, providing both feedback and diagnostic information.[37]

Weber studied successful reading achievement in four inner-city
ghetto schools. Although he acknowledged that nonschool factors can
contribute to success or failure in beginning reading, he argued that a
great difference in reaching achievement can result from the school's
effectiveness in teaching beginning reading. Weber found that forceful leadership, a pleasant and happy atmosphere, a strong emphasis
on reading, additional reading personnel, use of a phonics subskill approach, individualization, and careful evaluation of pupils' progress
contributed to successful reading programs. He believed that the attitude and approaches of the faculty, combined with a purposeful and
pleasurable learning environment and a well-structured reading program, were responsible for improved reading achievement in these
four inner-city ghetto schools.

The New York State Office of Education Performance Review identified at least four factors under the control of the schools that contributed to a successful reading program. They were effective use of
reading time, much positive reinforcement, extensive evaluations of
pupils, and high expectations.[39]

Investigations of the CRAFT Project indicated that efficient use of
time in reading instruction may be a relevant factor in successful programs. Thus, when a considerable amount of time was spent on activities that required little or no reading, the effect on reading achievement tended to be unfavorable; the amount of time spent in actual

reading activities was positively correlated with achievement for all methods.[40] This study suggests that neither the method used nor the amount of time allocated on the class schedule was related to achievement, but the time spent in actual reading activities was related to achievement.

From the studies investigated in this chapter, we must now attempt to distill the characteristics that appear to contribute to success in reading programs. Perhaps, at the risk of overgeneralizing, one may draw some tentative conclusions. At the organizational level, the evidence points to a district that has strong administrative leadership, cooperation, and involvement of staff in planning a coordinated reading program. An expectation of success permeates the educational enterprise. Further, the successful district is one in which fiscal resources are predominantly invested in personnel rather than facilities: pupil-teacher ratios are acceptable; aides assist in individualized instruction; and there is often a reading specialist or program coordinator.

At the instructional level, the variables may not be as neatly defined as one might wish, and it is clear that no one method of reading instruction is consistently superior. Certain characteristics of instruction are important, however: the successful programs break the reading task into subskills or units that are specifically sequenced; and the student moves through these units at an individual pace and must attain mastery of each before going on to the next. The continuous feedback resulting from such a system reinforces the student and provides a diagnostic aid for the instructor.

PRACTICAL IMPLICATIONS FOR READING INSTRUCTION

The current debate concerning the holistic versus the subskill approach may be somewhat overdrawn and may have established a false dichotomy, especially if one realizes that many teachers are eclectic in their approach to reading instruction. Furthermore, despite the claims of some teachers regarding their adherence to a particular approach to reading, there may be a significant gap between what they say and what they do.

Our problem may be reduced to one of focus, emphasis, and sequence. Regardless of which size unit one uses for beginning reading, one must also include units at the other end of the scale.

As Richard Venezky points out: "almost all methods for teaching

reading include letter-sound learning somewhere in the teaching sequence, although the amount and exact placement of this training account for the central disagreement between methods."[41] This view was
expressed in an article by Harry Singer, S. Jay Samuels, and Jean
Spiroff, who state: "While this study has demonstrated that for the
purpose of teaching children to identify a word it is best to present that
word in isolation . . . the child [also] needs to get ample practice
reading meaningful and interesting material in context so that he will
develop strategies for using semantic and syntactic constraints in
passages as aids in word identification."[42]

A major point made by critics of the subskill approach is that fractionating the reading process interferes with the essential characteristic of reading, which is comprehension. This point is well taken. Many
teachers who use the subskill approach have lost sight of the fact that
the approach is simply a means to an end. In many classrooms there
has been a displacement of goals, and the means have become ends. In
the subskill approach, care must be taken to prevent the subskills from
becoming the focal point of instruction. Once again, perhaps, the
point should be made that it is important for the child to get ample
practice reading meaningful and interesting material in context.

We agree with the critics of the subskill approach that too much
emphasis can be placed on these subordinate skills. The critics probably are in error, however, in failing to recognize the importance of
subskills in the developmental sequence of skill attainment. Just because fluent readers are able to determine the meaning on a printed
page is no reason to believe that beginning readers can do the same or
that we can transfer the sophisticated strategies of the fluent reader to
the beginning reader. Downing shares this view: "It seems quite unlikely that the learning-to-read process is directly derivable from the
behavior observed in a fluent reader as is assumed in the theories of
Smith and Goodman."[43]

Both the advocates of holistic and subskill approaches recognize
that reading is comprised of subordinate skills. There is a problem,
however, concerning who determines which subskills should be taught
and when they should be introduced. According to one school of
thought, when the student encounters a problem, the teacher should
analyze the nature of the difficulty and remedy it. This approach
places the teacher in the role of a troubleshooter. Thus, the particular
subskills that are taught are determined by the student, that is, by an

analysis of the student's weaknesses, and the skills are introduced after the problem is uncovered. According to the other school of thought, certain subskills must be mastered in the reading acquisition process, and these skills can be taught routinely before the student shows signs of having a problem. Thus, with this approach, it is the teacher or curriculum expert who determines a priori which skills are to be taught and when.

Many critics of the subskill approach suggest that meaningful reading material should be given to a child and that subskills should be taught when the student asks for help or shows evidence of needing particular skills. The shortcomings of this approach become obvious when one realizes the logistical and managerial problems facing the teacher with a large number of students. With regard to this last point, it is important to realize that many students do not know what kind of help to request, and a good number of teachers are not sufficiently trained to pinpoint the cause of the student's difficulty. Even when the teacher is able to diagnose accurately the cause of the problem, the managerial problems of providing individual help are so large as to make the system difficult to operate, if not unworkable. It would seem more manageable to assume on a priori grounds that beginning readers require certain subskills, which would be taught routinely to students. For those students who fail to master these skills, additional time could be allocated, and different methods could be tried.

We made the point earlier in this chapter that the adverse relationship between holistic and subskill approaches may not exist. Both approaches recognize there are subskills. Subskill approaches start with smaller units and move to larger and more complex units. The holistic approach, on the other hand, begins with the larger unit and moves to smaller units. Thus, one of the important factors differentiating the two approaches is that of sequencing. In considering this factor, we must think about which tasks and which unit size one would use to start instruction and how one would program the sequence of skills to be taught as the student progresses in skill. Another similarity between the two approaches is that both recognize the importance of diagnosis of difficulty in reading and the need to remedy the problem. The subskill approach, however, attempts to reduce the number of students who will experience difficulties in reading by teaching the prerequisite skills before a problem appears.

In summary, we must keep in mind that reading is a developmental skill, and, while the goal of reading is to acquire meaning, there are certain prerequisites. One important prerequisite is the development of decoding skills. These skills must be brought beyond the level of mere accuracy to the level of automaticity. When these skills become automatic, the student is able to decode the printed symbols without the aid of attention, thereby freeing attention for the all-important task of processing meaning.

NOTES

1. John Downing, "The Child's Understanding of the Function and Processes of Communication," unpublished paper, University of Victoria, Canada, 1977, 25-26.

2. Mitford M. Mathews, *Teaching to Read: Historically Considered* (Chicago: University of Chicago Press, 1966).

3. Rudolf Flesch, *Why Johnny Can't Read and What You Can Do About It* (New York: Harper and Row, 1955).

4. Mathews, *Teaching to Read,* 37-43.

5. Kenneth A. Goodman, "Acquiring Literacy Is Natural: Who Skilled Cock Robin," paper presented at Sixth World Reading Congress, Singapore, August 1976.

6. Kenneth A. Goodman, "Behind the Eye: What Happens in Reading," in *Theoretical Models and Processes in Reading,* ed. Harry Singer and Robert Ruddell, 2d ed. (Newark, Del.: International Reading Association, 1976), 494.

7. Kenneth A. Goodman and Yelta Goodman, "Learning to Read Is Natural," paper presented at Conference on Theory and Practice of Beginning Reading Instruction, Pittsburgh, April 1976, 21.

8. *Ibid.*

9. Frank Smith, *Understanding Reading: A Psycholinguistic Analysis of Reading and Learning to Read* (New York: Holt, Rinehart, and Winston, 1971), 3.

10. Charles C. Fries, *Linguistics and Reading* (New York: Holt, Rinehart, and Winston, 1963).

11. Eric H. Lenneberg, *Biological Foundations of Language* (New York: John Wiley and Sons, 1967), 125-187.

12. William N. Dember and James Jenkins, *General Psychology: Modeling Behavior and Experience* (Englewood Cliffs, N.J.: Prentice-Hall, 1970).

13. Arthur W. Staats and Carolyn K. Staats, *Complex Human Behavior* (New York: Holt, Rinehart, and Winston, 1963).

14. William L. Bryan and Noble Harter, "Studies in the Physiology and Psychology of the Telegraphic Language," *Psychological Review* 4 (January 1897): 27-53.

15. John T. Guthrie, "Models of Reading and Reading Disability," *Journal of Educational Psychology* 65 (August 1973): 9-18.

16. Ernest R. Hilgard and Donald G. Marquis, *Conditioning and Learning,* 2d ed. (New York: Appleton-Century-Crofts, 1961).

17. S. Jay Samuels, "Effect of Distinctive Feature Training on Paired Associate Learning," *Journal of Educational Psychology* 64 (April 1973): 164-170.

18. Robert M. Gagné, "The Acquisition of Knowledge," *Psychological Review* 69 (No. 4, 1962): 355-365.

19. Frank Smith, *Psycholinguistics and Reading* (New York: Holt, Rinehart, and Winston, 1973).

20. Gabrielle Marchbanks and Harry Levin, "Cues by Which Children Recognize Words," *Journal of Educational Psychology* 56 (April 1965): 57-62; S. Jay Samuels and Wendell F. Jeffrey, "Discriminability of Words, and Letter Cues Used in Learning to Read," *ibid.*, 57 (December 1966): 337-340.

21. Stan E. Taylor, Helen Frackenpohl, and J. L. Pettee, *Grade Level Norms for the Components of the Fundamental Reading Skill* (Huntington, N.Y.: Educational Developmental Laboratories, Inc., 1960).

22. David LaBerge and S. Jay Samuels, "Toward a Theory of Automatic Information Processing in Reading," *Cognitive Psychology* 6 (April 1974): 293-323.

23. Eleanor J. Gibson and Lynne Guinet, "The Perception of Inflections in Brief Visual Presentations of Words," *Journal of Verbal Learning and Verbal Behavior* 10 (April 1971): 182-189.

24. Donald Shankweiler and Isabelle Y. Liberman, "Misreading: A Search for Causes," in *Language by Ear and by Eye*, ed. J.F. Kavanagh and Ignatius G. Mattingly (Cambridge, Mass.: M.I.T. Press, 1972), 293-317.

25. *Ibid.*, 298.

26. Harold Stevenson, *The Natural Way to Reading: A How-to Method for Parents of Slow Learners, Dyslexic, and Learning Disabled Children* (Boston: Little, Brown, 1974), 20.

27. Mariam L. Goldberg, *The Effects of Various Approaches to Beginning Reading*, Final Report, Beginning Reading Project (New York: Teachers College, Columbia University, 1973).

28. Harry F. Silberman, *Exploratory Research in a Beginning Reading Program* (Santa Monica, Calif.: System Development Corp., 1964), 430-432.

29. Dina Feitelson, "Israel," in *Comparative Reading*, ed. John Downing (New York: Macmillan, 1973).

30. *Ibid.*, 432-433.

31. Wendel E. Jeffrey and S. Jay Samuels, "Effect of Method of Reading Training on Initial Learning and Transfer," *Journal of Verbal Learning and Verbal Behavior* 6 (June 1967): 354-358.

32. Carol N. Bishop, "Transfer Effects of Word and Letter Training in Reading," *ibid.*, 3 (June 1964): 215-221.

33. John E. Bowers et al., *Final Report Identifying, Validating, and Multi-Media Packaging of Effective Reading Programs* (Palo Alto, Calif.: American Institutes for Research, 1974).

34. George Weber, *Inner-City Children Can Be Taught to Read: Four Successful Schools* (Washington, D.C.: Council for Basic Education, 1971).

35. New York State Office of Education, *School Factors Influencing Reading Achievement: A Performance Review* (Albany: New York State Office of Education, 1974).

36. Albert J. Harris and Bernice L. Serwer, "The CRAFT Project: Instructional Time in Reading Research," *Reading Research Quarterly* 2 (Fall 1966): 27-56.

37. Bowers *et al.*, *Final Report*.

38. Weber, *Inner-City Children Can Be Taught to Read*.

39. New York State Office of Education, *School Factors Influencing Reading Achievement*.

40. Harris and Serwer, "The CRAFT Project."

41. Richard Venezky, *Language and Cognition in Reading*, Technical Report No. 188, University of Wisconsin-Madison (Washington, D.C.: U.S. Office of Education, 1972), 19.

42. Harry Singer, S. Jay Samuels, and Jean Spiroff, "Effects of Pictures and Contextual Conditions on Learning to Read," *Reading Research Quarterly* 9 (No. 4, 1974): 566.

43. Downing, "The Child's Understanding of the Function and Processes of Communication," 33.

3. Models of Reading: What Are the Implications for Instruction in Comprehension?

Michael L. Kamil

Improvements in reading instruction require documented research grounded in rigorous theory. This has not always been true of attempted improvements. It is fortunate, however, that relatively new reading models provide appropriate bases for the formation and testing of instructional questions on comprehension. The purpose of this chapter is to show how instructional questions about comprehension can be derived and answered according to various models of reading.

There has recently been an increased interest in the explanation of underlying processes in education in contrast to earlier interest in the description of processes. Out of explanatory search have come different theories and models of reading behavior,[1] but, unfortunately, distinctions between models and theories have become blurred. Thus, before the models and their implications for instruction in comprehension are presented, it is important to focus on some of the differences between theories and models.

Ernest Nagel lists three major components of a theory: "an abstract calculus that is the logical skeleton of the explanatory system, and that 'implicitly defines' the basic notions of the system, a set of rules that in effect assigns an empirical content to the abstract calculus by relating it to the concrete materials of observation and experiment, and an in-

Several colleagues provided helpful assistance during the preparation of this chapter. I would like to thank Anna Sanford, Raymond G. Hanson, Alden J. Moe, and Mary Beth Marr for reading and commenting on draft versions of this work.

terpretation or model for the abstract calculus which supplies some flesh for the skeleton structure in terms of more or less familiar conceptual or visualizable materials."[2]

A model is typically a part of or adjunct to a theory. Roy Lachman has distinguished four roles for models:[3]

1. "Representational." This function generally provides a means for talking about or conceiving the basic data (and interrelationships) that underly the model. It is important here to remember that this is an analogical usage. The models are not believed to be direct representations, but they are to be taken as *similar* representations.

2. "Inferential." Lachman states that the rules by which predictions are made from a theory are another function of models. The most common type of inferential model is the mathematical model. The rules of inference used in the original domain from which the model is taken are to be used in the new context. For mathematical models, the rules of inference are the rules of mathematical calculus and logic.

3. "Interpretational." Theoretical terms and definition must be linked to observational data. Models often serve this function by showing how to apply the theory. A theory may be explained and tested in terms of the model.

4. "Visualization." Lachman indicates that this may be the most common of modular functions. A familiar example is that of atomic elements consisting of nuclei and particles orbiting around them. In psychology, the "lavatory cistern" model of Donald Broadbent[4] to account for attention processes fulfills this visualizing function rather graphically.

What is most salient about the four functions listed by Lachman is that they do not involve explanation—a task reserved for theories. Theories are testable; models are the vehicles for verification. It is also important to note that there may be many models that can be applied to the same theory or set of data.[5] To help evaluate alternative models, Lachman lists three criteria:

1. *Deployability*—Can the model be brought to bear on the theoretical phenomena?

2. *Scope*—Does the model cover *all* the theoretical phenomena?

3. *Precision*—Is the model specific with regard to the theoretical phenomena?[6]

A fourth criterion should be added; it is usually known as Occam's razor. That is, all things being equal, a simpler model is to be preferred to a more complex one.

A major deficit in research on teaching has been a lack of a widely supported theory of instruction in spite of a few recent attempts to develop theory.[7] Interest in systematic instructional psychology is a relatively recent phenomenon and is necessary for instructional theory building.[8] Support from instructional psychology has been critical, but has not led to wide acceptance of the new theories, which remain unfamiliar to practitioners. This situation is unfortunate because theory of instruction is prerequisite (logically, if not actually) for asking meaningful questions about instruction and teaching.

The theory of instruction proposed in this chapter is based on an assumption that a single theory of instruction is sufficient for model building required in each content area, and, with an appropriate theory of instruction, a model of a content area (such as reading) will answer questions about teaching and learning in that area. Most of the production of models in education has been in reading.

In this chapter an attempt is made to show how models of reading can be used to generate questions and answers about instruction in comprehension. Because it is not always possible to separate decoding from comprehension, the discussion will refer to both word recognition and comprehension. Following is the general plan for the remainder of the chapter. First, it will present a preliminary theory of instruction. Second, it will generate instructional questions based on the theory of instruction. Third, it will describe several models of reading. Fourth, it will compare and contrast the models with regard to the ways in which the questions are answered. Of specific interest will be the emphasis on comprehension, even though word recognition skills cannot be ignored. Finally, it will discuss some residual concerns about comprehension that are not specifically dealt with elsewhere.

A PRELIMINARY THEORY OF INSTRUCTION

As noted earlier, there have been only a few attempts to generate theories of instruction. The proposed theory is not meant to be taken as a better example or a more refined product than others; rather, it is designed to show how a theory and a model for the theory can be coordinated to generate (and sometimes answer) questions about instruction. In this particular instance, the major focus is on comprehension processes in reading. To the extent that it is an adequate theory of instruction, however, it will work for any content area. It is only required that an appropriate model for the content area be found to instantiate the abstract constructs of the theory and to generate instructional questions. The theory will be specified by definition, boundary conditions on the definitions, and evaluation procedures for the theoretical constructs.

Definitions

Definitions are the basic elements of a theory. They are not testable. They are, rather, assumptions that will take on substance in the context of the entire theory.

1. *Learning is cognitive restructuring.* This definition presupposes the existence of cognitive structures; it does not specify the form of those structures. A model will be used to dictate what the structures are and how they can be changed. Implicit in this definition is a corollary: if no restructuring takes place, no learning has occurred. This definition is then typically referred to as practice.

2. *Instruction is arranging the environment so that learning can occur.* The major implication of this definition is that instruction must be observable. (Observability, as used here, refers to a strict sense of *potential* observability.) Some aspect of the environment *must* be changed in order for instruction to occur. If no environmental change takes place, instruction is not taking place. It is not implied, however, that learning must take place if instruction occurs. The two are not reflexively related.

3. *Performance is observable behavior.* Performance is different from learning since performance is observable, and learning is not. Performance may be used, however, to infer learning. That is, learning is a hypothetical construct that can be used to account for changes in performance.

Boundary Conditions

Boundary conditions are the limits within which definitions of the theory function. Thus, boundary conditions limit the scope of the very general definitions. As with definitions, boundary conditions are not testable. They are meant to clarify the definitions.

1. *Changes in performance do not always reflect learning.* The literature of learning research is filled with examples of differences between learning and performance. Such phenomena as spontaneous recovery, where high performance levels are seen after rest periods, would suggest that some other factors may mask true learning. There could be any number of other reasons for changes in performance that

do not reflect learning, for example, inattention, reminiscence, and even "luck."

2. *Instruction does not have to result in learning or changes in performance.* Perhaps the most obvious condition in which this boundary condition holds true is when the environment is restructured irrelevantly. That is, instruction may be given that is irrelevant to the desired outcome. It may also be the case that ceiling effects could prevent learning or changes in performance. Thus, instruction may result in a previously learned skill. Performance might be limited by some physical or physiological limits on abilities. There is also the possibility that the instruction may be developmentally inappropriate or faulty in one of a large number of other ways.

3. *Learning can take place in the absence of directed instruction.* This boundary condition is meant to account for the situations in which learning is self-directed or is indirect. To be specific, the environment can be manipulated in any of a number of ways for learning to take place. When someone else arranges the environment, it is called teaching. When the environment is arranged by oneself, the process may be called studying or exploration. Discovery learning (or instruction that uses discovery learning) may involve indirect instruction.

Evaluation Procedures

Specification of evaluation procedures is necessary in a theory to limit the scope of testing procedures. That is, evaluation procedures will limit the domain of evidence that can be brought to bear on the theory. Thus, the specification of evaluation procedures further clarifies the definitions and boundary conditions.

1. *Evaluation procedures are dictated by the distinction between learning and performance.* Evaluation must always deal first with performance and is accomplished by using converging operations. In short, if enough care is used in measuring performance, statements *can* be made about learning.

2. *Successful instruction is measured by the change in a learner from a naive state to a learned state.* To determine whether instruction has been successful, it is necessary that a full description of both the naive and learned states be available, though an individual probably is never totally naive with regard to a specific skill.[9] Also required here are evaluation techniques appropriate to the kind of change expected. To state the matter simply, global instruction can be mea-

sured by global evaluation techniques; specific short instruction will require finer grained measures. Finally, it is important to note that memory (and forgetting) play key roles in learning. While this is a boundary condition on learning, it is most apparent in measuring performance.

QUESTIONS ABOUT INSTRUCTION DERIVED FROM THEORY OF INSTRUCTION

The preliminary theory of instruction is not complete or final, but is intended to illustrate how instructional questions should be derived. That is, the definitions must be made clear and used inferentially to generate hypotheses (questions) that are testable. Research efforts require that questions be solidly based. Answers can then be clearly communicated to practitioners. The theory must be used in conjunction with a model of the specific content of instruction to provide the concrete materials for research. It is likely that many content areas will have similar models and thus similar teaching strategies. Such overlap in instructional methodology is not, however, a requirement in the systematic development of theory; it is one very likely possibility.

1. *What is restructured?* Since learning is cognitive restructuring, the first question a model must answer is: what are the basic units that instruction must deal with? Cognitive psychology provides a rather long list of possibilities, all of which have documented histories. For example, the units might be schemata,[10] networks of associations,[11] lists, [12] gestalten,[13] or processes.[14]

2. *What should the content of instruction be?* Here, again, the model must clarify a number of specific areas before instruction can be arranged. For example, the model must specify whether the content area is made up of component skills or processes, that is, whether the skills are hierarchically, sequentially, or randomly related. (See Chapter 2 of the present volume.)

3. *What should be the format of instruction?* Specific issues are, for example, whether learning should be inductive or deductive, the amount of practice and repetition that are necessary, and, the types of motivation and reinforcement. Most of these questions will be answered by the model for the content, but some may be dictated by external concerns (for example, the purpose of the instruction in the case of inductive versus deductive).

4. *When should instruction be given?* Two major issues should be addressed in this context: developmental consideration and sequencing of the subject matter. The content model will once more be able to dictate appropriate practices for instruction.

5. *How should instruction be evaluated?* The theory has determined that performance must be evaluated and that learning can be inferred. The content model will specify the skills of processes to be measured and assign relative importance to them. Further, the distinction between aptitude and achievement will rest on those specifications.

6. *Miscellaneous questions.* In the interest of showing how the theory will have to be expanded to provide *complete* explanation of instruction, there are at least a few other questions that will have to be dealt with. *What is the role of individual differences in instruction?* Individual differences will include such phenomena as differences in learning rate, learning style, and disabilities and remediation. *What is the role of social dynamics in instruction?* Urie Bronfenbrenner has cogently pointed out the need to make ecological validity a focus in research.[15] For similar reasons the social dynamics in a classroom (or other instructional setting) cannot be overlooked.

MODELS OF READING

Four models of reading are presented in this section. The models were chosen from a large number of reading models because they represent differences in emphasis. Extensive discussions of some of these and others can be found in several sources.[16] No attempt is made to evaluate the models since that has been done elsewhere.[17] The intent of this discussion is not to elaborate a complete or "final" model but to show how different models provide different answers to instructional questions about comprehension. Reading models should not exist in a vacuum, insulated from practice on the one hand and divorced from theory and data on the other.

Most of these models can be described as either "top-down" or "bottom-up" models,[18] designations that refer to the initiation of the reading process. If the act of reading is initiated by the visual (printed) stimuli, the processing is referred to as "bottom-up." When a reader generates hypotheses to be verified by the printed material, the term "top-down" is applied. These are not necessarily mutually exclusive processes.

The Gough Model

Philip Gough proposes a serial model with a set of linear, independent stages of processing.[19] In Lachman's terms, Gough's model fulfills the role of visualization. It is represented in Figure 3-1.

In this model, reading proceeds letter by letter to word formation and then to phonemic representations. Since the processing stages are assumed to be serial, no stage can be bypassed. Lexical units are grouped into sentential forms to be interpreted by Merlin, the magical processor of syntactic and semantic information. Interpreted sentences are stored in TPWSGWTAU (The Place Where Sentences Go When They Are Understood).

Most of Gough's discussion focuses on word recognition and subsequent lexical interpretation. Higher-level comprehension processes are not discussed at length, but are assigned to vaguely defined processors like Merlin and TPWSGWTAU. Gough's contention is that those processors are not well defined outside the reading process so as to be useful (at present levels of knowledge) in reading models. Gough suggests that as these processes become more sharply delineated by research they can be incorporated in the model.

This model is almost prototypical of the "bottom-up" variety since Gough specifically rejects "top-down" processing; that is, he does not believe that readers can use guessing strategies to facilitate reading. The remainder of Gough's model deals with the production of a vocalized reading response, which will not be considered in this chapter.

The LaBerge and Samuels Model

The model of David LaBerge and S. Jay Samuels is the first of the reading models to use the concept of automaticity.[20] (It should be noted that LaBerge and Samuels write about a *theory* of automaticity, not a model.) Automaticity theory assumes that reading is divided into two general skills: word recognition or decoding and comprehension.

It is further assumed that attention is required to perform either skill. Moreover, only a limited (and fixed) amount of attention is available to be allocated for these processes. Until decoding is "automated" (that is, until it requires little or no attention), comprehension suffers. As decoding comes to require less attention, more attention can be diverted to comprehension processes.

A representation of the model is given in Figure 3-2. There are three

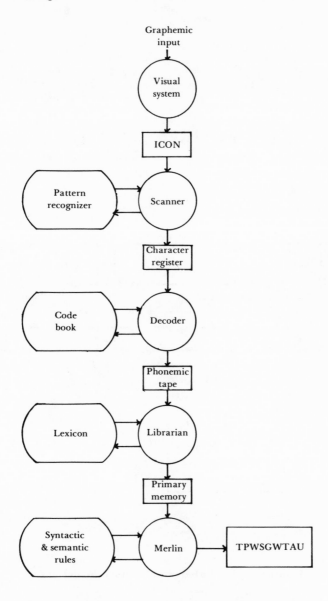

Figure 3-1. The Gough Model (1972)

Source: Philip B. Gough, "One Second of Reading," in *Language by Ear and by Eye,* ed. James F. Kavanagh and Ignatius G. Mattingly (Cambridge, Mass.: MIT Press, 1972), 345. Reprinted with permission.

Key:

VM	Visual Memory	sp	spelling pattern code
PM	Phonological Memory	v(w)	visual word code
RS	Response System	p(sp)	phonological spelling pattern code
EM	Episodic Memory	p(w)	phonological word code
		r(w)	response word code
		r(s)	response syllable code
		e	temporal spatial event code
		c	episodic code

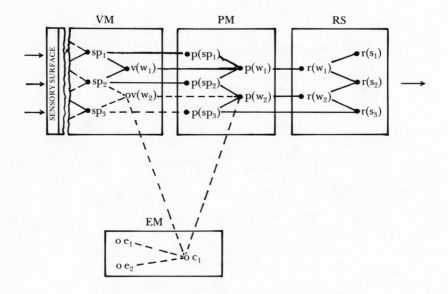

Figure 3-2. The LaBerge and Samuels Model (1974)

Source: David LaBerge and S. Jay Samuels, "Toward a Theory of Automatic Information Processing in Reading," *Cognitive Psychology* 6 (April 1974): 305. Reprinted with permission.

stages that are strictly relevant to reading: visual feature detectors and recognizers; phonological interpreters; and semantic interpreters. In each stage, units are processed singly or in common groups or clusters.

Some stages can be bypassed, even though the model is conceived as linear and hierarchical. For example, word patterns do not have to be phonologically interpreted in order to be assigned meanings. Such meanings might be assigned from episodic memory as indicated in Figure 3-2.

This model is also of the "bottom-up" variety. It assumes that *all* reading must be initiated by a visual input and terminated by a semantic interpretation (or some other response based on that semantic interpretation). David Rumelhart has pointed out, however, that this model is not as strictly "bottom-up" as that proposed by Gough.[21] The possibility of bypassing some of the processing stages prevents the LaBerge and Samuels model from being a fully serial model. It is not, however, a model that has "top-down" capabilities.

The Goodman Model

Kenneth Goodman's model is actually included only as a comparison or reference point.[22] It consists of three "proficiency levels," roughly corresponding to skill levels of readers. Goodman maintains that at the highest level of proficiency the focus is always on meaning, decoding is "automatic," and reading is structured by oral language. A representation of each of the three levels is given in Figure 3-3.

In this extreme form, Goodman's model is almost a strict "top-down" process. There is very little cue usage from the graphic input. The actual processes underlying decoding to meaning are not specified, but it is assumed that they are the same as or similar to those in oral language.

The Rumelhart Model

David Rumelhart has generated a computer-based model utilizing what he terms "interactive stages."[23] A schematic representation is given in Figure 3-4. What is unique about Rumelhart's model is its provisions for "top-down" as well as "bottom-up" processing. Reading can proceed in either fashion or both. A reader could begin with graphemic input to guide the extraction of meaning, or, alternatively, he could assume features and proceed to meaning (hypotheses) first, moving to verification of features and word patterns later.

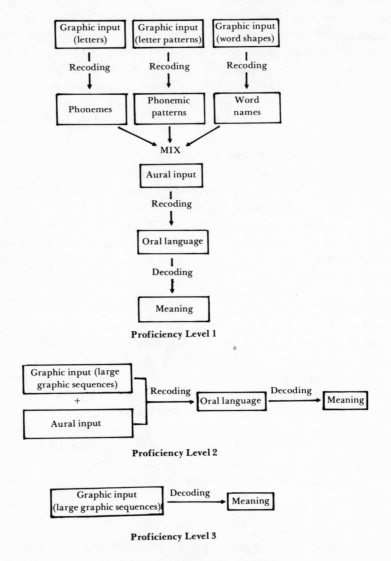

Proficiency Level 1

Proficiency Level 2

Proficiency Level 3

Figure 3-3. The Goodman Model

Source: Kenneth S. Goodman, *The Psycholinguistic Nature of the Reading Process* (Detroit, Mich.: Wayne State University Press, 1968), 17-19. Reprinted with permission. Professor Goodman has noted that his current views of the reading process are best represented in "The Reading Process," in *Language and Reading: Sixth Western Symposium on Learning,* ed. Sandra S. Smiley and John C. Towner (Bellingham, Wash.: Western Washington State College, 1975), 19-28.

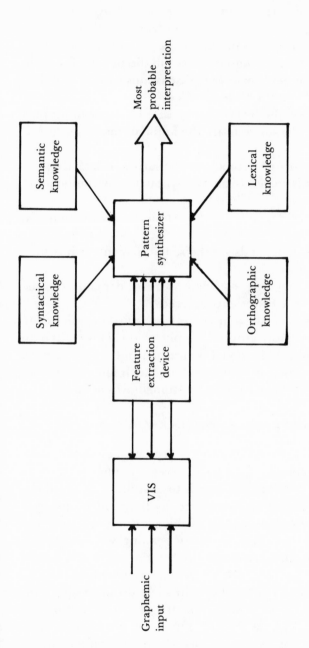

Figure 3-4. The Rumelhart Model

Source: David E. Rumelhart, *Toward an Interactive Model of Reading* (San Diego: Center for Human Information Processing, University of California at San Diego, 1976).

In addition to the interactive nature of the processing stages, it is assumed that processing of text is done in parallel rather than serially. The final important feature of Rumelhart's model is that the units of meaning are fully specified as schemata.[24] A full discussion of schema theory is not appropriate here; extensive discussions can be found in Rumelhart and Ortony[25] and in Anderson.[26]

For Rumelhart's model, the interactive nature of the reading process is illustrated by what he suggests are the foundations of his model. He believes:

1. Perception of letters often depends on the surrounding letters.

2. Perception of words depends on the syntactic environments in which they are encountered.

3. Perception of words depends on the semantic environments in which they are encountered.

4. Perception of snytax depends on the semantic context in which word strings are encountered.

5. Interpretation of meaning of what is read depends on the general context in which the text is encountered.

These statements demonstrate that there is *very* little emphasis on "pure" word recognition. More emphasis is placed on *context* than on the isolated visual stimuli. This model is flexible, but, consequently, less precise in some regards than other models. Much interest in comprehension processes has been generated by Rumelhart's model.

INSTRUCTIONAL ISSUES ADDRESSED IN READING MODELS

At this point, an instructional theory has been proposed and questions derived from the theory delineated. Several models of reading have also been presented. What remains is to examine how the questions derived from the theory are answered by the models. Because none of the models is definitive, not all of the questions are answered by all of the models. A "perfect" model of reading will, of course, answer all instructional questions, but further research (and model making) will be necessary before such a model is developed.

One caution is in order. Highly skilled readers do not require instruction. When questions of instruction are at issue, it must be remembered that not all of the models represent what occurs with nonskilled or less proficient readers. Thus, the discussion and interpretations given below involve a certain amount of license.

Subskill and Holistic Approaches

Gough's model clearly assumes that reading is composed of subskills, Figure 3-1 reveals the nature of those skills. LaBerge and Samuels make the same assumption. In fact, this issue is treated in detail by Samuels and Schachter in the present volume (see Chapter 2). They point out that this may be a false issue. Goodman, however, clearly emphasizes the holistic nature of the reading process. At proficiency level 3, no subskills are discernible. Rumelhart's position is that the skills are at best interactive. This can be taken to mean that reading can be *either* a component skill or holistic process.

There is some empirical evidence that both approaches have to be taught. Rebecca Barr has evidence that suggests that training in component skills (code emphasis) does not automatically transfer to holistic processing (meaning emphasis).[27] She indicates that transfer skills need to be taught specifically.

Decoding and Comprehension

Gough's solution to the problem of decoding and comprehension is, again, clear. He assumes that it is most important to emphasize word recognition skills (decoding) before comprehension. This is true of all "bottom-up" models. Thus, LaBerge and Samuels also emphasize decoding for beginning instruction; comprehension only becomes important when decoding skills are automatic. Goodman emphasizes the priority of comprehension, even for beginning readers. His model stresses the importance of always extracting meaning. Rumelhart presumably emphasizes both decoding and comprehension as interactive processes.

Sequence of Skills

Again, both the Gough and the LaBerge and Samuels models specify sequencing of skills. Gough assumes the skills are linear; LaBerge and Samuels assume they are hierarchical. LaBerge and Samuels prescribe intensive practice in word recognition before any instruction in comprehension.

The other two models stress comprehension, with Goodman placing most emphasis on those processes. He suggests that meaning does not have an exact correspondence with decoded verbalizations (oral reading). He indicates, instead, that verifying "guesses" about the meaning of the text is the primary goal of reading. Rumelhart's model emphasizes the interactive nature of decoding and comprehension. It might suggest that instruction should proceed simultaneously in both word identification and "hypothesis testing." Such instruction would provide maximum mutual facilitation of the two processes.

The Question of Practice

Only the LaBerge and Samuels model specifies the amount of practice: intensive practice is necessary in decoding. Goodman recognizes the need for practice, but he seems to allow it to be nonintensive. Neither Gough nor Rumelhart specifies the levels of practice. One could assume, however, that some minimal level must be required for each skill.

Modalities in Teaching Reading

For Gough, the primary emphasis should be on the visual modality; the same is true for LaBerge and Samuels. In both cases, however, visual stimuli must be paired with auditory representations (for decoding). Goodman gives equal weight to auditory instruction (for example, in oral language) and to visual materials. Rumelhart also stresses both modalities to facilitate the interactive nature of the whole process.

It is probable that level of ability has much to do with the issue of modality. Accomplished readers may not always recode phonemically prior to lexical access. That is, reading may proceed on a hypothesis-testing basis. If so, relatively skilled readers may not need auditory instruction, and beginning readers may need instruction that combines modalities. (Combining modalities also guarantees higher levels of attentiveness during instruction for beginning readers.)

Familiarity of Materials

This may be another "nonissue" (such as the skills approach versus the holistic approach). In some ways, familiar material is always easier to deal with than nonfamiliar material. Gough's model does not specify a need for familiar text. LaBerge and Samuels argue that until decoding is automated, materials should be familiar. Goodman agrees with LaBerge and Samuels, stating specifically that the text should match a reader's oral language.

Remedial Strategies

There are specific models related to reading disabilities, for example, those of Morton Wiener and Ward Cromer[28] and of John

Guthrie.[29] For a true remedial instruction strategy, these remedial models would have to be used in conjunction with the theory of instruction. The models discussed in this chapter are not specifically concerned with problem readers. Consequently, the answers to the question of remedial strategies, are, at best, highly speculative.

The models of Gough and Rumelhart do not deal with remediation. LaBerge and Samuels suggest that the major cause of reading difficulty might be nonautomated decoding; the remedial strategy involves intensive work in decoding. For Goodman, the emphasis is on comprehension; if readers have little difficulty in comprehending, reading remediation should not be necessary.

COMPREHENSION ISSUES NOT CONSIDERED IN READING MODELS

All of the issues discussed in this section involve comprehension. They are residual but critical and reflect the fact that most reading models do not provide full descriptions of comprehension processes. The models most often assign comprehension to relatively undifferentiated processes labeled "meaning." This is, in turn, a simple function of the present lack of knowledge about cognitive processes in general and semantic processes in particular.

Since these issues have immediate implications for instruction, they cannot be ignored. The purpose of this section is not to generate definitive answers for these issues, but, rather, to define the issues more sharply so that future models of reading can focus on them. When this occurs, the theory of instruction will then allow definitive answers based on the models.

Is Comprehension Composed of Subskills?

The grestest hindrance to answering the above question is its dichotomous nature.[30] We must be concerned, on the one hand, with instructional practice and, on the other, with the "true" state of the world. Thus, when we address instructional concerns, we must give answers, regardless of the state of our knowledge. The present discussion must be tempered in light of this distinction.

Even a cursory examination of a scope and sequence chart from a basal reader will lead to the conclusion that comprehension is composed of subskills. For example, the scope and sequence chart accompanying the Scott, Foresman series includes more than twenty-five comprehension or study skills;[31] that of Lippincott includes twenty-one such skills.[32] Thus, the first answer to the question is that, regardless of the "true" state of affairs, instruction proceeds as if comprehension were composed of subskills. These "skills" have been used in such a large number of instructional programs that they have acquired greater status than research evidence would warrant.

To answer the question from the perspective of "true" states of affairs requires that the models be examined. The models discussed earlier assign comprehension to one or more processing stages. Gough ascribes comprehension to Merlin, although lexical access occurs prior to that stage. LaBerge and Samuels assign comprehension to semantic memory, but they do not address the issue of whether comprehension is specifically composed of subskills. Goodman makes the strongest case for holistic processing of comprehension. In any event, comprehension is almost always assumed to be one of the at least two skills required for reading. This is discussed at some length by Samuels and Schachter in Chapter 2 of the present volume.

The lack of an appropriate model of cognitive processes also is a hindrance to answering the question concerning subskills. Cognitive psychology provides models of cognitive structures, as discussed earlier. Such models are not, however, entirely relevant since the issue of subskills could involve strategies for combining, retrieving, or creating new structures. For example, Piagetian theorists might argue that assimilation and accommodation are comprehension subskills. Other theorists involved with schemata might argue for processes like elaboration and instantiation,[33] but these processes are so general that it is questionable whether they can be justly referred to as comprehension skills.

A further consideration involves the methodology used to investigate comprehension skills. The measures used are frequently factor analytic or correlational, but simple correlations do not allow conclusions to be made about reading subskills. There are, however, techniques for statistically adjusting obtained scores.[34]

Until research provides appropriate answers, instructional decisions must be based on pragmatic concerns rather than solid evidence. It is not possible to make definitive statements based on the state of affairs in the real world. It is also not possible to call a halt to instruction in comprehension. For the present, this instruction must proceed as if there were subskills, which will provide for variety in instruction and may allow for students' success in the subskill areas.

Can Comprehension Be Taught?

This question is related to the first question. If an accurate description of comprehension is not available, effective instruction is difficult at best. Most teachers would say that comprehension can be taught; some theorists and researchers would disagree. This reflects the same dichotomy between instructional practice and real knowledge referred to in the previous discussion.

This issue is, theoretically, similar to the debate between Plato and Aristotle over epistemology.[35] Plato maintained that a person could not "learn" something if he did not already have the "essence" of the thing.[36] Aristotle suggested that people learned by induction from many examples. In this manner, learning can take place in the absence of the general concept.

Much contemporary instructional methodology simply involves practice in comprehending. Some examples might help to illustrate this point. Suppose a child has difficulty in establishing or detecting main ideas. What are the common practices to teach or reinforce the skill? If the child has some ability, the teacher is in fairly good shape. He might begin by having a student give a title for a picture. The child could then be given practice in selecting titles for passages or be asked what the passage is about or what word or phrase best describes the passage.

If a child has difficulty detecting sequence, the remedies are also fairly common. For example, cartoon strips are cut into separate boxes and given to the child to put in the proper order. A paragraph might be separated into sentences and given to the child to reconstruct. The same can be done with sentences or words. A student might be asked to relate events in a story in order.

All of these examples have one thing in common: the student must have at least some rudimentary level of the skill in question. If a student cannot perform a task, the task is held constant, and the materials are changed until a level is found at which the child can perform. The illusion of teaching is a progression from easy to harder materials. The distinction between the content of comprehension and the process of comprehension is thus blurred in most instruction. Rather than teaching transfer skills, teachers concentrate on particular examples of comprehension, not on the generalizable process.

Analogy and modeling have been often used to "teach" comprehension, but they do not solve the problem of differentiating practice from teaching. Weimer has reviewed evidence that even perceptual processes are subject to the Platonic notions.[37]

It is unfortunate that the question of whether comprehension can be taught is also unanswerable. For purposes of instruction, teachers must act as if it can be taught. They must be careful, however, to try to teach process rather than content. Theoreticians should continue to deal with the problem, even though no totally new answers (or decisions) have been forthcoming in the two thousand years since Plato and Aristotle proposed their answers.

Is Reading Comprehension the Same as Oral Language Comprehension?

Again, there are two types of answers: instructional and theoretical. Most beginning reading proceeds by assuming that reading comprehension is similar to oral language comprehension; that is, children are taught to decode spelling patterns to sound.[38] The assumption is that the child can monitor the resulting message as if it were oral language.

The answers are not, theoretically, completely clear. Gough, for example, suggests that auditory recoding always takes place. Thus, the comprehension processes occur in the same way for visual or auditory input. LaBerge and Samuels point out that phonemic recoding can be bypassed, but they do not indicate whether that necessitates a different type of semantic memory from the one evoked by phonemically recoded stimuli. Goodman is emphatic in contending that comprehension is a single process. While Rumelhart does not specifically address the issue, one would assume that the interactive nature of the model dictates a single comprehension process.

Other theorists have contended that reading comprehension is the same as oral language comprehension.[39] Ronald Carver suggests that oral language may even be the limiting factor in reading comprehension.[40] Glenn Kleiman, however, has indicated that phonemic recoding is an optional form of processing print.[41] One might infer that there are alternative forms of comprehension.

As models elaborate comprehension processes more fully, the answer to this question will become clearer. The weight of evidence seems presently to favor a single semantic processing device. There are processes involved in comprehension that are definitely different in reading and in listening. For example, memory load is reduced when the stimulus is text. It is also probably true that there is a greater regularity in syntax in text than in speech. The implications of these differences, however, are not clear.

Instruction will continue to assume that reading comprehension is the same as oral language comprehension for beginning readers. It may be that reliance on oral language comprehension decreases as reading proficiency increases. This would be likely under both Goodman's and Rumelhart's notions of hypothesis generation and confirmation. Carver seems to reject this notion, but he specifically excludes speed reading, skimming, or studying.[42] We are thus still left with two different answers to this question—one instructional, the other theoretical.

What Is the Role of Questioning in Instruction in Reading Comprehension?

This question emphasizes instructional practices more than the other questions considered in this section. There are two aspects to the question: the first involves taxonomic classification of questions, and the second the use of interspersed questions to enhance learning from text. (The latter aspect also includes the use of advance organizers.)

The most popular questioning strategies have been based on the taxonomies developed by Benjamin Bloom[43] and Thomas Barrett.[44] Barrett's taxonomy has four levels of questions—literal, inferential, evaluation, and appreciation—which are ordered hierarchically. Morris Sanders has pointed out that the form of the question is not always related to the difficulty that it poses for a student.[45] For example, "why" questions are often assumed to be more difficult than "what" questions. If the author has stated "why," the answer may be relatively simple to obtain.

P. David Pearson[46] and Pearson and Tom Nicholson[47] have argued for the necessity for some important distinctions that are obscured in the traditional taxonomies. The first distinction is between script and text. A script is similar to a schema;[48] it contains background information, both specific and general, that the individual "knows." The text is the printed material. A reader can derive information from the text and combine it with information in his or her script. An orthogonal distinction is whether the information obtained is explicit or implicit. Simple syntactic parsing of the text will yield explicit information; anything else is implicit.

For any question, the answer is either textual or cognitive and either implicit or explicit. These distinctions yield four types: first, textually explicit, where the answer is contained verbatim in the discourse; second, textually implicit, where the answer must be obtained by inference from the discourse; third, cognitively explicit, where the answer is contained verbatim in the individual's store of knowledge; fourth, cognitively implicit, where the answer must be obtained by inference from the discourse. (It is very difficult, however, to determine whether an answer is truly cognitively explicit.) Given these distinctions, instruction can be directed where it will yield the best results.[49] Thus, a student's cognitive structures can be elaborated if they are deficient. If the student has difficulty with explicit comprehension, perhaps work with grammatical analyses might help. What is most important, these distinctions highlight aspects of comprehension obscured in other taxonomies.

The use of questions is one way to evaluate the degree to which a reader has organized the material he has read. Advance organizers have been shown to increase memory (comprehension?) for text when used appropriately.[50] Richard Anderson, Rand Spiro, and Mark Anderson have pointed out that the theoretical justification for advance organizers is flimsy.[51]

Richard Anderson favors the Socratic method for changing schemata.[52] He paints a pessimistic picture of the didactic, expository teaching methods. His conclusion is that the questioning aspect of the Socratic method will allow schemata to be changed more efficiently.

Thus, the role of questions in instruction is to aid readers in organizing material. The greater the organization, the better the memory for the material. What is yet unresolved about the role of questions is their precise format and content. Research has, however, given some definition to those issues.

SUMMARY

This chapter has attempted to show how an instructional theory can be used with models of reading to raise (and sometimes answer) questions about instruction in comprehension. More precise answers will be available when a highly articulated theory of instruction and "complete" models of reading are available. The residual issues discussed in the last section emphasize the need for continued research and theorizing. It is, at the same time, imperative that preliminary answers to the instructional questions be given to practitioners. The educational enterprise cannot wait for absolutely definitive answers.

NOTES

1. Some recent work on this matter is discussed in Richard E. Snow, "Theory Construction for Research on Teaching," in *Second Handbook of Research on Teaching*, ed. Robert M. W. Travers (Chicago: Rand McNally, 1973), 77-112. Additional discussion may be found in Robert Glaser and Lauren B. Resnick, "Instructional Psychology," *Annual Review of Psychology* 23 (1972): 207-276.

2. Ernest Nagel, *The Structure of Science: Problems in the Logic of Scientific Explanation* (New York: Harcourt, Brace and World, 1961), 90.

3. Roy Lachman, "The Model in Theory Construction," *Psychological Review* 67 (March 1960): 113-129.

4. The imagery value of the phrase "lavatory cistern" should be obvious. It appears in Donald E. Broadbent, "A Mechanical Model for Human Attention and Immediate Memory," *ibid.*, 64 (May 1957): 205-215.

5. Morris R. Cohen and Ernest Nagel, "The Nature of a Logical or Mathematical System," in *Readings in the Philosophy of Science*, ed. Herbert Feigl and May Brodbeck (New York: Appleton-Century-Crofts, 1953), 129-147.

6. Lachman, "The Model in Theory Construction."

7. Some of the works that have dealt with this issue (more or less successfully) include: Jerome S. Bruner, *Toward a Theory of Instruction* (Cambridge, Mass.: Belknap Press of Harvard University Press, 1966); *Theories of Learning and Instruction*, Sixty-third Yearbook of the National Society for the Study of Education, Part I, ed. Ernest R. Hilgard (Chicago: University of Chicago Press, 1964); *Theories of Instruction*, ed. James B. Macdonald and Robert R. Leeper (Washington, D.C.: Association for Supervision and Curriculum Development, 1965); Guy J. Groen and Richard C. Atkinson, "Modes for Optimizing the Learning Process," *Psychological Bulletin* 66 (October 1966): 309-320; and Richard C. Atkinson and J. A. Paulson, "An Approach to the Psychology of Instruction," *ibid.*, 78 (July 1972): 49-61.

8. Glaser and Resnick, "Instructional Psychology."

9. This issue was debated in a more general form by Aristotle and Plato. Two thousand years later, there are still no definitive answers. Contemporary positions in psycholinguistics are examined in this light by Walter B. Weimer, "Psycholinguistics and Plato's Paradoxes of the Meno," *American Psychologist* 28 (January 1973): 15-33.

10. The best-known schema theorist is, of course, Jean Piaget. A good discussion of his notions of schemata can be found in John H. Flavell, *The Developmental Psychology of Jean Piaget* (New York: Van Nostrand, 1963). Recent work by Anderson and by Rumelhart and Ortony also helps define the concept of schema. See Richard C. Anderson, "The Notion of Schemata and the Educational Enterprise," in *Schooling and the Acquisition of Knowledge*, ed. *id.*, Rand J. Spiro, and William E. Montague

(Hillsdale, N.J.: Erlbaum, 1976); David E. Rumelhart and Andrew Ortony, "The Representation of Knowledge in Memory," *ibid.*

11. John R. Anderson and Gordon B. Bower, *Human Associative Memory* (Washington, D.C.: V. H. Winston and Sons, 1973).

12. Edward E. Smith, Edward J. Shoben, and Lance J. Rips, "Structure and Process in Semantic Memory," *Psychological Review* 81 (May 1974): 214-241.

13. See, for example, Wolfgang Kohler, *Gestalt Psychology* (New York: Liveright Publishing Corp., 1947), 80-101.

14. Philip B. Gough, "One Second of Reading," in *Language by Ear and by Eye,* ed. James F. Kavanagh and Ignatius G. Mattingly (Cambridge, Mass.: M.I.T. Press, 1972).

15. Urie Bronfenbrenner, "The Experimental Ecology of Educational Research," *Educational Researcher* 5 (October 1976): 5-15.

16. Among these sources are: *Theoretical Models and Processes of Reading,* ed. Harry Singer and Robert B. Ruddell (Newark, Del.: International Reading Association, 1970; 2d ed., 1976); *The Literature of Research in Reading with Emphasis on Models,* ed. Frederick B. Davis (New Brunswick, N.J.: Graduate School of Education, Rutgers University, 1971).

17. A general discussion closely related to the present topic can be found in Michael L. Kamil, "Alternative Models in Reading Comprehension," paper presented to the International Reading Association, Miami Beach, 1977. Application of evaluation criteria to a specific model may be found in P. David Pearson and Michael L. Kamil, "What Hath Carver Raud? A Reaction to Carver's 'Toward a Theory of Reading Comprehension and Reading,' " *Reading Research Quarterly* 13 (1977-78): 92-115.

18. The terms "top-down" and "bottom-up" are used rather widely by contemporary cognitive psychologists. They provide a convenient way of indicating whether processing must proceed with the external stimulus first (bottom-up) or whether processing of the external stimulus can be facilitated by internally generated hypotheses (top-down).

19. Gough, "One Second of Reading."

20. David LaBerge and S. Jay Samuels, "Toward a Theory of Automatic Information Processing in Reading," *Cognitive Psychology* 6 (April 1974): 293-332.

21. David E. Rumelhart, *Toward an Interactive Model of Reading,* Technical Report No. 56 (San Diego: Center for Human Information Processing, University of California at San Diego, 1976).

22. Kenneth S. Goodman, "The Psycholinguistic Nature of the Reading Process," in *The Psycholinguistic Nature of the Reading Process,* ed. *id.* (Detroit, Mich.: Wayne State University Press, 1968).

23. Rumelhart, *Toward an Interactive Model of Reading.*

24. Rumelhart and Ortony, "Representation of Knowledge in Memory," define schemata as "cognitive templates." They may be loosely taken as cognitive structures for coding and storing information and are sometimes referred to as scripts or frames.

25. *Ibid.*

26. Anderson, "The Notion of Schemata and the Educational Enterprise."

27. Rebecca Barr, "The Effect of Instruction on Pupil Reading Strategies," *Reading Research Quarterly* 10 (No. 4, 1974): 555-582.

28. Morton Wiener and Ward Cromer, "Reading and Reading Difficulty: A Conceptual Analysis," *Harvard Educational Review* 37 (Fall 1967): 620-643.

29. John T. Guthrie, "Models of Reading and Reading Disability," *Journal of Educational Psychology* 65 (August 1973): 9-18.

30. I wish to acknowledge the contribution of P. David Pearson to the discussion in this section.

31. Helen Robinson *et al.*, *The New Open Highways Program, Prereading—Book 8, Scope and Sequence Chart* (Glenview, Ill.: Scott, Foresman, 1976).

32. Glenn McCracken and Charles Walcutt, *Basic Reading Series, Grades 1-8, Scope and Sequence Chart* (Philadelphia, Pa.: J. B. Lippincott, 1975).

33. See, for example, Richard C. Anderson *et al.*, *Instantiation of General Terms*, Technical Report No. 10 (Urbana, Ill.: Laboratory for Cognitive Studies in Education, 1976).

34. Robert L. Schreiner, Albert N. Hieronymous, and Robert Forsyth, "Differential Measurement of Reading Abilities at the Elementary School Level," *Reading Research Quarterly* 5 (Fall 1969): 84-99.

35. Weimer, "Psycholinguistics and Plato's Paradoxes of the Meno."

36. *Ibid.*, 16.

37. *Ibid.*, 19-25.

38. The major exception is the McDade Non-Oral Reading Method. See James McDade, "A Hypothesis for Non-Oral Reading: Argument, Experiment, and Results," *Journal of Educational Research* 30 (March 1937): 489-503.

39. Thomas G. Sticht *et al.*, *Auding and Reading* (Alexandria, Va.: Human Resources Research Organization, 1974).

40. Ronald P. Carver, "Toward a Theory of Reading Comprehension and Reading," *Reading Research Quarterly* 13 (1977-78): 8-63.

41. Glenn Kleiman, "Speech Recoding in Reading," *Journal of Verbal Learning and Verbal Behavior* 14 (August 1975): 323-339.

42. Carver, "Toward a Theory of Reading Comprehension and Reading."

43. *Taxonomy of Educational Objectives: Handbook 1, Cognitive Domain*, ed. Benjamin S. Bloom (New York: David McKay, 1956).

44. A full statement of the Barrett taxonomy may be found in Theodore Clymer, "What Is Reading? Some Current Concepts," in *Innovation and Change in Reading Instruction*, Sixty-seventh Yearbook of the National Society for the Study of Education, Part II, ed. Helen M. Robinson (Chicago: University of Chicago Press, 1968).

45. Morris M. Sanders, *Classroom Questions* (New York: Harper and Row, 1966).

46. P. David Pearson, *Reading Comprehension* (New York: Holt, Rinehart and Winston, forthcoming).

47. *Id.* and Tom Nicholson, "Scripts, Text, and Questions," paper presented to the National Reading Conference, Atlanta, Georgia, 1976.

48. The usage of script or frame or schema seems to be idiosyncratic; the concepts are roughly interchangeable.

49. This statement assumes, for the sake of argument, that comprehension can be taught.

50. John P. Rickards, "Processing Effects of Advance Organizers Interspersed in Text," *Reading Research Quarterly* 11 (No. 4, 1975-76): 599-622.

51. Richard C. Anderson, Rand J. Spiro, and Mark C. Anderson, *Schemata as Scaffolding for the Representation of Information in Connected Discourse,* Technical Report No. 24 (Urbana, Ill.: Center for the Study of Reading, 1977).

52. Anderson, "The Notion of Schemata and the Educational Enterprise."

4. Two Approaches to Reading Assessment: A Comparison of Apples and Oranges

Richard L. Venezky

Measuring the effectiveness of educational programs has for almost a century been a major concern of school administrators, educational psychologists, and legislators. And yet, while our ability to collect, store, and analyze evaluative data has improved by quantum jumps during this period, our competence in defining what and whom to measure and how to interpret the outcomes of such assessments has inched only slightly forward since the observational evaluations of Joseph Rice[1] and the school surveys of the early 1900s. Schools are complex entities which, unlike agriculture or industrial production, have goals that are seldom defined precisely. But even when goals are simplified to such measurable qualities as student achievement, the relationship between input and output remains obscure.

In agriculture the deployment of fixed amounts of seed, fertilizer, water, and pest controllers at a given location will produce a predictable yield with surprisingly low variation from year to year. But in schooling only the foolhardy will venture such exacting predictions of the results of particular resource allocations. An aide, or a new set of mathematics books, or a reading specialist is added to a school not because a transfer function predicts precise benefits, but because someone believes—on the basis of subjective data—that the chances are good that some benefit will accrue from the addition.

But while some communities will accept on faith the wisdom of current school practices, most will not; neither will the United States Congress nor the funding agencies that are asked to contribute more and more to the costs of education. Federal educational agencies, in particular, have been adamant, if not obsessive, in their demands for educational evaluation. The Title I program, for example, which became law in 1965, required pre- and posttesting for achievement in even the first year of use of Title I funds. (That this practice is not only based on unrealistic expectations, but is also counterproductive to the goals of the Title I program has yet to lead to a change in the program.)

From the congressional mandates, and from the studies funded by the Office of Education and National Institute of Education, among others, a variety of different approaches to educational evaluation has emerged. The purpose of this chapter is to juxtapose two of these approaches. One is a highly visible and expensive testing program that employs sophisticated measurement techniques, samples its subjects nationally, and announces its results at press conferences. The other, which is represented by less than a handful of recent studies that have appeared in occasional papers, reports of state departments of instruction, and other marginally accessible organs, concentrates on schools rather than students and employs questionnaires and other subjective data-gathering techniques. The two approaches are so different in intent, methodology, and results that they seem as incomparable as apples and oranges. And yet there is, I believe, a benefit to be gained from such a comparison because each methodology has something to offer the other.

The first approach, which is exemplified here by the National Assessment of Educational Progress, demonstrates that exact methods and massive accumulations of data do not always lead to usable results, especially when interpretation of results is an afterthought. The second approach demonstrates that, if a study asks the right questions, even its suspicious methodology and paucity of data can yield important suggestions for educational planners. The challenge in comparing these methodologies is to find relationships that will assist each to do its job more effectively.

THE FIRST METHOD: WIDE-SCALE TESTING

At 2 p.m. EDT on September 21, 1976, the Education Commission of the States issued a news release entitled "It's a Fact—Johnny, Age 9, Is Reading Better."[2] Datelined Washington, D.C., the release begins

"Who says Johnny—and Mary—can't read? Contrary to popular opinion, Johnny and Mary, at age 9 at least, are reading better than their counterparts of a few years ago." In the four-page text that follows, the nationwide reading surveys done by the National Assessment of Educational Progress (NAEP) in 1971 and 1975 are compared and discussed. At the end of the release, the director of the NNAEP is quoted as saying that "special programs at the elementary level are paying off."[3]

With the dismal reports on literacy that continue to emanate from most of America's major urban areas, from the military, and from the college entrance examinations, some good news on reading should certainly be welcomed. But is the report of the NAEP really good news? Does it show that special programs at the elementary level are paying off? And is the approach to evaluation of the NAEP the best one available for assessing schooling?

The answers to these questions are exceedingly complex and are bound up not only in the goals and processes of reading instruction, but also in the methods and management of the NAEP itself. It will not be possible in the space available here to treat all of these issues fully. My purpose is, instead, to probe just far enough beyond the figures and interpretations that have been offered to uncover the more basic problems with the effort of the NAEP, and then to present, in contrast, a totally dissimilar yet highly promising approach to educational assessment.

Interpretation of Scores

First, does the report of the NAEP really bring good news? It does if we accept the premise that any *statistically significant* increase in reading ability qualifies as "good news." The facts are as follows. Of the three age levels surveyed—nine, thirteen, and seventeen—and of the three major abilities assayed within each age level—literal comprehension, inferential comprehension, and study skills—there were three statistically significant changes in ability: nine-year-olds improved overall, nine-year-olds improved in study skills, and thirteen-year-olds declined in study skills.[4] No group improved significantly in any comprehension skill, although the direction of change for all students at the nine-year-old level for the two comprehension skills was positive.

At first glance these appear to be encouraging changes, but for a public that has been led to believe that the nation's schools do a dismal job of teaching reading and that "progress is our most important product," even the assumption that any statistically significant increase is welcomed does not convert the report to unqualified good news. With hundreds of millions of dollars pumped into Title I, educational television, Right to Read, and other literacy-oriented programs over the past ten years, the payoff appears to be far below expectation. Compounding this pessimism is the finding of the NAEP that the subject population that most needs help — that of the economically depressed inner-urban areas — showed no significant improvement in any skill at any age level. Though most special programs in reading are aimed at these areas, students there continued to score an average of about ten percentage points below the national average at each age level.

The only bright spot seems to be the progress shown by nine-year-old blacks, who improved in all skills, but who nevertheless remain, like students in inner-urban areas, ten or more percentage points below the national average. But to decide whether or not even this improvement is good news brings us to the heart of the matter.

The differences in scores by themselves, whether positive or negative, whether statistically significant or not, are meaningful only when compared to desired performance levels and anticipated changes. We can attach no more meaning to an inferential comprehension score of 61.730 percent correct for nine-year-olds than we can to an average wing-beat rate of 650 strokes per minute for a particular species of hummingbirds.

In both cases we need to know what a *sufficient* level of performance is before we can interpret the value of the measure. For the hummingbird, we need, for example, an estimate of the minimum flap rate required for remaining airborne while extracting nectar. For the particular inferential comprehension items used in the tests of the NAEP, we need from local educational agencies estimates of how well their students are expected to do, based on their own instructional objectives. Similarly, to assign values to changes in abilities over time, we need to know how desirable a change is.

To improve reading scores requires investments of resources. Resources for education are scarce and, therefore, must be expended where they are needed most. If nine-year-olds are doing well enough on inferential comprehension, then we should not, in general, invest further resources in improving this ability, nor should we weep when the ability fails to show a significant improvement from one testing period to the next. On the other hand, when the abilities of some group, such as the inner-urban poor, are considered to be lower than what is desired *by some standard,* we expect that additional resources will be allocated to change the situation. And, if so, we anticipate improvements. Although conditions can be conceived in which abilities might improve without changes in methods or allocations of resources, significant improvements are generally anticipated only where changes are made in an effort to effect improvement.

In other words, when the NAEP reports that nine-year-olds scored 67.00 percent correct on study skills, we do not know whether to cheer because we are not sure what score represents adequate study skill ability for nine-year-olds. Furthermore, an increase in study skill ability, although usually welcomed, is equally uninterpretable without knowing either what goal we desire for study skills or what effort we have made to achieve this goal. To determine what study skill ability is adequate or desirable for different age levels requires extraordinary industry and tact, and, no matter what conclusions are reached, they are sure to evoke opposition. And yet shirking from this task out of fear of disapproval is undeserving of our sympathy. Superintendents, principals, and teachers are required to make similar decisions every year in the selection of curricular materials and in the setting of instructional goals. And the army is currently doing the same in defining reading skill levels for each military occupational specialty, a procedure that the NAEP should observe closely.

If the goal of literacy instruction is to prepare students for social, educational, and occupational roles in society, then somehow the nature of these roles and their demands on literacy should be defined. The alternative is to continue to treat literacy as a rarified abstraction, too elusive for a precise definition, and too exalted for an imprecise one. This might guarantee continued employment for those who traffic in academic debates over literacy, but will do the nation as a whole no good.

Statistical versus Educational Significance

The problems above are only the first in interpreting the data of the NAEP. Another major difficulty is the confusion that the announcement of the NAEP perpetuates between statistical significance and educational significance. Statistical significance, for the NAEP, is a difference from one testing period to the next that is at least twice as large as the estimate of the standard error of the difference. For the nine-year-olds, this was a total change of 1.216 percentage points, that is, a change from 63.979 percent correct in 1971 to 65.195 percent correct in 1975. With a change standard error of .545, this percentage difference is significant at a .05 confidence level but not at a .01 level. For the NAEP, statistical significance is synonymous with educational significance.

Educators, on the other hand, will find it extremely difficult to assign educational significance to such a small absolute change, but might be willing to give the NAEP the benefit of the doubt if they had high confidence in the validity of the reading test items. On this question, however, educators should have their most serious doubts about the NAEP. The original reading objectives and test items (exercises) were developed by a commercial publisher under contract to the NAEP. These items were supplemented with additional items developed by independent writers. After the reading assessment in 1971, however, the staff of the NAEP attempted a post hoc reclassification of the test items into eight groups or themes (for example, word meanings, visual aids, critical reading). The original reading objectives were apparently quietly laid to rest.

For the more recent assessment, the theme approach has been abandoned in favor of another ad hoc classification, namely, literal comprehension, inferential comprehension, and study skills. Without a close inspection of the test items, it is impossible to determine what skills are actually being assessed. Frequent alterations in nomenclature by the staff of the NAEP do not, however, impart a sense of confidence in the original selection of items.

In summary, we do not know what skills the items test, we do not know what levels of performance to expect on the items, regardless of how they are grouped, and, therefore, we do not know the educational significance of any particular score or change in score.

Background Variables

Given the concerns just stated, the conclusion attributed to the director of the NAEP "that special programs at the elementary level are paying off" needs to be examined. From a casual observer, unfettered from the constraints of scientific rigor, such a conclusion could be accepted. But from an organization that has consumed nearly $40 million in federal and private monies to provide objective, quantitative approaches to the issue of program effectiveness, such a statement borders on the irresponsible. *No cause and effect relationship between special programs like Title I and the reading abilities of nine-year-olds is deducible from the data of the NAEP.*

Sampling procedures of the NAEP ignore such background and demographic variables as type of school, attendance in special programs, and per capita expenditure on education. These procedures concentrate instead, on variables that are, for the most part, of value only for archiving: sex, race, geographical locations, and so forth. For demographers and statisticians these variables are foursquare in the center of traditional sampling procedures. But we do not design special reading programs just for males or for females, just for blacks or for whites, or just for the southeastern sector of the United States. It is difficult to imagine, therefore, what educational decisions are to be made from such data.

In short, no evidence from the surveys of the NAEP shows that children who participated in special programs improved their reading abilities any more than those who did not. And it is yet unfortunate that the NAEP was created exactly for this purpose, namely, to assist in determining what effects on learning the vast governmental expenditures on education have made.

Comptroller General's Report

In view of these limitations, there seems to be no justification for the tone of the press release cited at the beginning of this section. The release probably would have been more accurate if it bore the title "Johnny, Age 9 or 13 or 17, is not comprehending better." But these criticisms are not the first that have been made of the NAEP.

After seven years of work and almost $40 million in federal and private support, the NAEP has come under strong criticism from another source. The comptroller general's office, after surveying local, state, and national educational organizations, along with government officials involved in educational decision making, concluded: "National Assessment results have been of limited usefulness to education decision-makers, researchers, and practitioners. This has prevented the project from achieving its basic goal."[5] The specific criticisms in the comptroller general's report strike at the heart of the

procedures of the NAEP. On the one hand, though the scores in traditional subject areas and their changes over time are of greatest interest
at the state and local level, they are reported here only on a regional
and national basis. Because of this policy, state and local educational
agencies indicate that "They have not used and do not plan to use National Assessment data for resource allocation purposes."[6] On the
other hand, the data are too general, require too long to collect and
analyze, and are based on too few variables on students' background
and on demography to be of concern to decisionmakers at the national
level. "Although all the officials we interviewed at HEW, research
organizations, and test publishing firms were aware of the National
Assessment, very few indicated that they had used project data and
few could cite any use for the data as it is currently collected and
presented."[7]

The comptroller general's report also criticized the NAEP for not
interpreting its own data and for not relating its results to accepted
performance standards—criticisms discussed earlier in this chapter.

Positive Aspects

Given these negative aspects of the NAEP, what should happen
now? The NAEP itself seems to have seen its fate tied closely to the
type of news it carries, hoping however unconsciously that if we kill the
messenger who brings bad news, we would look with favor upon one
who brought good news. For this reason it attempted to overemphasize
the positive aspects of the data it collected. But this seems shortsighted
because the comptroller general's report also related a highly positive
aspect of the NAEP, that of developing and implementing a model for
objective-referenced assessment.

Forty or more state educational agencies are now using items or
techniques of the NAEP in their own assessment programs, and extensive efforts are apparently being made to provide similar services to
local educational agencies. By establishing thorough procedures for
selecting and validating objective test items that cover a wider range of
abilities than typical standardized achievement tests, the NAEP has
provided for the first time an alternative to norm-referenced tests. For
this accomplishment alone the NAEP may be able to justify its existence.

In addition, the NAEP has expressed a willingness to reconsider its testing procedures and has asked a number of professional organizations for assistance in correcting many of the deficiencies mentioned in the comptroller general's report.

Even with this willingness for self-inspection, however, the effort of the NAEP should move away from costly and marginally useful national surveys of the contemporary type and toward a service mission of exploring testing procedures, assisting local and state agencies in developing and administering their own assessments, and in providing specialized assessments on request from national agencies. Certainly the purblind accumulation of educational statistics without reference to specific decisions that require such data cannot be afforded.

But before we suggest removing the NAEP completely from national surveys, we might consider what this organization could learn from a highly dissimilar approach to reading assessment.

THE SECOND METHOD: CASE STUDY

Background

The second methodology is the case study approach whereby schools are examined in depth to uncover factors that might account for students' achievement (or lack of it). This approach is a natural successor to the school survey that was used in the nineteenth and early twentieth centuries to initiate school reform. Horace Mann and Henry Barnard were probably the first Americans to use school survey data to coerce communities into appropriating funds for school improvement.[8] The schoolhouses of the early and middle nineteenth century were so inadequate for schooling and so decrepit physically that the mere exposure of their conditions was sufficient to embarrass communities into action.[9] Achievement data were not required then; nor were they needed in the late 1800s by Joseph Mayer Rice to convince Americans that the prevailing methods of instruction in most public schools were unscientific and dehumanizing.[10]

Rice, a pediatrician who studied educational methodology in Germany, undertook a study of the public school system of the United States under the auspices of a popular journal, *The Forum,* in 1892. In a period of a little over five months, Rice observed more than twelve hundred teachers in classrooms in thirty-six cities. His observations, published first as a series of articles in *The Forum* and then in book

form, contributed not only to John Dewey's educational reform movement of the early twentieth century but also the methodology of classroom observation and of school management analysis.[11]

School surveys done in the first quarter of the twentieth century,
although usually restricted to a single city or state, drew upon Rice's
methodology and were, in general, undertaken for the same goal of
educational reform.[12]

Recent Case Studies

The studies of immediate interest to this chapter descend naturally
from the Mann-Barnard-Rice tradition, with Rice being the most important antecedent. What is different today, however, is that both the
physical and the instructional conditions have improved (generally) to
the point where a mere exposure of particular school conditions is no
longer adequate for stirring up the instincts to reform or provoking
the taxpayer into increased school expenditures.[13] Achievement, particularly in reading and to a lesser degree in mathematics, interests the
public and the various local, state, and federal agencies the most.
Thus, survey and case study methodologies have been forced to incor-
porate achievement in one or both of these topics as selection factors.

The new case study approach is included in the following: George
Weber's study, carried out by the Council for Basic Education, Washington, D.C.;[14] the study by the New York State Education Department, carried out by the State Education Department;[15] the study by
the Michigan Department of Education, carried out by Education
Turnkey Systems, Inc., for the Michigan Department of Education;[16]
and Ghita Wilder's study, a component of the Educational Testing
Service (ETS) study of compensatory reading programs.[17] In the
studies by Weber and by the ETS, expectations were based on grade-
level norms; in the other three studies, they were based on more complicated formulas that compared actual achievement to predicted
achievement, on the basis of either students' background variables or
achievement scores in earlier grades. Schools so identified were then
studied in depth, using observations of classrooms and interviews with
teachers, specialists, and administrators. Finally, those factors attended to by the observation and interview instruments that were
unique to either the high-or low-achieving schools were isolated. The
intent of these studies has generally been to identify alterable (that is,
trainable) factors that are needed for successful schooling. In Weber's
study, however, the goal was simply to demonstrate that schools with

students predominantly from the lowest socioeconomic areas can succeed in teaching reading.

In his study, Weber initially identified ninety-five inner-urban schools that drew their students primarily from poorer families and claimed to be teaching reading successfully. Of these, four met both criteria of the study: they were in predominantly lower-economic, inner-city areas, and they were successful in teaching reading as measured not by a standardized test but by a special test made up from the vocabularies and life experiences of students similar to those in the sample schools. These four schools were then visited, the teachers and administrators were interviewed, and reading classes were observed. From these observations a number of features were abstracted that were common to the four successful schools. (Two of these schools were in Manhattan, one was in Kansas City, Missouri, and one was in Los Angeles; all were achieving at approximately the level of the typical school attended by students from families with average incomes. Each had 80 to 90 percent black and Puerto Rican enrollment and drew its students from the lowest economic levels.)

The first common characteristic of the successful schools was strong leadership for reading improvement. This usually came from the principal, but in one school derived from a specialist.

The second characteristic was that all the successful schools had high expectations for their students. This atmosphere reflected a belief that the children could learn to read and that they could be as successful as children from more advantaged areas. (This attitude is crucial for success in teaching reading. Reading is not a high-level cognitive skill; it is not atomic physics or statistics. Children with IQs as low as 80 typically are placed in mainstream reading programs. Reading can be acquired by practically anyone who is given the proper opportunity to learn.)

The third characteristic was a good atmosphere. This quality is difficult to define precisely. One senses it when he walks into a school and sees children's work everywhere rather than in carefully delineated lines on the available bulletin boards. One senses it when he sees children moving from group to group and room to room in a reasonably orderly fashion but not marching with the teacher's ruler over their heads. One senses it when he sees the principal, the assistant principal, the janitor, and the other school personnel interacting frequently with students.

The fourth characteristic was a strong emphasis on reading. It was clear to parents, to teachers, and to everyone else who walked into the schools that reading was important and that resources were made available for it.

The fifth essential characteristic was the presence of extra personnel within the schools to help with reading, and the sixth was a high degree of individualization. Individualization implied in the most general sense attention to individual needs. It did not mean that a teacher worked only with one child at a time. To individualize, a teacher must assess where each child needs help and modify instruction to meet these individual needs. This may result in a variety of groups with different reading abilities or in groups that combine different levels of ability.

A seventh characteristic was careful assessment of students' progress, based on both formal and informal means. And, finally, but perhaps as important as any other characteristic, the four schools took three to nine years to implement their programs. The average school required about five years to achieve a major change in its reading program.

The other studies of successful schools have revealed similar results. The one in New York State, for example, reported that the successful schools studied there had better teacher rapport, better reporting methods, better control by teachers, more extensive use of materials, more regrouping during reading periods, and stronger school leadership than the unsuccessful schools.

In the study by Wilder, which analyzed five high-achieving "outlier" schools from an initial sample of 741, the following common characteristics were found: reading was the top priority among the school's activities, which was reflected by either the amount of time devoted to reading activities or the amount of money allocated for reading materials; effective leadership specific to reading was evident; reading programs gave careful attention to basic skills; schools exhibited a relative breadth of reading materials; teachers frequently exchanged ideas about reading.

Summary and Criticisms

The picture revealed by these studies of successful reading programs is one of successful schools. There was strong curricular leadership (usually from the principal), specialists and other aides were frequently available, there was good in-service training, the staff exhibited positive attitudes toward the children, there was a high degree of individualization, cooperation was present among teachers, there was flexibility in instructional methods, and the reading programs were carefully planned. Central to all of these virtues are people: principals, teachers, and reading specialists who perform as professional educators and who are equipped to make educational decisions.

It should also be pointed out, however, that these studies generally have concentrated on small numbers of schools, have utilized subjective evaluation techniques, and have dealt with imprecisely defined variables, such as leadership, cross-fertilization, and atmosphere. Strong leadership, for example, might be exemplified by the "tight ship" approach whereby all decisions are made and enforced from the top, or it might be through effective delegation of power with a more widely distributed decision-making and enforcing procedure. It cannot be determined from the studies reviewed here which of these leads to higher achievement among students, although most educators would assume that the former approach would be considerably less successful than the latter. Further specific criticisms could be made of the two methodologies reviewed here, but it may be more helpful to examine how they might relate to each other for their mutual improvement.

RELATIONSHIPS

Even with the tentative nature of the case study results, the NAEP might consider incorporating some of them into its methodology. The most obvious beginning point is in stratification variables. The NAEP currently utilizes such factors as sex, geographic location, and race in selecting subjects. But the case studies indicate that school factors such as leadership, priority given to reading, attitude of staff toward children, role of teachers in decision making, and allocation of resources determine exceptional achievement. The NAEP might develop interview questionnaires, such as those used in the New York State study, to assess these variables and then include the results as either factors for selecting subjects or as background variables for post hoc analyses.

This would be a major departure from current practices of the NAEP and would involve variables that cannot be assessed with the same precision as sex, race, or achievement. Relating achievement to alterable school variables on a national scale fits, nevertheless, within the mandate of the NAEP. If this is done successfully, the NAEP would make a major contribution to our understanding of schooling, because attention would be concentrated on variables that schools and school systems could, with appropriate resources, alter.

Knowing as we do from current survey results that females gained somewhat more or less in a particular reading skill over a four-year period tells us nothing that is usable in allocating reading funds or in developing new programs for reading instruction. But if degree of individualization were shown to relate significantly to success in reading, particularly in inner-urban schools, or attitude toward children, or any of the other variables isolated in the case studies, then at least an entry point for improvement will have been identified. Even with the imprecision that is sure to exist in the definition and assessment of these school factors, and even after refinement of current instruments, their inclusion in a national survey seems advisable.

If school factors were assessed with the same degree of planning and development of instruments as the NAEP now exerts for the development of achievement tests, then a variety of different variables, including types of special reading programs, could be included in the NAEP records. This would be an important step toward realizing one of the original motivations for creating the NAEP, that is, determining the effects of special programs on reading achievement.

At the present time educational surveyors show a strong propensity for assessing what can be measured reliably, regardless of whether or not such variables relate logically to differences in achievement or are under control of a school system. They are searching for answers to a problem, not where the answers most likely will be found, but where the light is best.

The NAEP might continue to assess achievement as it has done in the past, perhaps with attempts to relate its items to recognizable reading skills and its scores to instructional expectations. Even if this were accomplished, however, the value of the NAEP's assessment data to governmental bodies and educational planners would still be limited. So long as every major segment of the population is not reading at a desired criterion level or is not moving steadily and uniformly toward that level, decisions about allocation of resources and about programs will need to be made, and these decisions will require information on what is working and what is not.

This means that someone will need to know which programs, processes, or procedures are producing desired results and which are not. If the NAEP does not furnish this information, some other group will be commissioned to do so. The choice seems to be between a well-tried testing procedure that produces reliable, but not totally useful results, and a somewhat unsure and perhaps even suspicious procedure that, if it is successfully implemented, could produce extremely important data for reading improvement, but, if it fails, would leave us no worse off than we are now.

On the other hand, case study methodology can profit from some of the experience of the NAEP, even in those instances where the NAEP has not been overly successful. The case studies discussed here have all treated reading as an integral process by utilizing a single reading score for each subject at each testing point. But reading is not taught as a single process; nor are there empirical data that suggest that it should be treated as such. It is conceivable, for example, that certain school practices are beneficial for acquiring basic, mechanical skills such as decoding, but are less helpful for comprehension. The importance of the priority variable would suggest that what a school emphasizes most determines what is acquired best by its students. Since curricular emphasis often changes across grades, schools assessed at the lower grade levels, such as in the studies conducted by Weber and New York State, might not appear so successful if assessed at higher grade levels. Case studies need to take this into account both by partitioning of reading into subcomponents and by testing at several—if not all—grade levels. Whether the reading skills of the NAEP or some other group of skills are chosen is probably not as important as the distinction between a single score and multiple scores.

But whatever the defects in current case studies, they still represent a promising approach to educational assessment and are a refreshing complement to the traditional survey of educational statistics. No matter how educational achievement might change over time or what it might correlate with, there is scant hope of affecting major changes in educational outcomes until the process of education is understood. And this can be done only by direct inspection of the educational apparatus, including its facilities, its managers, its organizational procedures, and its primary participants, the students and teachers. The current case study methodology does not attend reliably to all of these entities, but it is the most promising approach in use today for analyzing such systems.

NOTES

1. Joseph M. Rice, *The Public-School System of the United States* (New York: Arno Press, 1969; first published by Century Co., New York, 1893).

2. Most of the material in this section has been adapted from my article, "NAEP—Should We Kill the Messenger Who Brings Bad News?" *Reading Teacher* 30 (April 1977): 750-755.

3. "It's a Fact—Johnny, Age 9, Is Reading Better," news release from the Education Commission of the States, Denver, Colorado, September 21, 1976, 4.

4. *Reading in America: A Perspective on Two Assessments,* Reading Report No. 06-4-01 (Denver, Colorado: National Assessment of Educational Progress, 1976), xi.

5. Comptroller General of the United States, *The National Assessment of Educational Progress: Its Results Need to Be Made More Useful,* Report to the Congress (Washington, D.C.: U.S. Government Printing Office, 1976), ii.

6. *Ibid.,* 24.

7. *Ibid.*

8. *Henry Barnard's School Architecture,* ed. Jean McClintock and Robert McClintock (New York: Teachers College Press, 1971), 10-28.

9. A startling case in point is found in the *Annual Report of the Superintendent (Hon. Samuel Young) of Common Schools [of New York], Made to the Legislature January 13, 1844:* "The whole number of school-houses visited and inspected by the county superintendents during the year was 9,368: . . . of these 3,160 were found in good repair; 2,870 in ordinary and comfortable repair, and 3,319 in bad repair, or totally unfit for school purposes . . . . The number furnished with a single privy is, 1,810; those with privies containing separate apartments for male and female pupils, 1,012; while the number of those not furnished with *any privy* whatever, is 6,423." (Cited in *Henry Barnard's School Architecture,* ed. McClintock and McClintock, 377.)

10. But, of course, achievement tests are a product of the twentieth century and hence were not available to Barnard or Rice.

11. The following statement from the preface to Rice's collected school reports *(The Public-School System of the United States,* 5) shows concerns not distinctly different from the school analysis procedures of today: "When one has gained a considerable amount of experience in investigating schools, much can be learned of the school system of any city during fifteen minutes spent in the ABC class of almost any school visited at random. The appearance of the room, the attitude of the teacher toward the child, the manner in which recitation is conducted, the character of the busy-work, and the answers to a dozen questions put to the teacher concerning the general scope of her work, the teachers' meetings she attends, as well as what she does generally to improve her own mind, will frequently suffice to give a key to the whole situation."

12. David Tyack, *The One Best System: A History of American Urban Education* (Cambridge, Mass.: Harvard University Press, 1974).

13. Reading may still be an exception to this hypothesis, although generally one has to create an air of underachievement, as did Rudolf Flesch (*Why Johnny Can't*

Read and What You Can Do About It [New York: Harper and Row, 1955]), before condemning the current instructional techniques and advocating new ones.

14. George Weber, *Inner-city Children Can Be Taught to Read: Four Successful Schools* (Washington, D.C.: Council for Basic Education, 1971).

15. New York State Education Department, "Reading Achievement Related to Educational and Environmental Conditions in 12 New York City Elementary Schools" (New York: University of the State of New York, Division of Education Evaluation, 1974, mimeo).

16. Michigan Department of Education, *Michigan Cost-effectiveness Study: An Executive Summary* (Lansing: Department of Education, 1974).

17. Ghita Wilder, "Exemplary Practices in Reading Comprehension Instruction," unpublished manuscript, Educational Testing Service, Princeton, N.J., n.d. Two other studies are relevant to the issues raised here, but have not been included in this review. One, Brian Cane and Jane Smithers, *The Roots of Reading* (Slough, Bucks: National Foundation for Educational Research in England and Wales, 1971), reports on a case study of twelve British infant schools in deprived areas, but was not included because the school systems and subjects' age levels differed markedly from those in studies of the U.S. The other is a study of three high-achieving and three low-achieving schools in Delaware, carried out by the Research and Planning Group in the Delaware Department of Public Instruction. This study attempted to assess many more variables than the other studies reported here, but the results have not yet been made publicly available.

5. Reading and the Affective Domain

Ken L. Dulin

Educators today use the terms "affect" and "affective" extensively. And yet, like so many other perfectly good words, in particular the esoteric kinds of words so often used in talking about the abstract ideas in the field of education, these words can sometimes end up meaning very little simply because they mean so very much. Thus, an overall introduction to the term "affect" is probably in order.

DEFINING THE TERM "AFFECT"

In general education, for example, the terms "affective education" and "affective learning" are used very broadly. At times they refer to any educational experiences involved in the development of certain "values," "attitudes," or "feelings" considered desirable by those who plan such programs. At other times they refer to a particular teaching technique or strategy deemed somehow more "humane," "humanitarian," or "democratic" than our old-fashioned, traditional, teacher-centered ones.

But even within a single curricular area, such as the one being dealt with in this book, no real consistency of definition for these terms can be found. Everyone in the field of reading is in favor of affect, it seems, but, once we become the least bit behavioral in describing our current curricular concerns or our current research interests, we often find ourselves talking about very different things.

Affect as Attitude toward Reading

Probably the most common use of "affect" by those in the field of reading is in relation to concerns over the presence or absence, usually in young readers, of a favorable attitude toward reading; that is, most of us seem to share a feeling that all children should "like" or "respect" reading and see it as a pleasurable, worthwhile activity. Thus, from this point of view, "affective" goals are ordinarily concerned with how best we can instill this liking or respect for reading in our students, usually by employing or by not employing certain classroom practices, certain teaching behaviors, or certain pedagogical approaches. Book reports are "out," and games and uninterrupted Sustained Silent Reading (a leisure reading program in which both students and teachers take a certain amount of time out of each day to read) are "in," the better to convince students that reading is a pleasurable, satisfying activity, one to be respected and admired throughout their lives, the same as we, their models and their mentors, respect and admire it. In short, most of us feel that reading should be seen as a "good" thing. That, then, is one approach.

Affect as Motivation to Read

The second meaning of "affect" as used in the literature of reading is closely related to attitudes toward reading, but is even more direct and immediate in its application. Not only are we all concerned that our students *perceive* reading as a good, worthwhile activity, but also that they move immediately into *doing* some of it. Thus, teachers and students of education flock eagerly to convention presentations with titles like "Motivating the Reluctant Reader" or "How to Get Your Students to Read More and Like It." All forms of bribery—the awarding of points, presents, or grades for reading—seem to be acceptable, if they work, at least for the moment.

The immediate motivation to read, then, and how to promote it constitute a second major dimension of the overall term "affect" as it relates to reading.

Affect as Preference for Certain Reading Materials

A third use of "affect" relates to *what* individual readers or groups of readers like to read. Thus, there is a continuous assessment of readers' constantly changing preferences within and among various types of reading materials. Librarians and those who are professionally involved in the field of reading turn out survey after survey. The publishing industry maintains an almost day-by-day sales record of specific titles. And many teachers administer informal surveys, questionnaires, and checklists of reading preferences to their classes every school term.

In short, then, the "what" of reading, particularly as it relates to voluntary, self-selected reading activities, is considered by most people in the field of reading to be part of the total picture of affect and reading.

Affect as Specific Response to Reading

A fourth use of "affect" concerns specific responses of readers to particular *characteristics* of reading materials, both with regard to such elusive qualities as style, mood, and tone and to more literal qualities such as person, point of view, and characterization. At its most esoteric level, this aspect of affect and reading deals with literary "taste" or "appreciation" and at its most pragmatic level with the response of readers to propaganda techniques, to persuasive devices, or even, as in advertising research, to page format, to print characteristics, or to the presence or absence of particular "appeals" to certain groups of readers.

Within the professional literature of reading, this aspect of affect and reading is usually discussed under the rubric "critical" or "creative" reading. In reality, however, relatively little serious study of this level of reading response has been attempted by professional educators in the field of reading, and what few research findings do exist have come primarily from research in the fields of speech, journalism, and advertising.

Summary of the Four Faces of Affect

The purpose of this short introduction has been to define the four major ways in which "affect" is generally used among those in the field of reading education: to refer to the overall, long-term *attitudes* individuals and groups hold toward reading; to refer to the levels of immediate *motivation* to read operating within individuals and groups at particular times and under particular conditions; to refer to the patterns of *preference* for particular reading materials operative among certain readers or groups of readers; and to refer to the particular patterns of emotional or affective *response* that occur when readers are confronted with various characteristics of style or print format within reading materials. Figure 5-1 illustrates this model.

As attitude toward reading	As motivation to reading	As preferences within reading	As response to reading

Figure 5-1. The Four Definitions of Affect as Related to Reading

It must be admitted that a much finer and more detailed conceptual classification could have been attempted. Certain personality types, for example, undoubtedly react differently to the same reading materials, and individuals undoubtedly react differently to identical reading materials when they are encountered at different times and under different conditions. An effort could possibly have been made to account for these sorts of interactions. Little is known, however, about the subtleties of these interactions, and thus we are probably better off dealing with the more general model presented above. It is on the basis of this model that this analysis will proceed.

ATTITUDE TOWARD READING

As previously noted, probably the primary reason most of us in the field of reading are so eager to develop strong, positive attitudes toward reading in our students is simply because we feel this is a "good" thing to do. Most of us like reading, and we would like to pass some of this feeling along to others. Thus, our basic motivation here is cultural, in almost the anthropological sense of the term. As members of a reading "class," we wish to initiate others into that class. We hope, thereby, that their membership in that class will be pleasurable and personally fulfilling and that they will, in turn, pass on membership in it to others. At times this pursuit of new proselytes becomes somewhat frantic, as when we readers see the existence of our class threatened, which happened a decade or two ago when Marshall McLuhan's dire predictions of a retreat from the domination of print in communication briefly set us on guard. Overall, however, we are fairly comfortable, since reading and the teaching of reading are quite clearly institutionalized into our accepted systems of schooling and child rearing, and thus most of our activities related to "passing on the torch" can be warm, fairly relaxed, and comfortable.

In addition, however, other good reasons for building relatively positive attitudes toward reading exist, at least for young readers who are still pursuing their basic educations; these reasons are practical, economic, and pragmatic. Reading, like all other acquired, developed skills, flourishes with practice. People who read regularly and heavily become skilled at reading, and so the development of warm, positive attitudes toward leisure reading can be seen simply as good pedagogical insurance for the growth of strong capabilities and competencies in reading, and thus clearly an important goal for instruction as well as for acculturation.

Finally, in addition to both of the points above, is the simple fact that reading is one of the best, if not the best, ways in which to learn, particularly if that learning is abstract and ordered or exotic and vicarious. Learners who combine a strong reading skill with a knowledge of how and where to secure the reading matter they desire need never reinvent the wheel or rediscover fire; the combined, accumulated knowledge of all civilizations is available to them, simply by scanning the right page.

Thus, we can marshal cultural, pedagogical, and practical reasons for fostering strong, positive attitudes toward reading in our students. But how do we do this?

Building Positive Attitudes toward Reading

Through identification. One way we can build strong positive attitudes toward reading in our students is by demonstrating that we ourselves enjoy, respect, and profit from reading. This can be done in a variety of ways — by sharing our own reading experiences with them, by encouraging them to share their reading experiences with us and with each other, and by creating in our classrooms an atmosphere that shows that reading is an important and useful part of our adult lives.

Identification is one of the most commonly neglected of all the opportunities teachers have for influencing young readers' attitudes toward books and reading. All too many teachers, particularly at the secondary level, approach their classes with goals related to content areas rather than with a concern for their students' broad development of positive educational skills and attitudes. Within almost every group in a classroom are a few individuals who feel a close identity with the teacher; thus, if all teachers were to share their enthusiasm for reading with each group, almost every student would at some time within the school day be touched by this enthusiasm.

Within the school, some of the most potent examples of identification are those staff members least automatically identified with reading: athletic coaches, music directors, art teachers, shop teachers, and so on. Quite often these are the people with whom students lacking in adult reading models identify; for this reason, their enthusiasm for reading can be highly effective among those who most need such an influence. To be fully effective, of course, this idea of spreading enthusiasm for reading by way of identification must extend beyond the school. Parents, too, should try to share their participation in and enjoyment of reading with their children, but this must be done in an informal, noncoercive way. An even more effective use of identification would be for public figures, particularly the entertainers, musicians, and athletes who are so often the personal heroes of many young people, to exhibit their reading habits.

Through rewards. Another approach to building positive attitudes toward reading is to provide rewards — grades, social approval, or concrete reinforcement.

To do this, we must overcome our Puritan belief that virtue and all other good things are necessarily their own reward; for many adults, parents and teachers alike, this can be a difficult thing to do. Once we ourselves have internalized our own attitudes about an activity, it often bothers us that others may have to be enticed into doing it. What we often forget, of course, is that at some time in the past we, too, were probably rewarded in some way for doing what we now do because of purely intrinsic motivation.

But, whether we like it or not, reward does work and is, therefore, a good way to start youngsters reading on their own. It is to be hoped that social and other nonmaterial rewards will be enough for most students most of the time, and perhaps for all students eventually. We should not, however, automatically rule out the more concrete kinds of rewards as useful tools in building attitudes, at least at times.

The opposite side of the reward coin is punishment. It should go without saying that if strong, positive attitudes toward reading are desired, then reading should never be used as punishment. This admonition is not always followed, however. Far too often, reading is used as punishment, particularly in schools. Edgy, fidgety classes are still threatened with having to read in place of recess, and long, tedious reading and writing tasks are still assigned to "settle down" (that is, punish in advance) a class.

Through successful experiences. Easier for us to take, but still honored more in the breach than in the practice, is the idea that "nothing succeeds like success," whether that success is measured in extended learning, heightened attitudes toward an activity, or both. We all quickly come to enjoy, and to hold positive attitudes toward, those things we do comfortably, easily, effectively, and well. Reading is no exception to this rule. Perhaps the aforementioned adage should be changed only slightly to: "Nothing succeeds like *perceived* success," that is, results perceived by the *learner* as well as the teacher. This is why self-scoring reading exercises and self-evaluated reading experiences are so much more motivating to a pupil than is approval or praise by the teacher, even though the teacher may feel at times that even a small degree of improvement is worthy of praise. Thus, to a student, "success" is whatever he or she sees as success, not what we may deem to be successful.

What this means to teachers, then, is that they must provide successful reading experiences for every student if they are truly concerned about fostering positive attitudes toward reading. Rather than "challenging" students daily, by always giving them reading tasks just a little beyond their comfortable accomplishment, they should provide more opportunities for fairly easily attainable success. This success should be obvious enough for the students themselves to perceive it easily, rather than depending on the teacher to judge it so.

Through adapting to students' individual needs in reading. To provide successful reading experiences for every student, and thus to foster positive attitudes toward reading, it is necessary to move on to another principle: the recognition of students' individual differences in needs, interests, and preferences in reading materials. Just as there is rarely complete unanimity in preferences for sports, hobbies, or foods among groups of people, so are there usually great variations in the kinds of reading materials different individuals find interesting and fulfilling. It is true that a few overall age-related and sex-related patterns of preference do exist, such as girls in the upper grades in elementary schools liking dog and horse stories and boys in junior high schools enjoying World War II adventures. Most of these statistically distilled results of interest inventory data, however, come from, and in turn apply only to, the large "average" group of readers of any age. Thus, they should be considered only as broad guidelines, not as specific rules for establishing individual reading programs and classroom activities. As will be dealt with in more detail later, reading interests derive from human interests, and they vary to exactly the same degree that human personalities do.

More easily defined than the ranges of interest in reading materials, however, is the issue of difficulty of reading. The middle 80 percent of any classroom group of readers will range in reading ability up to as many as ten grade levels, and thus self-perceived success for every student is an impossible goal unless the reading materials reflect these differences. This is particularly true if they are "required," "accountable for," reading materials that must be read and then used in completing assigned learning tasks.

A final success-related point about reading materials concerns *rate* of reading. Students with considerable ability read faster as well as better than those with less ability. Thus, the amount of reading, in terms of the required number of pages per period, must be adjusted for different readers if they are to be successful. This is particularly true at the high school level, where students in the 90th percentile will be reading approximately twice as fast as those in the 10th percentile. Even in the lower grades, however, the observed differences in the rate of reading are quite substantial. Thus, teachers at all grade levels should take these differences into account when making reading assignments.

Through building the habit of reading. Where does all this lead, as attitudes toward reading develop through the grades? If all goes well, it leads to the point where reading comes to be as *habitual* as eating, drinking, and sleeping. But how do we get the attitude toward reading to this point?

To answer the question simply, the habit of regular reading develops just as do all other habits, through daily or almost daily practice. Thus, teachers and parents who want reading to become a daily habit of their students and children should establish a pattern of daily reading and then adhere to it. This is particularly important when the school provides the major force for building positive attitudes toward reading. If homes do not reward or reinforce reading and do not provide a structure within which reading time is a normal, everyday consideration, then only the school can do it. If time for reading is not provided by the school, none will exist, and neither the habit of reading daily nor the attitude that it is an important and useful daily activity will develop.

The Measurement of Reading Attitude

How do we know where we are in the building of attitudes toward reading? Probably our best theoretical model for assessing our progress is the well-known taxonomy of objectives in the affective domain developed by David Krathwohl, Benjamin Bloom, and Bertram Masia.[1] This taxonomy posits five different stages in the development of an attitude, with the progression of these stages running from psychologically "outside" the individual to "inside" the individual. These stages are: attending; responding; valuing; organization; characterization. Though there are actually hypothesized substeps as well, the major divisions of the hierarchy are probably the most useful to us.

Thus, as individuals move up the steps of this ladder, they move from "attending," or simply "noticing" reading as part of their surroundings, to "responding" to it in a positive way, to "valuing" it, perhaps even to the degree of extending it to others as a positive value, to "organizing" it into their life-styles, and finally to internalizing it into their own personality makeups or "character."

Should we then expect all readers to achieve the final fifth stage? We probably should not, though they certainly ought to have the opportunity to do so if their overall complex of personal abilities, interests, and aptitudes is compatible with their doing so. A more realistic goal for the majority of Americans is probably the attainment of at least the third level — accepting reading as a worthwhile "value" to be honored, respected, and passed on in a favorable light to others.

Many experimental instruments have been developed to "measure" attitudes toward reading. The best is probably the Mikulecky Behavioral Reading Attitude Measure,[2] a short twenty-item paper-and-pencil inventory built directly around the taxonomy referred to above. But even without resorting to any kind of score-producing instrument, the hierarchy suggested in this model can be extremely useful. Simple observation of classroom behavior, particularly when coupled with informal interviewing techniques, can usually provide the teacher with insight into the pupil's position in the hierarchy, but its most useful contribution is probably that of providing a *mental model* of attitude development for the teacher, rather than establishing a set of exact, discrete steps.

For attitude development, then, we do have an available model. But what about the second definition of affect — immediate motivation — as it relates to reading?

MOTIVATION TO READ

In approaching this problem, we face a series of questions. Rather than simply asking "What motivates people to read?" we must also ask "What people, what kind of reading, and when?" Motivations to read will obviously be as numerous as the number of combinations and permutations possible between and among all these factors. Despite this, however, attempts have been made at dividing up, even if in an admittedly artificial way, the various reasons why various people read various materials at various times.

Wilbur Schramm, for example, attempted the following "typology" of reading motivation during the 1950s:[3]

1. *Compulsive ritualistic reading.* This term referred to reading that was so habitual and internalized as to be almost "automatic," like reading the newspaper over breakfast or leafing through a magazine in a dentist's waiting room. For this sort of reading, the content of the material is almost inconsequential; the activity of reading is what provides the security or solace desired.

2. *Reading for respite.* This is the ultimate in escapist reading. The content is almost completely divorced from the reader's real life. Consequently, little learning or retention is involved.

3. *Reading for a sense of personal security.* Here is reading for "borrowed success experiences" in which readers identify with the characters in a story or article to the degree that they psychologically share in those characters' exploits, deeds, successes, and personal triumphs.

4. *Reading for a sense of social security in a changing world.* In this type of reading one reinforces his own attitudes, beliefs, and judgments, and thus he is reassured that his own values are indeed still the "right" ones. Particularly when the reader is selecting nonfiction reading, this motive is often a dominant one.

5. *Reading for vicarious experiences.* Schramm defines this sort of reading as similar to the third type above, but its subject matter is more exotic. The reader might, for example, share in Lindbergh's transatlantic flight or scale Mount Everest with Tenzing and Hillary.

6. *Reading for social contact.* In this type of reading one reads

about interesting public personalities in such a way and to such a depth as to feel he "knows" them. He is thus vicariously involved in their lives. "Society" columns in local, regional, or national newspapers provide such reading material.

7. *Reading for aesthetic experience.* Certain characteristics of several of the preceding types are included in this sort of reading, although it is more penetrating and perhaps provides more insight for the reader. Schramm's definition of this type is less detailed than those of the other types of reading.

8. *Reading as a value in society.* Reading of this kind is pursued simply because it is felt to be a "good" thing, something to be done by all well-educated people. Here again Schramm's definition is lacking in detail.

9. *Reading as a tool for daily living.* Clearly informational and pragmatic, this sort of reading includes weather reports, stock market quotations, and so forth.

10. *Reading as a tool for self-improvement.* Information on how to do one's work better or how to raise one's family more successfully are examples of such reading. Here the techniques for self-improvement are probably more important than the insights or self-discoveries made by the reader.

11. *Reading as a device for scanning the horizon.* Included in this category are general news reading or informational reading, that is, materials dealing with the trends and directions of social movements, rather than with their daily progress.

12. *Reading for interpretation.* Schramm defined this as reading to acquire an understanding of what the day-to-day news means. As a result of such reading one can, for example, effectively evaluate current public policies.

There are, of course, weaknesses in Schramm's "typology," particularly in terms of the discreteness of the various types, even at a theoretical level. His pattern—that of moving from those reading activities whose reward is most immediate to those whose reward is most delayed or long term—probably holds. His apparent goal of creating an even dozen types may have led him, however, into more divisions than were really there. Also, one could substitute a phrase like "information seeking" for "reading" in each case and still fulfill the hierarchical goal of immediate to delayed reward. Many of the needs implicit in Schramm's list, in fact, are today probably far more easily and effectively met through televiewing than through reading. Social contact, for example, is achieved more fully through the regular viewing of talk shows than through reading, and even "Harlequin Romances" do not provide the vicarious experiences and perhaps even the personal security that soap operas do.

Overall, however, Schramm's list is still valuable to us because it provides a tremendous range of motives for reading. Of more importance to teachers would be a "model" or "pattern" or "formula" through which they could gauge the motivational appeal a particular reading activity might have for their students. Here, too, Schramm makes a contribution.

Motivation as a Ratio between Expected Reward and Expected Effort

In discussing reading choices, Schramm developed a concept and a model he described as "the fraction of selection."[4] With very little adaptation his approach can be transformed into a workable model, illustrated below, for considering motivation to read per se.

$$\text{motivation} = \frac{\text{expectation of reward to be gained}}{\text{expectation of effort to be expended}}$$

This model suggests to the teacher that motivation to read can be viewed simply as a fraction, the numerator of which is the amount of reward the student expects from the proffered piece of reading, and the denominator of which is the amount of effort, or "work," the student expects that piece of reading to entail. The value of the fraction, then, or the student's motivation to do the reading, like all fractions, can be increased in either of two ways: by raising the value of the numerator or by lowering the value of the denominator. In the classroom the teacher can increase desire (emphasize the possibilities of reward), decrease anticipated effort to be expended, or at times do both simultaneously.

Raising Expected Reward

The goal of most "introductory" or "readiness" activities carried out in the presentation of a new reading assignment to an individual or a group should stress the expected reward. By setting the stage for the reading activity — by posing questions, by relating the topics dealt with in the story to the students' experiences and interests, or simply by exhibiting enthusiasm for the story—the teacher is raising the numerator of the motivational fraction. The reading material becomes more valuable simply because there is more to be gained from it.

On the other hand, by introducing some of the difficult concepts or words to be dealt with or by pointing out and preparing the students for some of the challenging parts of the reading selection, the teacher is lowering the denominator. Thus, the total ratio is now worth more because it calls for relatively less effort.

This model could be extended even farther to cover the most extreme situations of low reading motivation a teacher faces: asking students to read especially difficult textbooks, to do follow-up research or reference reading in the library, or to make detailed stylistic analyses of literary works. Increasing the expected reward could go so far as to promise extrinsic reinforcements, such as grades, prizes, or release from some other school obligation. Decreasing the expected effort could go so far as the simplification of the material, such as providing study guides and outlines to be followed during the reading or giving specific help on certain tasks. Viewed this way, then, Schramm's initial model takes on overall pedagogical significance; it becomes almost an affective lesson plan, an overall schema for delineating the interplay between positive and negative forces for all classroom activities, as well as for reading.

It should be noted that many of the ways in which the expected reward is raised or the expected effort is lowered work in a complementary manner; that is, many of these procedures *both* raise the level of expected gains and lower the level of expected toil. A good introduction to a reading assignment, for example, can provide students with additional reasons for reading while at the same time preparing them for a more comfortable, less demanding reading experience.

Summary

The two major points in this section are based on the ideas of Wilbur Schramm. First, people are motivated to read for a variety of reasons, some automatic, habitual, and downright banal, and others more intellectual, more "cultural," and more in harmony with what professionals in the field consider the "higher" potentials of reading. Second, immediate motivation to read can be expressed as a ratio, a manipulable relationship between two factors: the reader's expectation of reward and expectation of effort to be expended in the reading task. To the teacher of reading, the second point is by far the more useful and valuable one.

PREFERENCES WITHIN READING MATERIALS

Here, too, as with immediate motivaton to reading, exact delineation of precise patterns of behavior is impossible. Preferences for various print media and reading topics are related to the reader's age, sex, skill, total background of experience, total complex of personal skills and abilities in reading, and total range of intellectual and psychological interests.

This is not to say, of course, that certain fairly consistent overall age-related or sex-related patterns of preference do not exist. They do, and much survey literature exists to document these patterns.[5]

Voluntary reading peaks during the junior high school years, with boys preferring adventure, mystery, and sports stories and girls preferring romance, animal stories, and career stories. As for exact titles, however, it is almost impossible to keep up with the field. Every year hundreds of new books appear, and each new favorite pushes an older best-seller out of the limelight.

We can say, however, that most readers like to read about things they know about, things they are curious about, or things they have dreamed about or fantasized about. In short, reading interests are based on human interests, and thus the best model for predicting interest patterns in reading would be one that deals with interest patterns in life. It is fortunate that we have such a model, even though it has rarely been suggested for this purpose: Abraham Maslow's hierarchy of human needs.[6]

Maslow's Hierarchy as a Predictor of Reading Interests

Maslow's hierarchy consists of five "stages" or "levels" hypothesized as covering the individual's total range of physical and psychological needs, and it suggests that some of these needs are more "basic" than others. The hierarchy can be conceived of as a triangle (as below), with the needs nearer the base, the most essential, and those higher on the triangle, the more "advanced" or "cultivated."

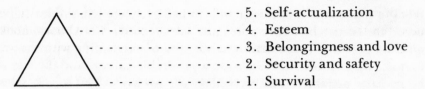

- - - - - - - - - - - - - - - - 5. Self-actualization
- - - - - - - - - - - - - - - 4. Esteem
- - - - - - - - - - - - - - 3. Belongingness and love
- - - - - - - - - - - - - 2. Security and safety
- - - - - - - - - - - - 1. Survival

Level 1: Survival needs. A person at this level feels a most powerful need for food, water, sleep, oxygen, and sex for reproductive purposes. He is thus said "to live by bread alone," as he can think of little else.

Level 2: Security and safety needs. At this level a person has already had the needs of the first level satisfied. Now he wants protection from uncertainty, a safe and secure environment that provides a sense of order.

Level 3: Belongingness and love needs. Once the needs of the first and second levels are satisfied, the needs of the third level gain greater potency. Wanting love, affection, and belongingness, the person seeks a place in a social group. He seeks love in terms of being "deeply understood and deeply accepted." The desire to be part of and accepted by the group is a pronounced characteristic of people operating at this level.

Level 4: Esteem needs. The needs for self-respect and to be held in esteem by other people are involved at this level. There is a strong desire for confidence, competence, mastery, adequacy, achievement, independence, and freedom. Respect from others involves the need for prestige, recognition, acceptance, attention, status, reputation, and appreciation.

Level 5: Self-actualization and cognitive needs. Maslow describes this level of need "as the desire to become more what one is, to become everything that one is capable of becoming." Self-actualizing people have satisfied, in large measure, the first four of Maslow's hierarchy of needs. Now they appreciate beauty, are at peace with themselves, and tend to be honest, "complete" people who enjoy life fully. They usually search for justice, perfection, individuality, and self-sufficiency. Maslow has suggested that there may be, in addition, higher cognitive "needs to know" that become operative when the other basic needs are met. Thus, the search to know for the sake of knowledge itself would characterize people operating at this level.

Anyone familiar with the relative sales records for various kinds of reading materials in America will immediately see the similarity between the hierarchy above and those sales records. Cookbooks, books on child care and home maintenance, and books dealing with the way to make money, the way to pursue a profitable career, and the way to be sexually attractive and well liked are always at the top in sales. Books related to love, adventure, and social success follow. Last in sales, and thus smallest in readership, are those books dealing with religion, philosophy, and aesthetics, the "needs to know" end of Maslow's hierarchy. In other words, in reading interests as well as in life, most people begin with the basics and then branch out or rise above them. The majority of us, however, rarely get beyond the middle levels.

From the point of view of teachers eager to encourage and motivate wide reading by their students, the implications of these generalizations are clear. In order to get unmotivated students to read, teachers must offer them reading materials dealing with the more basic areas of human needs. In order to motivate fairly interested students, teachers must expand the tastes of these students into books dealing with Maslow's higher levels of human needs.

We must, of course, be realistic. Just as there will probably never be as broad a base of attendance at the ballet or the symphony as there is at the musical comedy or the rock concert, there will also probably never be as many people who enjoy the classics in literature as who read how-to books, popular fiction, and current social commentary. Maslow's hierarchy does, however, provide a model and a direction. Most of us in reading would rather have our students read anything than read nothing, simply because of our strong conviction that this reading will help build and reinforce their general reading skill. Thus, we can start with books dealing with the basic needs and build from there. If we finally succeed in leading our students to "better" materials (or if, as happens so often, they themselves are led later in life to these materials), they will be skilled enough to deal successfully with them.

Summary

We can make two generalizations about readers' patterns of preference and how to capitalize upon them. For younger readers, particularly those still mastering basic reading skills, we should select material that deals directly with experiences and activities with which they are familiar and knowledgeable. For older readers, we can use Maslow's hierarchy as a model, beginning with materials related to the most basic human needs and then gradually nudging their reading tastes upward. Again, reading anything is better than reading nothing, at least from a pedagogical point of view, since continued growth in reading skill is necessary if one is ever to enjoy fine literature.

SPECIFIC AFFECTIVE RESPONSE TO READING MATERIALS

As noted earlier, this final aspect of the term "affect" as it relates to reading is undoubtedly the least truly researched of all the possible meanings of the term, even though this aspect is popular in terms of pedagogical and social theory about the nature of reading and reading response. Practically every literary critic and, indeed, almost all teachers of reading or literature have their own private conceptions of just what readers do or do not respond to as they deal with literary materials.

In education, the terms "critical" or "creative" reading are used to deal with this topic, but even within the profession there is no clear agreement as to just what these labels denote. In literature classes, for example, teachers usually urge their students to respond emotionally to reading: to the rhythm of the language; to the nuances of denotation and connotation attached to the author's words; to tone, to point of view, or even to certain symbols supposedly present in much good writing. Here, the teacher will probably advise the student to let himself go, to let the author carry him away on the wings of his words. Thus, highly responsive, although perhaps stylized, reading response is being called for and cultivated.

In social studies classes, or perhaps in home economics classes, however, if "wise consumerism" is the current topic under study, teachers give their students the opposite advice. Propaganda techniques will be pointed out, the verbal "tricks" or "appeals" of the advertising copywriter will be noted and analyzed, and the overall reading strategies advocated will be antithetical to those encouraged in literature classes. Students will be advised not to be taken in and not to allow themselves to be emotionally moved by the verbal trappings of the message. They should be cool, rational readers, not emotionally responsive ones. In this case, then, "suspended judgment," not "suspended disbelief," is being called for, even though in both cases the teacher's topic of the day may be referred to as "critical" reading.

Probably the best model we have available for encompassing these two divergent approaches to affective response to reading is Barrett's taxonomy of reading comprehension,[7] outlined in skeleton form below:

Barrett's Taxonomy of Reading Comprehension

1.0 Literal recognition or recall
    1.1 Recognition or recall of details
    1.2 Recognition or recall of main ideas
    1.3 Recognition or recall of sequence
    1.4 Recognition or recall of comparisons
    1.5 Recognition or recall of cause and effect
    1.6 Recognition or recall of relationships
    1.7 Recognition or recall of character traits

2.0 Inference
    2.1 Inferring supporting details
    2.2 Inferring the main idea
    2.3 Inferring sequence
    2.4 Inferring comparisons
    2.5 Inferring cause-and-effect relationships
    2.6 Inferring character traits
    2.7 Predicting outcomes
    2.8 Inferring about figurative language

3.0 Evaluation
    3.1 Judgments of reality or fantasy
    3.2 Judgments of fact or opinion
    3.3 Judgments of adequacy or validity
    3.4 Judgments of appropriateness
    3.5 Judgments of worth, desirability, and acceptability

4.0 Appreciation
    4.1 Emotional response to the content
    4.2 Identification with characters or incidents
    4.3 Reactions to the author's use of language
    4.4 Imagery

The above listing is, of course, only a bare outline of the complete taxonomy. Every serious student of reading will profit from a careful perusal of the author's full original statement, which includes suggestions both for framing questions and for designing classroom activities intended to develop readers' skills in each of the categories listed. The taxonomy shows us several ways in which both of the two major approaches to critical reading can be dealt with.

The third and fourth parts of the taxonomy, in particular, account for affective response, at least insofar as fairly young readers are concerned. What is most lacking in this model is the specificity needed to explain mature readers' responses to the various stylistic devices used by authors. In "inferring character traits," for example, we probably need to go beyond this broad category to determine exactly which elements in the reading passage cause us to infer that particular personality traits are present in the literary characters. Do their names draw forth certain affective overtones of meaning from within us? Do certain speech patterns found within the characters' dialogue (such as dialect, slang, or idioms commonly associated with particular occupations or social settings) elicit specific affective overtones as we read them?

In terms of this definition of affect as it relates to reading, then, the conclusions are clear. We need much more research and study before we can really begin to understand mature reading response and to decide how best to develop it in our students. Barrett's model can be helpful, but only as a beginning.

In truth, this is probably one of the areas in research on the reading process where most of us in the field are not well enough equipped, either conceptually or methodologically, to do the kind of research that is needed. For this job, we need the help and advice of psychologists, sociologists, and anthropologists, as well as of scholars in more closely related fields, such as linguistics and literary criticism. Reading viewed at this level is essentially thinking, and so we must consider all the variables associated with that process, not just those usually considered to be part of reading.

NOTES

1. David R. Krathwohl, Benjamin S. Bloom, and Bertram B. Masia, *Taxonomy of Educational Objectives, the Classification of Educational Goals, Handbook II: Affective Domain* (New York: David McKay, 1956).

2. Larry J. Mikulecky, "The Developing, Field Testing, and Initial Norming of a Secondary/Adult Level Reading Attitude Measure That Is Behaviorally Oriented and Based on Krathwohl's Taxonomy of the Affective Domain," unpublished dissertation, University of Wisconsin, 1976.

3. Wilbur Schramm, "Why Adults Read," in *Adult Reading*, Fifty-fifth Yearbook of the National Society for the Study of Education, Part II, ed. Nelson B. Henry (Chicago: University of Chicago Press, 1956), 79-81.

4. *Ibid.*, 64.

5. Alan C. Purves and Richard Beach, *Literature and the Reader: Research in Response to Literature, Reading Interests, and the Teaching of Literature* (Urbana, Ill.: National Council of Teachers of English, 1972).

6. Abraham Maslow, "A Theory of Human Motivation," *Psychological Review* 50 (July 1943): 374-396.

7. A full statement of the taxonomy developed by Thomas C. Barrett appears in Theodore Clymer, "What Is 'Reading'? Some Current Concepts," in *Innovation and Change in Reading Instruction*, Sixty-seventh Yearbook of the National Society for the Study of Education, Part II, ed. Helen M. Robinson (Chicago: University of Chicago Press, 1968), 19-23.

6. Current Issues in Secondary School Reading Instruction

Eugene H. Cramer

The major educational reform movement of the mid-1970s has focused on the American high school.[1] Many shortcomings in the education of American adolescents have been attributed to inadequacies of high school educational programs. Chief among these is the charge that high schools are not preparing students to be responsible, mature citizens in an age beset with problems.

Educational authorities and the general public have decried the apparent decline in educational achievement of high school students. Clifton Fadiman, in addressing a conference of the Council for Basic Education in St. Louis, expressed the concern that "student achievement has now declined to a point that may endanger our whole social structure."[2] At the same conference, Dr. John Porter expressed doubt that schools would be able to give occupational and vocational training to students who most need it because they "Can't read and write well enough to pass a simple eighth-grade examination."[3] The pessimism of these and other educational authorities is echoed by the general public. In the Eighth Annual Gallup Poll of the Public's Attitudes toward the Public Schools, conducted in April 1976, 59 percent of the sample indicated a belief that a decline in national test scores of students in recent years means that the quality of education is declining, 51 percent thought that devoting more attention to the teaching of basic skills would do most to improve the overall quality of public school education, and 65 percent favored requiring students to pass a standard nationwide examination in order to get a high school diploma.[4]

Another indication of the public's dissatisfaction with high school achievement levels has been manifested in the courts. "Peter Doe," an eighteen-year-old graduate of a San Francisco high school, filed a $1 million suit against the public schools in 1972, contending that although he received a diploma, he is unable to read adequately.[5] In January 1977, the parents of Edward Donohue filed notice of intention to sue the School District of Copaigue, New York, alleging that their son received a high school diploma although he could not read beyond the fourth-grade level.[6] In both of these cases the high school graduates contended that they could not read or write well enough to cope with job application forms and basic occupational requirements.

A growing conviction that high school programs should prepare graduates for occupations was also reflected in the 1976 Gallup Poll. To the question, "Do you think that the school curriculum should give more emphasis, or less emphasis, to careers and career preparation in high school?" 80 percent of the national sample responded, "More emphasis."[7] Thomas Sticht anticipated this national trend with his book, *Reading for Working,* in which he concluded that secondary schools should develop functional literacy curricula that will help high school students develop not only their academic skills but also their career and occupational skills.[8]

In response to the criticism of educational authorities and the demands of citizens, many high schools have developed various models of remedial or corrective reading programs for students whose reading skills appear to be below expectations. Such programs have been given various labels: compensatory, alternative, innovative, remedial, and so forth. While some programs have been successful, most appear to be ineffectual, inefficient stopgap measures.

It is the purpose of this chapter to examine a cluster of exceedingly complex issues surrounding reading instruction in junior and senior high schools. In light of increasing pressures for secondary school reform, particularly in the basic skill of reading, the first section of the chapter examines currently available data on reading achievement levels and discusses implications of variously conceived standards of reading competency. The second section contains a description of the reading needs of secondary school students, including development of higher-level reading skills and a review of the current status of research in secondary school reading. In the third section, various ideas, suggestions, methods, and programs for improving reading instruction in secondary schools are presented. The fourth section deals with the content teacher's role in reading instruction, including an account of the current status of state certification requirements in reading for secondary teachers. The final section reemphasizes current needs and makes suggestions for future directions in the improvement of reading instruction at the secondary school level. Because other chapters of this book deal specifically with remedial reading and with affective dimensions of reading instruction, these important topics are not included in this chapter.

HISTORICAL PERSPECTIVE

Professionals in reading have long recommended that reading instruction be included as a regular part of the high school curriculum. One of the earliest formal statements to that effect was made in 1925 by the National Committee on Reading in the Twenty-fourth Yearbook of the National Society for the Study of Education.[9] The committee took the position that pupils must be made aware of the relationship between reading and all other activities of school life from the very beginning of their reading instruction through the middle grades and into junior and senior high school. They expressed the view that the mere mastery of the mechanics of reading, the development of good oral reading habits, and the motivation of interests in good literature were no longer appropriate aims for education in a rapidly changing society. Accordingly, the committee recommended that reading objectives needed to be broadened to "prepare pupils to engage effectively in all essential school and life activities that involve reading."[10] Despite enormous technological and sociological changes over the past fifty years, which have brought our country from the horse-and-buggy age to the space age, equivalent changes have not occurred in reading education. Thus, the statement of the committee in 1925 would be, with minor changes, equally desirable as a charge to the schools today.

The specific aims set forth by the National Committee on Reading as appropriate for junior and senior high school students included the following: to extend the experiences of students and to increase their intellectual understanding through wide reading, both work-type and recreational, of books, articles, magazines, and newspapers appropriate to each subject that was studied; to help students acquire the highest possible standards of personal taste and values for the wholesome use of reading in leisure activities and public life; to lead students to high levels of critical reading skills that are involved in reading for various purposes; to give special individual or group instruction in basic reading skills as the need exists; to improve oral reading skills in performance situations, both in class and in public; and to develop high levels of skill in ability to use books and library resources most effectively.[11] Again, with the exception of the development of oral reading skills, the aims established in 1925 appear to be substantially those expressed most often today as admirable objectives for the development of reading skills, habits, and attitudes in our junior and senior high school students.

The National Committee on Reading formulated goals for reading instruction that were based notably upon Edward L. Thorndike's conclusion that reading is thinking and upon other earlier work such as that of Edmund Burke Huey.[12] These goals have changed remarkably little in the intervening years. For example, present-day reading specialists and investigators tend to agree that higher-level reading skills need to be taught beyond the elementary school years into the junior and senior high school years. Although goals have remained fairly constant, methods of instruction and division of responsibility for meeting the goals have engendered considerable disagreement. A number of these issues will be discussed in later sections of this chapter. In the Sixty-seventh Yearbook of the National Society for the Study of Education, issued in 1968, Helen Robinson summarized the then, and now, current problems involved in any serious attempt to improve the teaching of reading at all levels: "The attack on the problems of (a) understanding the reading process, (b) learning how to teach higher-level reading skills, (c) developing effective teaching and learning sequences, and (d) determining the various roles of the teacher is a large order for the next decade."[13]

The next decade is nearly over, and the "large order" specified by Robinson is far from being fulfilled. In fact, in the mid-1970s there are a growing public dissatisfaction with levels of reading achievement and a weakening of public confidence in the ability of schools to overcome the deficiencies.

CURRENT LITERACY ASSESSMENTS

College Entrance Test Scores

The source of much public concern over reading achievement levels in the high schools is a year-by-year decline of college entrance examination scores over the past decade. Verbal scores on the Scholastic Aptitude Test of the College Entrance Examination Board have moved down from a national average of 473 in 1964-65 to 434 in 1974-75, almost double the rate of decline of mathematics scores on the same test. The average test scores for each year in verbal and mathematics achievement of the total national group are shown in Table 6-1.

Table 6-1

Average Test Scores on the College Entrance Examination Board's
Scholastic Aptitude Test, Men and Women Combined

Year	Verbal	Mathematics
1964-65	473	496
1965-66	471	496
1966-67	467	496
1967-68	466	494
1968-69	462	491
1969-70	460	488
1970-71	454	487
1971-72	450	482
1972-73	443	481
1973-74	440	478
1974-75	434	472

Source: Adapted from ACTivity, newsletter of the American College Testing Program, 14 (December 1976): 5.

Similar declines in scores are evident in the American College Testing Program's ACT results. Over the past eleven years average scores in English, mathematics, social studies, and the composite have, with few exceptions, moved downward, while the average scores have remained at about the same level in the natural sciences. The sharpest decline was in the social studies, and there was a moderate decline in the English and mathematics scores. Table 6-2 shows average scores over the period 1964-1975 for the English, mathematics, social studies, natural sciences, and composite sections of the ACT test.

Table 6-2

Average Test Scores in the ACT Assessment Program
Men and Women Combined

Year	English	Mathe-matics	Social studies	Natural sciences	Composite
1964-65	18.7	19.6	20.6	20.4	19.9
1965-66	19.1	19.5	20.5	20.5	20.0
1966-67	18.5	18.7	19.6	20.1	19.4
1967-68	18.1	18.3	19.4	19.8	19.0
1968-69	18.4	19.2	19.4	20.0	19.4
1969-70	18.1	19.5	19.3	20.5	19.5
1970-71	17.7	18.7	18.3	20.2	18.9
1971-72	17.6	18.6	18.4	20.3	18.8
1972-73	17.8	18.8	18.1	20.5	18.9
1973-74	17.6	18.1	17.9	20.6	18.7
1974-75	17.3	17.4	17.1	20.8	18.3

Source: Adapted from *ACTivity,* newsletter of the American College Testing Program, 14 (December 1976): 5.

That the decline in college entrance test scores has caused some consternation is an understatement. The issue has aroused much emotion, and many possible explanations for the decline have been made. The ACT program directors instituted a comprehensive search into the phenomenon and suggest that there is some factual evidence to support at least two theoretical explanations. The first is that the pool of students planning to enter college today has changed from what it was a decade ago. More students from the lower half of their graduating classes have entered the pool, thus depressing the average scores. The second explanation is that high school students today are weaker academically than their counterparts of a decade ago. Various explanations are cited for this change: widespread use of elective courses, lowered demands and expectations by teachers, and a more "open" classroom atmosphere permitting students a greater degree of self-direction than occurred in the past.[14]

National Assessment of Educational Progress (NAEP)

The withering of public confidence does not seem to be entirely justified, however. Despite the decline of average scores on college entrance examination, data from the NAEP indicate that the reading abilities of high school students were about the same in 1971 and 1975.[15] The NAEP test assessed general reading skills of three age groups: nine-, thirteen-, and seventeen-year-olds in 1971 and 1975.

All three age levels did well on literal comprehension questions, but thirteen- and seventeen-year-olds had more difficulty in items that required the use of inferential reading skills. In reference skill items, nine-year-olds improved by 2.2 percentage points, thirteen-year-olds declined slightly, and seventeen-year-olds remained about the same as their counterparts in 1971.[16] Roger Farr noted that, while overall reading achievement is really better than the public believes, the NAEP scores suggest that high schools could do more to get students involved in reading and to help them develop higher levels of reading skills.[17]

Other Literacy Assessments

Although the data presented by the NAEP indicate no serious reading decline among the overall national sample, it is true that certain groups of students in various areas of the country fall well below the norms on standardized reading tests. For example, results of reading test scores, published annually in a number of major cities, show wide variation in average scores from school to school within a single system. Furthermore, studies of reading achievement in Georgia by Bernice Cooper in 1974 and in Kentucky by Wallace Ramsey twelve years earlier indicated an apparent lag in achievement in reading skills from elementary school years to upper grades and high school years.[18] In Cooper's study, which involved 30,000 pupils in the fourth through the twelfth grades, black children showed a mean comprehension deficit of 1.2 grade levels in the fourth grade and a deficit of 5.3 by the twelfth grade; white children lagged 0.2 grade levels in the seventh grade and 2.2 in the twelfth. Cooper noted the increased lag in both groups and concluded that there is a necessity for sustained, sequential reading instruction throughout the secondary school years. Ramsey's study included over half of the fourth- and eighth-grade pupils in Kentucky in 1962. He noted relatively small gains in scores among eighth graders and also concluded that the results might mean that reading instruction should be continued throughout the secondary school years.

Paul Diederich surveyed the research from 1960 to 1970 on the deficit in functional literacy and inferred from it that "the data base does not exist for adequate estimates of this deficit in terms of any criterion of meeting individual needs and social needs."[19] He noted, however, that if the reading grade level of 5.0 is accepted as adequate,

12 million persons over fourteen years of age fall below; if that of grade 8.0, 45 million fall below.[20]

STANDARDS OF LITERACY

Since the passage of the Adult Education Act of 1966, there has been renewed interest in the problems of defining and measuring literacy. A number of terms have been coined to indicate literacy levels: functional literacy, survival literacy, minimal competence, career literacy, and adult performance level, to name a few. The problem with this proliferation of terms was alluded to by Diederich in the study citied above. What criterion level is to be used to signify that literacy has been attained? In past years, literacy was linked to number of years spent in school. Such a criterion is useless without some knowledge of reading skill attained by an individual during those years. Two separate investigators have recently attempted to establish criteria of literacy that will have more meaningful application and wider currency.

In an attempt to provide the type of theoretical rationale necessary for determining adequate levels of literacy, William Powell has delineated three literacy levels that are based on standardized reading grade-level equivalents: a preliteracy level, a basic literacy level, and a career literacy level.[21] He asserts that a reading grade-level ability of 7.5 is the lowest level at which an individual will have a minimal choice of occupation.

The American College Testing program announced in October 1976 the availability of an Adult Performance Level (ACT-APL) Survey that focuses on the reading abilities adults are expected to possess in order to function in their daily lives. After four years of research and development, the new instrument is available in two forms: high school and adult. Thomas W. Mann, director of the ACT-APL project, defined functional competency on the basis of research studies as "the ability of an adult to apply skills to several major areas of knowledge that are important to adult functioning: consumer economic, occupations, health, community resources, and government and law."[22] The position of ACT is that basic reading ability, as it has been measured in the past with standardized reading tests that assess grade-level reading achievement, is not a useful criterion for determining basic literacy. For this reason, the ACT-APL test assesses an individual's ability to apply reading skills to everyday adult reading situations by including items about job notices, tax forms, retail shopping information, traffic regulations, health notices, and the like. National norms are being established, presumably in response to recent court cases and public indignation about so-called "illiterate" high school graduates. By using an instrument such as the ACT-APL test, a school system would have sufficient information to award or withhold a high school diploma. Implications of competency testing of this sort, however, need to be examined carefully. What, for example, can be done to assure equivalent standards for different students from different school districts and different states? What will happen to those who do not meet standards of minimal competence? Will current conceptions of minimal career literacy remain sufficient to enable high school graduates to cope with the rapidly changing requirements of our technological society?

In summary, the current national concern about the "reading problem" is focused on levels of literacy. At one extreme are high school graduates who do not read well enough to perform the most basic operations considered essential to successful life as adults. At the other extreme is the seeming lack of higher-level reading skills essential to the successful pursuit of academic endeavors. An examination of the higher-level skills will demonstrate that these are not unrelated extremes, but, rather, points along a continuum.

HIGHER-LEVEL READING SKILLS

The statement of goals of the National Committee on Reading in 1925 was explicit in making junior and senior high school teachers responsible for helping students to develop their reading skills in each of the content areas.[23] Although the slogan had not yet been coined, it was clear that the authors regarded every teacher as a teacher of reading. Further, they implied that reading was to be viewed as a process "subservient to the real interests and larger purposes for which pupils read."[24] Throughout their report, the authors emphasized that reading was not a separate curricular activity but a tool for experiencing and interpreting subject matter in all fields. Despite their insistence that the reading process be regarded as a tool, the committee enjoined subject-matter teachers "to keep the reading skills sufficiently in the foreground that they may be improved and refined."[25]

In the past few decades, an enormous amount of research and program development has been devoted to the teaching of beginning reading skills. Research studies into beginning reading processes and instructional methods have been estimated to outnumber those dealing with the upper grades by a ratio of six to one.[26] Some reading authorities are now saying that, although there is the ever present possibility of further improvement in beginning reading instructional methods, large gains have already been made.[27] Diederich, for example, ventures the opinion that " it seems reasonably safe to say that we *do know* how to get practically all children past the initial stages of learning to read."[28]

If these opinions are valid, then the focus of research should be shifted to questions related to teaching higher-level reading skills. Getting children past the initial stages of beginning reading, or basic decoding, has not yielded to easy or simplistic treatments. Similarly, the complex process of leading pupils to their full potential in higher-level reading skills will require a massive national effort in basic research and in the development of programs and materials.

Research into Content-Area Reading

Central to all discussion of content-area reading instruction is comprehension. Many models and conceptualizations of reading comprehension have been formulated. It is not the intent, nor is it within the scope of this chapter, however, to examine the complexities of reading comprehension in great detail. A minimal definition of comprehension is that it involves the process by which a reader gets the thought of what he is reading. Various studies of the underlying factors of reading comprehension have been conducted over the past several decades by such investigators as Edward Thorndike, I. A. Richards, Frederick Davis, Jack Holmes, and others.[29] These studies have led to the general understanding that reading comprehension is apparently influenced by a reader's knowledge of word meanings, his ability to reason, his grasp of syntactic elements, his rate of reading, and his purpose for reading. Despite a growing body of information about reading comprehension, however, it remains a process that is but dimly understood, both psychologically and physiologically.

Without a much clearer delineation of the interrelationships involved in the process of reading comprehension, the teaching of high-level reading skills must remain largely the intuitive operation that it is at present. Diederich and his colleagues reviewed an inclusive collection of research studies dealing with the nature and extent of the current deficit in functional literacy, the effectiveness of different methods of teaching reading, and the training of teachers of reading.[30] Of the 15,000 documents collected and reviewed, only 480 were ultimately selected as meeting such standards of research that their conclusions could be studied to "find out what was known for sure about reading and what further research was needed."[31]

Chief among the conclusions drawn by Diederich are the following. First, no solid evidence exists to restrict the teaching methods of any reasonably informed, perceptive teacher at any level, since some literature supports and other literature challenges all reading instructional methods used in the last decade. Second, research studies on beginning reading should be curtailed, and those dealing with higher levels of reading should be emphasized. Third, standards of conducting and reporting research in reading must be raised. Fourth, the national reading problem is, in effect, a problem of thinking or comprehension over which the schools have little control.

Anyone who is concerned with the development of higher-level reading skills will find the implications of Diederich's conclusions enormous. His first conclusion is consistent with earlier ones reported by Guy Bond and Robert Dykstra and by Jeanne Chall.[32] The vast amount of research data collected over the years points to no single beginning reading method as being superior to the others. As Diederich avers, "With allowance for the percentage of failure that seems unavoidable in all human enterprises, it seems reasonably safe to say that we *do know* how to get practically all children past the initial stages of learning to read. Above grade 3, in fact, traces of any initial advantage of one method over another are hardly to be found."[33]

Diederich's second and third conclusions bear directly upon the major contention of this chapter. In regard to his second point, curtailing research on beginning reading and concentrating on those dealing with higher-level reading skills may do much to alleviate the reading problem. Research on higher-level reading skills is lacking in both quantity and quality. In regard to his third point, Diederich and his associates reviewed at one stage of their research 612 studies dealing with reading methods. They ranked each study according to three criteria: representativeness, treatment, and measurement. Of these studies, only 265 were judged to be "acceptable" according to the above criteria. Of the acceptable studies, 80 percent were concerned with methods of reading instruction for the first through the sixth grades, 15 percent with the seventh through the twelfth grades, and the remaining 5 percent with college and adult levels.[34] It is clear, therefore, that research studies into methods of instruction in higher-level reading skills are greatly overshadowed by those dealing with the lower grade levels. This trend must be reversed, and the resultant research must be carefully designed, conducted, and reported.

Diederich's fourth conclusion — that the national "reading problem" is in reality a thinking or comprehension problem — has sociological, psychological, and economic implications that range far beyond the scope of this chapter. It seems unlikely, however, that the problem will be resolved by the current emphasis on research into beginning reading methods. But massive and rigorous research effort into higher-level reading skills and methods of teaching them could have a profound effect on solving our reading problem.

General Investigations into Secondary School Reading Instruction

Not only has the amount of research into secondary school reading instruction been disproportionately low, but what has been done has not been concerned with higher-level reading skills. Investigators have studied, instead, such things as differential reading achievement between adolescent boys and girls, effects of special, compensatory reading projects or programs, and the predictability of entrance examination scores as related to academic achievement. It is difficult to generalize from such investigations because of a lack of information regarding research design, treatment, selection of subjects, measurement procedures, and so forth.

Following are some representative general research studies into secondary school reading done in the past few years.

Harry Singer noted that the reading achievement of girls is markedly higher in the early, formative years and that junior high school girls maintain an edge in rate and vocabulary over their male counterparts.[35] Naomi Sinks and Marvin Powell, however, reported no difference in reading achievement among adolescent males and females in their study.[36] It should be noted that contradictory or equivocal results are not unusual in studies dealing with reading achievement based on sexual differences.

In the area of special compensatory reading projects or programs, Mary Harris and Fred Ream reported on the results of a summer ses-sion course designed to increase students' commitment to improving their study habits and techniques. The subjects were high school students, both volunteers and nonvolunteers, from English and geometry classes. Treatment was described as a number of specially designed lessons. Summer school grades were used as the criterion. When grades were compared with a control group, no significant difference was noted, but a trend toward higher grade point average was apparent for the reading improvement group.[37]

In another reading improvement study, Wayne Gwaltney randomly assigned sixty high school sophomores and juniors to three sections in a seven-week course. A variety of instructional materials was used. No significant difference was reported among the groups that were given a pretest, a posttest, and a delayed posttest after ten weeks.[38]

In a specially designed reading improvement program for Indian students who were problem readers, Robert Alley and his colleagues used tangible rewards and instructor-selected activities in eight reinforcement areas. After twelve weeks of instruction in classes of fifteen to twenty students who met daily for fifty minutes, the sixty-five ninth graders and thirty-nine eleventh graders showed a mean increase on standardized reading measures of 1.2 years.[39]

Richard Sinatra reported the results of a summer reading improvement program that also utilized a point reinforcing system. Subjects were nineteen white students and seventeen black students in the eighth, ninth, and tenth grades. The program involved three teachers and a staff of seven, allowing the students to be divided into five reading groups. A mean growth in reading grade level of 1.4 years was reported, along with an increase of twenty-two words per minute in reading rate. It was also reported, however, that eleven students dropped out of the program before it was completed.[40]

In the preceding three studies it is not clear whether gains in reading were made because of rewards, the form of special instruction, or some combination of the two factors.

Another general study dealt with the predictability of scores on a high school entrance examination. Maureen Murphy observed three measures of academic performances of students over a four-year period and compared them with students' scores on an entrance examination. The relationships were significant for regularly admitted groups but not for a special compensatory group. Murphy reasons that the entrance examination is a reliable predictor of academic success for regularly admitted students but that some other measure is needed to predict accurately the academic success of students from economically depressed areas who are admitted on a special basis.[41]

A few general studies dealing with reading comprehension have been done in the past several years. Typical of these are the following three.

Maurice Williams and Virginia Stevens investigated the ability to summarize the main idea of a paragraph and to find the topic sentence. They found that, when trained with example exercises, both elementary and secondary pupils improved in these abilities, that secondary pupils were more proficient than elementary pupils, and that both groups had most difficulty when the topic sentence was placed in the middle of a paragraph.[42]

The use of instructional objectives as directions to learners was studied by Robert Kaplan and Ernst Rothkopf. Variables were the length of the passage and the amount of objective-relevant content. Increased performance resulted from the use of objectives as directions. Mastery of any objective decreased with the number of objective-relevant sentences, and specifically stated objectives resulted in greater intentional learning than generally stated objectives.[43]

Priscilla Galloway compared the ability of eleventh-grade students with the ability of teachers to comprehend subject-matter textbooks. Teachers outperformed students in all comparisons, but there were differences in the degree of performance on different types of material. Students improved when tests were given in context; teachers did not. Both students and teachers had most difficulty with selections from literature.[44]

The preceding research studies have been presented as typical of general investigations into secondary school reading. I contend that, even when they are most rigorously conducted, most studies fall far short of what is most needed: direct investigation of higher-level reading processes and instructional methods for increasing the proficiency of high school students in using them.

Investigations into Content-Area Reading

Harold Herber and Margaret Early pointed out the scarcity of research into methods of teaching reading as an integral part of a content-area curriculum.[45] They estimated that a mere one-fourth of all research on secondary school reading is directed toward the teaching of reading skills; the rest is concerned with a variety of tangential matters.

One of the most extensive reviews of the research on reading in content areas is the publication of the International Reading Association, *Reading in the Content Areas.*[46] Research on the teaching of reading skills in English, mathematics, science, and social studies is reported at length, with sections devoted to possible applications of the findings. It is worthy of note that all of the authors point out the scarcity of research in their particular fields. Herber, writing on social studies, is perhaps the most vehement: "The paucity of research on methods of teaching reading as an integral part of the social studies curriculum is almost appalling."[47] Each of the contributors to the book, however, enthusiastically accepts the responsibility for incorporating instruction in reading skills into the subject-matter curriculum. Their papers generally support the position that students' achievement is improved if instruction in reading skills is integrated with instruction in content.[48]

A problem that is frequently investigated in research in content-area reading is the readability of textbooks. A number of recent readability studies support the investigation by Margaret Janz and Edwin Smith who reported that many high school students with average intellectual ability have difficulty comprehending their content-area textbooks.[49] Keith Kennedy found this to be true for textbooks in science.[50] Milton Jacobson asked his students to underline words they did not understand in their physics and chemistry textbooks. He found that the least popular physics text was the most difficult for students to read, although difficulty was not considered by the state agency responsible for selecting textbooks.[51] In a well-designed study, Regis Wiegand calculated the readability levels of mathematics textbooks for the eighth through the twelfth grades and administered standardized reading tests to the students who used them. He concluded that the median readability levels of the textbooks were above the reading levels of the students.[52] Robert Aukerman, measuring the readability levels of sixty-six literature anthologies, discovered that few could be read independently by underachieving readers. Thus, he estimated that approximately three million students cannot read their assigned literature textbooks.[53]

Russell Burgett reported on a number of studies dealing with reading comprehension in the content areas.[54] He feels that reading comprehension is influenced most strongly by four major factors: vocabulary, sentence and paragraph structure, reading rate, and the purpose for which the reader is reading. These and other higher-level reading skills are discussed in the next section.

There are, of course, many more investigations into content-area reading than can be discussed here. The common view regarding research into the teaching of reading at the junior and senior high school levels is, however, that not enough has been done, that little of what has been done is of sufficient quality to be useful, and that too much of it is peripheral.

Reading Needs of Secondary Pupils

On the basis of reviews of research, personal observations, and opinions gathered from colleagues, I have compiled the following list of the reading needs of secondary school students. There are several potential uses for such a list. It could serve as a guide for content-area teachers to select and devise appropriate teaching materials and strategies for improving the reading skills of their students. It could enable investigators or teachers to locate areas of critical weakness in students' higher-level reading skills. It could be employed as a syllabus in a reading methods course for preservice secondary school content-area teachers. It could act as a reminder of the great number of complex skills required of a mature reader, thereby serving as an overview of secondary reading skills.

Word Reading Skills

Basic to all reading is the ability to cope with unfamiliar words encountered in print. Mature readers favor the use of contextual clues and structural analysis to solve the problem. Beginning readers, on the contrary, frequently employ phonic analysis to unlock from print a word that is contained in their listening-speaking vocabulary. Phonic analysis is, however, of questionable value to the mature reader for whom unfamiliar printed words are not likely to be in the aural-oral vocabulary. Junior and senior high school students need direct instruction and considerable practice in the use of contextual and structural analysis. Secondary school students need to become conscious of words, aware of their multiple meanings, and sensitive to the subtle shadings of meaning brought about by an author's choice of words. Instruction and practice in use of the dictionary are also vital to a mature reader for those times when other methods of recognizing and choosing the appropriate word are inadequate.

Sentence Reading Skills

Students encounter a confusing array of syntactic possibilities in their subject-matter reading. They need to be introduced to absolute and relative terms, inverted word orders, the conventions of punctuation, double negatives, multiple embeddings, and heavy passive use, to name a few. Audrey Edwards found that the position and construction of relative clauses and the structure of independent clauses affected students' reading comprehension scores.[55] Roy O'Donnell reported a seemingly higher correlation between reading comprehension and the ability to recognize structural relationships of words in sentences than there is between reading comprehension and the ability to verbalize knowledge of terminology and rules.[56] Studies such as these emphasize the need for teachers to become aware of the needs of students in order for them to develop sentence reading skills.

Paragraph Reading Skills

Locating topic sentences, identifying main ideas and details, and recognizing transitional words and phrases are reading skills needed by mature readers. A study by Sister Mary Conception Tomkowicz in 1959 produced some evidence that direct teaching of paragraph patterns was of significant value in improving reading comprehension of eighth-grade students.[57] There have been a few other studies in this area, all suggesting that knowledge of paragraph structure has a beneficial effect on reading comprehension.[58] Further research is needed, particularly in the areas of teachers' knowledge of paragraph structure and of methods and materials for developing students' awareness of these structural elements.

Book Reading Skills

Students need a wide variety of book reading skills to become more effective readers. They include knowledge and use of the various parts of a book: title page, headings and subheadings, appendixes, glossaries, indexes, and typographical aids. Further, students can be instructed in techniques of sampling, browsing, and selection. While no research studies were located that test only book reading skills, they were included as an element in a comprehensive research project by Iver Moe and Frank Nania that deals with study skills for superior students in secondary school. One of their conclusions was that students' reading rate and flexibility had substantially improved three months after the teaching cycle ended.[59] It is not possible, of course, to infer that knowledge of the parts of a book had any effect in this study. Since skills in book reading are included in many texts on reading methods and in books on improving the ability to study, it would seem that some research is needed to justify their inclusion.

Reference and Library Reading Skills

Classification systems, in locating materials, skills, use of special reference works, and other devices employed by mature readers can and should be taught to high school students. They are probably best taught, however, as a process subordinate to a larger purpose. Thus, when a student genuinely needs or desires to use the library, the learning involved will be less troublesome than when it is a part of the typical "library unit" appended to many English and social studies classes.

Study Skills

Efficient study systems, beneficial study habits, techniques of memorizing, and principles of associating new knowledge with old can be taught within content-area classes. For many students, reading a chapter in a textbook and studying that chapter mean the same thing. A great amount of information about the psychology of learning is available in the research literature. Most high school students and many of their teachers are not, however, aware of this body of knowledge. This is most unfortunate since the principles of learning are immediately useful in a high school student's life, as well as later.

Purpose and Rate of Reading

Mature, skilled readers are able to adjust their rate of reading to a predetermined purpose.[60] Too many students and some other adults, however, read all materials at one constant rate. Thomas Lackman found that a reader's purpose for reading influenced the rate of reading; the mean reading time for subjects who had to select and defend their choice of prequestions was significantly faster than the mean reading time for subjects receiving other treatment or instructions.[61] When a reader has a purpose for reading, he is more likely to read faster and comprehend more. The principle of flexibility of reading rate to match purpose for reading is one that can be practiced in most content-area classes.

Content-Area Reading Skills

Each content area has a number of reading skills unique to it. Science, literature, and social studies, for example, all have special vocabularies. Reading map symbols in earth science classes, translating story problems to mathematical symbols in arithmetic classes, or following recipes in cooking classes are but a few special situations involving content-area reading. Content-area teachers can help students by listing and describing the types of reading skills to be emphasized in their respective areas.

Critical and Evaluative Reading Skills

To follow an author's line of argument, to detect fallacies in reasoning, to infer an author's intention, tone, or persuasive strategy, and to judge the value of a piece of writing are among the highest reading skills. Content-area teachers can help their students to improve such skills through skillful questioning techniques and by requiring the comparative reading of wider ranges of materials. By constantly challenging students to inquire about causes, motives, results, and purposes, teachers will help them become critical consumers of what they read both in school and out.[62]

Creative and Appreciational Reading Skills

Mature readers respond emotionally to an author's use of language, to descriptions of characters and events, and to the mental imagery aroused by a passage. Their reading creates, devises, assembles, or produces ideas, actions, and products. At the same time that content-area teachers are fostering their students' creative and appreciational reading habits, they are also increasing their awareness of the range and scope of the content area. A number of publications are available to help content-area teachers plan activities and projects to encourage creative and appreciational reading skills.[63]

CONTENT-AREA PROGRAMS, METHODS, AND INNOVATIONS

Current Status

Though there is a dearth of empirical data to support content-area teachers in the teaching of reading skills, an abundance of suggestions, methods, strategies, and innovations have been reported. The writers of the many reports seem to feel that an idea that has been tried and judged successful in one school will work equally well in other schools. In this section are listed but a few of the hundreds or such reports published within the last five years.

First are a few articles from the *Journal of Reading,* published by the International Reading Association, all of which are of the personal account or "how-to" variety. Jill Frankel's article is a "personal account of ideas implemented in the classroom, all the while integrating, integrating, integrating."[64] An article by Fred Lees, entitled "Mathematics and Reading," contains "specific suggestions for teaching students to read in mathematics courses."[65] John Carney's and William Losinger's article is headed "Reading and Content in Technical-Vocational Education."[66] Kenneth Ahrendt's and Shirley Haselton's article, "Essential Reading Skills in Bookkeeping," is described thus: "Every teacher a teacher of reading is a fine goal, but content area teachers often need specifics. The coauthors provide practical suggestions for the business education teacher to help make reading assignments worthwhile."[67] "Of course He Can Read—He's in High School," an article by R. Baird Shuman, contains some "ideas and approaches for helping disabled teenage readers."[68] A somewhat more ambitious article by Nicholas Criscuolo, entitled "An Interdisciplinary Approach to Reading," contains "a description of six content area reading programs on the secondary level."[69] W. John Harker noted the "embarrassment of riches" aspect of articles concerning the teaching of reading in secondary schools in his categorization of fifty-two such articles under sixteen headings.[70]

Further, several issues of the *English Journal,* published by the National Council of Teachers of English, have been entirely devoted to the teaching of reading in English classes. Most notable is the issue of November 1974, "Reading in the English Classroom," which includes editorials, feature articles, teaching ideas, and resource sections focusing on what English teachers can do about the "reading crisis." Most of the articles in the issue are written from a "humanness" point of view that reading is a holistic process and that readers are persons who read. It decries "simplistic skills development solutions" of workbooks, kits, and other technological devices.[71]

All of the foregoing seems an echo of Diederich's conclusion that "there is no solid evidence to restrict the teaching of a reasonably informed alert teacher of reading at any level."[72]

Evaluation of Innovations

At this point a number of issues converge to force a conclusion. First, there is increasing public demand for improvement in reading achievement, particularly in higher-level reading skills. Second, there is a lack of rigorous empirical studies into higher-level reading processes and appropriate instructional methods. Third, there is an almost unchecked flow of articles, lacking empirical support, that explain how to teach reading in secondary school content areas. The conclusion to be derived from the foregoing is that it is past time to subject promising innovations to critical evaluation procedures. Those that are found wanting must be discarded, and those that prove effective, according to the most rigorous empirical standards, should be disseminated.

Evaluating innovations in the teaching of reading is not a difficult task, but it is an exacting one. Over the years, a number of guidelines have been established for evaluating empirical studies.[73] The set presented here was devised by Willard Congreve.[74] With minor adaptations, the list is most appropriate to the evaluation of innovations in the teaching of higher-level reading skills.

Basic to the evaluation of instructional innovation is the innovator's sense of responsibility. Anyone who undertakes the task of improving reading instruction must be willing also to accept the following responsibilities: to conduct a comprehensive review of existing research literature dealing with the area under consideration; to choose appropriate evaluation instruments and procedures that will truly measure the effectiveness of the innovation; to consider carefully all aspects of the innovation, including both process and results, in constructing the rationale, the strategies and materials, and the instruments of measurement; and to report in detail *all* treatments, procedures, and outcomes. Without assurances that promising innovations in instructional methods in reading have successfully passed through such evaluation procedures, reading professionals may waste considerable time and money in fruitless efforts to duplicate unsound innovations.

SECONDARY TEACHERS AND READING INSTRUCTION

The idea that all content-area teachers are responsible for helping students to develop higher-level reading skills is at least fifty years old.[75] Only within the past decade, however, has the idea begun to gain wide acceptance among content-area teachers. In 1968 Wayne Otto surveyed junior and senior high school teachers in Wisconsin concerning their attitudes toward teaching reading in the content areas. These teachers agreed strongly on the following items: teaching of reading skills can be incorporated into content-area courses; any secondary school teachers who assigns reading should also teach his students how to read; and teaching reading is a necessary and legitimate part of teaching any content course in high school. They strongly disagreed on the following: in secondary school, the teaching of reading should be the responsibility solely of the reading teacher; only remedial reading should be included in the secondary school program; and teaching of reading removes all enjoyment from teaching at the secondary level.[76] Otto's study indicated that at least one group of teachers was willing to take on the responsibility of teaching reading in content classes.

After a review of selected reading research pertaining to content-area instruction, Walter Moore suggested in 1969 that all teachers can, to some extent, be involved in the teaching of reading and that some must be involved to a very high degree. Furthermore, administrators should also become acquainted with techniques for developing good reading habits in students.[77]

Although it was established that teachers should be teaching reading and that many of them were willing to do so, many authorities have felt that, for the most part, secondary school content teachers lack sufficient knowledge of reading and reading methods to function effectively as teachers of reading.[78]

Because of threatened or real lawsuits involving high school graduates who lack even minimal reading skills and of concerned parents and citizens who demand that school systems increase reading achievement levels, it has become apparent that classroom teachers must take more responsibility for teaching reading. Harold and Marcia Roeder made four recommendations for improving teachers' competency in instructional methods in reading: required courses on methods of teaching reading for all preservice teachers who plan to teach at the junior or senior high school level; in-service training in reading methods for experienced teachers' reading consultants to work with content-area teachers; and the true adoption by school systems and teacher-training institutions of the attitude that "every teacher is a teacher of reading."[79]

By 1975 Lois Bader was able to report that a trend was apparent from a survey of state certification requirements.[80] Out of fifty-one certification boards (fifty states and the District of Columbia), eighteen require preparation in reading methods, and 30 percent of those states without such requirements reported that these requirements were being strongly considered. Thus, 55 percent of fifty-one state teacher certification boards either have or are strongly considering a reading certification requirement for secondary teachers.

Professional reading organizations in several states without such a certification requirement are attempting to persuade their certification boards to adopt similar policies. An example of one such effort is an open letter to the New Jersey State Board of Education by the New Jersey Reading Teachers Association, which says in part: "We are not naive enough to believe that the proposed six credit requirement will cure all reading failure, but we sincerely believe that it will be helpful and that it is one of the many things practical and possible to do at this time. We are all limited by what is possible, and it is possible to change certification requirements."[81] If the trend toward certification of secondary teachers as teachers of reading continues to gather momentum, the long-deferred ideal of "every teacher a teacher of reading" may at last become a reality.

CONCLUSIONS

A number of complex and intertwining issues that surround reading instruction in secondary school have been discussed in this chapter. The demands for increased levels of reading achievement, presumably those involving higher-level reading processes of inference, evaluation, and appreciation, are counterbalanced by demands for basic literacy skills for all high school graduates that would enable them to enter occupations without further education. The scarcity of high-quality research on upper-level reading processes and instructional methods is confounded by a plethora of instructional innovations of unevaluated quality. And, finally, a note of cautious optimism about the apparent trend toward certification requirements in reading for all junior and senior high school teachers must be tempered by the realization that it has been more than fifty years since the idea was seriously formulated.

If demands for increased reading competence in both the higher-level reading area and the functional literacy area are to be satisfied within the next decade, a massive research and development effort is necessary. Public and private schools, colleges, and universities must coordinate their endeavors, funds must be gathered from business and government, and a base of enlightened theory must be established if true progress is to be made.

Is the goal of reading improvement worth such a massive effort? Aristotle held that reading is useful to the purposes of life in a variety of ways: in money-making, in the management of a household, in the acquisition of knowledge, and in political life. Enormous changes have taken place in the world since Aristotle's observation 2,300 years ago. And yet, despite our many and complex economic, sociological, environmental, political, and educational problems, people still read for the same basic purposes.

Beyond merely utilitarian purposes, however, Aristotle maintained that reading (and writing) should be studied because many other sorts of knowledge are acquired through them. "To be always seeking after the useful does not become free and exalted souls."[82] Today, many people read for information, for enlightenment, for entertainment, for stimulation, and for comfort. Thus, the dual purposes of reading—utility and recreation—have been recognized at least since the time of Aristotle.

If today more people can and do read, at ever-increasing levels of skills and appreciation, the goal of reading improvement is worth the effort.

NOTES

1. William Van Til, "Reform of the High School in the Mid-1970s," *Phi Delta Kappan* 56 (March 1975): 493-494.

2. "Highlights of the St. Louis Forum," *Council for Basic Education Bulletin* 21 (November 1976): 6.

3. *Ibid.*, 7-8.

4. George H. Gallup, "Eighth Annual Gallup Poll of the Public's Attitudes toward the Public Schools," *Phi Delta Kappan* 58 (October 1976): 187-200.

5. *Los Angeles Times,* November 23, 1972, 23.

6. *Chicago Sun-Times,* January 20, 1977, 9.

7. "Eighth Annual Gallup Poll," 191.

8. Thomas G. Sticht, *Reading for Working* (Washington, D.C.: Human Resources Research Organization, 1975).

9. *Report of the National Committee on Reading,* Twenty-fourth Yearbook of the National Society for the Study of Education, Part I, ed. Guy M. Whipple (Bloomington, Ill.: Public School Publishing Co., 1925), 97-140.

10. *Ibid.*, 9.

11. *Ibid.*, 65.

12. Edward L. Thorndike, "Reading as Reasoning: A Study of Mistakes in Paragraph Reading," *Journal of Educational Psychology* 8 (June 1917): 323-332; Edmund Burke Huey, *The Psychology and Pedagogy of Reading* (New York: Macmillan, 1908).

13. Helen M. Robinson, "The Next Decade," in *Innovation and Change in Reading Instruction,* Sixty-seventh Yearbook of the National Society for the Study of Education, Part II, ed. *id.* (Chicago: University of Chicago Press, 1968), 407.

14. "Declining Admission Test Scores," *American College Testing Program Research Report Series* 71 (January 1976).

15. "Education '76: A Mix of Ups and Downs," *National Assessment of Educational Progress Newsletter* 9 (December 1976): n.p. ("Spotlight" section).

16. *Ibid.*

17. *Ibid.*

18. Bernice Cooper, "An Analysis of the Reading Achievement of White and Negro Pupils in Certain Public Schools of Georgia," *School Review* 72 (Winter 1964): 462-471; Wallace Ramsey, "The Kentucky Reading Study," *Reading Teacher* 16 (December 1962): 178-181.

19. Paul B. Diederich, *Research 1960-1970 on the Reading Problem in the United States,* Part II (Princeton, N.J.: ERIC Clearinghouse on Tests, Measurement, and Evaluation, Educational Testing Service, 1973), 6.

20. *Ibid.*

21. William R. Powell *et al.,* "Specifying Basic Skills," Technical Report No. 2, DOE-UF Basic Skills Project, Contract No. R5-174 (Tallahassee, Fla.: Department of Education, 1976, mimeo).

22. "New ACT-APL Program Available in Both High School and Adult Form," *ACTivity,* newsletter of the American College Testing Program, 14 (October 1976): 2.

23. *Report of the National Committee on Reading,* ed. Whipple, 65.

24. *Ibid.,* 140.

25. *Ibid.*

26. Richard W. Burnett, "Reading in the Secondary School: Issues and Innovations," in *Teaching Reading Skills in Secondary Schools: Readings,* ed. Arthur V. Olson and Wilbur S. Ames (Scranton, Pa.: International Textbook Co., 1970), 11-17.

27. Jeanne Chall, "Reading Seems to Be Improving," *Instructor* 83 (February 1974): 44.

28. Diederich, *Research 1960-1970 on the Reading Problem,* Part II, 5.

29. For a discussion of these investigations, see *Theoretical Models and Processes of Reading,* ed. Harry Singer and Robert Ruddell (Newark, Del.: International Reading Association, 1971).

30. Diederich, *Research 1960-1970 on the Reading Problem,* Part II, 1.

31. *Ibid.,* 4.

32. Guy L. Bond and Robert Dykstra, "Interpreting the First Grade Studies," in *The First Grade Reading Studies: Findings of Individual Investigations,* ed. Russell G. Stauffer (Newark, Del.: International Reading Association, 1967); Jeanne Chall, *Learning to Read: The Great Debate* (New York: McGraw-Hill, 1967).

33. Diederich, *Research 1960-1970 on the Reading Problem,* Part II, 5-6.

34. *Ibid.,* 4.

35. Harry Singer, "Substrata-Factor Theory of Reading: Grade and Sex Differences at the Elementary School Level," in *Improvement of Reading through Classroom Practice,* ed. J. Allen Figurel, Proceedings of the International Reading Association (Newark, Del.: International Reading Association, 1964), 313-320.

36. Naomi B. Sinks and Marvin Powell, "Sex and Intelligence as Factors in Achievement in Reading in Grades 4 through 8," *Journal of Genetic Psychology* 106 (March 1965): 67-69.

37. Mary B. Harris and Fred Ream, "A Program to Improve Study Habits of High-School Students," *Psychology in the Schools* 9 (July 1972): 325-330.

38. Wayne K. Gwaltney, "An Evaluation of a Summer Reading Improvement Course for Disadvantaged High School Students," *Journal of Reading Behavior* 3 (Fall 1970-71): 14-21.

39. Robert D. Alley *et al.*, "A Reading Improvement Strategy," *Journal of American Indian Education* 13 (January 1974): 14-20.

40. Richard C. Sinatra, "Summer Reading Program on a Point Reinforcer System," *Journal of Reading* 16 (February 1973): 395-400.

41. Maureen C. Murphy, "Academic Implications of a High School Entrance Examination for Economically Disadvantaged and Other Students," *Journal of Educational Research* 67 (March 1974): 303-306.

42. Maurice Williams and Virginia M. Stevens, "Understanding Paragraph Structure," *Journal of Reading* 15 (April 1972): 513-516.

43. Robert Kaplan and Ernst Z. Rothkopf, "Instructional Objectives as Directions to Learners: Effect of Passage Length and Amount of Objective-relevant Content," *Journal of Educational Psychology* 66 (June 1974): 448-456.

44. Priscilla Galloway, "How Secondary Students and Teachers Read Textbooks," *Journal of Reading* 17 (December 1973): 216-219.

45. Harold L. Herber and Margaret J. Early, "From Research to Practice: Is There a Time Lag?" *ibid.*, 13 (December 1969): 191.

46. *Reading in the Content Areas,* ed. James L. Laffey (Newark, Del.: International Reading Association, 1972).

47. Harold L. Herber, "Reading in the Social Studies: Implications for Teaching and Research," *ibid.*, 202.

48. *Reading in the Content Areas,* ed. Laffey.

49. Margaret L. Janz and Edwin H. Smith, "Students' Reading Ability and the Readability of Secondary School Subjects," *Elementary English* 49 (April 1972): 622-624.

50. Keith Kennedy, "Reading Level Determination for Selected Texts," *Science Teacher* 41 (March 1974): 26-27.

51. Milton D. Jacobson, "Reading Difficulty of Physics and Chemistry Textbooks," *Educational and Psychological Measurement* 25 (Summer 1965): 449-457.

52. Regis B. Wiegand, "Pittsburgh Looks at the Readability of Mathematics Textbooks," *Journal of Reading* 11 (December 1967): 201-204.

53. Robert C. Aukerman, "Readability of Secondary School Literature Textbooks: A First Report," *English Journal* 54 (September 1965): 533-540.

54. Russell E. Burgett, "Reading Comprehension in the Content Fields" (Madison: Wisconsin Department of Public Instruction and the Wisconsin Right to Read Effort, 1976, mimeo), 1-6.

55. Audrey T. Edwards, "The Comprehension of Written Sentences Containing Relative Clauses," unpublished dissertation, Harvard University, 1969.

56. Roy C. O'Donnell, "A Study of the Correlation between Awareness of Structural Relationships in English and Ability in Reading Comprehension," *Journal of Experimental Education* 31 (March 1963): 313-316.

57. Sister Mary Conceptia Tomkowicz, "An Experimental Study of the Value of

Teaching Paragraph Patterns in the Improvement of Reading Comprehension,"
master's thesis, Cardinal Stritch College, 1959.

58. See, for example, Estella E. Reed, "An Investigation of the Relative Effect of
the Study of Syntax and Paragraph Structure on Reading Comprehension of Monolingual and Bilingual Pupils in Grade Seven," unpublished dissertation, Indiana
University, 1966; Maurice Williams and Virginia M. Stevens, "Understanding
Paragraph Structure," *Journal of Reading* 15 (April 1972): 513-516.

59. Iver L. Moe and Frank Nania, "Reading Deficiencies among Able Pupils," in
Improving Reading in Middle and Secondary Schools, ed. Lawrence E. Hafner (New
York: Macmillian, 1974), 172-185.

60. Thomas W. Lackman, "Effects upon Comprehension and Reading Rate under
Four Prequestion Conditions," unpublished dissertation, University of Delaware,
1970.

61. *Ibid.*

62. Robert Karlin, "Sequence in Thoughtful and Critical Reaction to What Is
Read," in *Improving Reading in Middle and Secondary Schools,* ed. Hafner,
115-121.

63. See, for example, Richard J. Smith and Thomas C. Barrett, *Teaching Reading
in the Middle Grades* (Reading, Mass.: Addison-Wesley, 1974), 84-94.

64. Jill C. Frankel, "Reading Skills through Social Studies Content and Student Involvement," *Journal of Reading* 18 (October 1974): 23-26.

65. Fred Lees, "Mathematics and Reading," *ibid.,* 19 (May 1976): 621-626.

66. John J. Carney and William Losinger, "Reading and Content in Technical-
Vocational Education," *ibid.,* 20 (October 1976): 14-17.

67. Kenneth M. Ahrendt and Shirley S. Haselton, "Essential Reading Skills in
Bookkeeping," *ibid.,* 16 (January 1973): 314-317.

68. R. Baird Shuman, "Of Course He Can Read—He's in High School," *ibid.,* 19
(October 1975): 36-42.

69. Nicholas P. Criscuolo, "An Interdisciplinary Approach to Reading," *ibid.*
(March 1976): 488-493.

70. W. John Harker, "Teaching Secondary Reading: Review of Sources," *ibid.,* 16
(November 1972): 149-155.

71. *English Journal* 63 (November 1974): entire issue.

72. Diederich, *Research 1960-1970 on the Reading Problem,* 4.

73. William J. Gephart, *Application of the Convergence Technique to Basic
Studies of the Reading Process,* Final Report, Project No. 8-0737, Grant No.
OEC-0-8-080737-4335 (Washington, D.C.: U.S. Office of Education, National
Center for Research and Development, 1970).

74. Willard J. Congreve, "Implementing and Evaluating the Use of Innovations,"
in *Innovation and Change in Reading Instruction,* ed. Robinson, 291-319.

75. *Report of the National Committee on Reading,* ed. Whipple, 97-140.

76. Wayne Otto, "Junior and Senior High School Teachers' Attitudes toward
Teaching Reading in the Content Areas," *Modern Language Journal* 52 (May 1968):
293-301.

77. Walter J. Moore, "What Does Research in Reading Reveal about Reading in
the Content Fields?" *English Journal* 58 (May 1969): 707-718.

78. Robert Karlin, "What Does Research in Reading Reveal about Reading and the High School Student?" *ibid.*, 386-395; Leonard S. Braam and James E. Walker, "Subject Teachers' Awareness of Reading Skills," *Journal of Reading* 16 (May 1973): 608-611.

79. Harold H. Roeder and Marcia A. Roeder, "1,000,000 Reasons for Improving Preparation of Secondary Teachers," *ibid.*, 17 (May 1974): 604-607.

80. Lois A. Bader, "Certification Requirements in Reading: A Trend," *ibid.*, 19 (December 1975): 237-240.

81. Edward B. Fry and Lillian R. Putnam, "Should All Teachers Take More Reading Courses?" *ibid.* (May 1976): 614-616.

82. Aristotle, *Politics and Poetics,* tr. Benjamin Jowett and S. H. Butcher (New York: Heritage Press, 1964), 271.

7. Language and Reading Acquisition for the English-Speaking Minority Student

Susanna Pflaum-Connor

There are many variations of the English language. When the speech of an identifiable group of people exhibits unique and consistent patterns of sound (phonology), grammar (syntax), and vocabulary, a dialect emerges. Dialects are perpetuated in isolated regional and social situations. Within a single geographic region a dialect may reflect the characteristics of the region, as well as special features of one or more social groups within the region. Dialects spoken by minority persons are referred to as nonstandard dialects. It is this nonstandard dialect, specifically the influence of nonstandard dialect on the process of learning to read, that is the major focus of this chapter.

Another concern is the effect that a second language has when one is learning to read and write. Many children in the United States speak another language and know little or no English when they begin their schooling. Often older pupils enter school at an even higher grade level with little or no mastery of the English language. It is expected that all of these children will learn to speak, read, and write fluent English. Today many schools also attempt to maintain and develop the non-English language learned earlier at the same time that they are trying to develop proficiency in English.

Nonstandard dialect and bilingualism are often incorrectly viewed as two sides of the same coin, but the contrasts of two dialects of one language are of an entirely different order than the contrasts between two languages. The differences between a standard and a nonstandard dialect are much finer than those between two languages, and the educational implications of this point are important. Some introduction to the distinctions between language and dialect might clarify the material in this chapter and in Chapter 8.

LINGUISTIC DISTINCTIONS BETWEEN LANGUAGE AND DIALECT

A consideration of two dialects shows that the contrasts lie in the different sounds (phonemes) used, in the different grammatical (syntactic) structures, and in different aspects of meaning (vocabulary). There are enough identifiable but distinct linguistic features in the speech of many blacks using American English to identify it as a dialect; this dialect, known as black English (BE), is often studied. There are phonological contrasts between BE and standard English (SE), the speech of educated, mainstream persons generalizable across geographic regions but with a few regional characteristics. For example, William Labov demonstrated the phonological contrasts between BE and SE by using lists of homonyms. Although *pit* and *pet* sound different in SE speech, they often sound the same in BE speech, especially in certain phonological contexts. In the same vein, *bold* and *bowl* may not differ in the speech of BE speakers. There are similar contrasts in syntactic features. For example, BE speakers often express habitual or iterative action with an uninflected *be* (He be asking me.), where SE speakers would express the same meaning with a phrase (He asks me over and over.).[1] Words (vocabulary) also have special meanings for BE speakers unknown to SE speakers. It is important to note that there are more similarities than differences between BE and SE. If this were not so, communication would be extremely difficult.

In comparison, bilingual speakers contend with entirely separate rules. Non-English-speaking schoolchildren learning English must learn not only some new sounds, but an awareness of allowable combinations of sounds in English. They must learn how words are ordered and how endings are added to words in English sentences. They must learn meanings of words and appropriate combinations of concepts in English. There are universal linguistic characteristics common to all language — for example, inclusion of subject and predicate roles in sentences — but communication in English for these youngsters and for adults cannot exist until they learn the rule systems and the phonology, syntax, and vocabulary of that language.

Table 7-1 depicts the contrast between using two dialects or using two languages by isolating the linguistic characteristics of dialects and languages as they would operate in idealized situations with adult speakers.

Table 7-1

Linguistic Knowledge of Two Adults Speaking in Dialects Contrasted with That of Two Adults Speaking Separate Languages (Bilingual)

Contrasts	Two dialects	Two languages
Phonological	Most phonemes the same in both	Many phonemes of one not in the other
	A few phonemes not used the same way	Some phonemes the same in both
	Intonation differs somewhat	Intonation patterns separate
	Rules for combining phonemes the same	Rules for combining phonemes differ
Syntactic	Basic rules the same	Very different rules at sentence level
	Slight variations in rules do not mask meaning	Sentence relationships marked by different rules
	Inflections (word endings) subject to slight changes	Inflections entirely separate
Vocabulary	Meanings of words the same	Separate sets of words
	Nuances of meaning may exist, often unique to a less prestigious dialect	Cognates may exist if languages are related
		Cognates may confuse rather than clarify

The table is an oversimplification in that it does not represent the language of a number of different groups of speakers: bilinguals whose English is nonstandard, bilinguals whose native language is nonstandard, monodialectal speakers who speak only a nonstandard dialect, or monodialectal speakers who speak only a standard dialect.

The educational implications of these variations are vast. Before undertaking analysis of these groups, however, it is necessary to examine the educational implications of simple dialect variation and bilingualism.

For each of these two major topics, which affect dialect-speaking and non-English-speaking children, the following questions are important: (a) Does the language variation cause an interference in learning to read so that major instructional adjustments are needed? (b) Do attitudes toward nonstandard dialects and languages other than English impede the learning process? (c) What adjustments are needed to develop literacy in English among the linguistic groups?

Dialect and reading are the major considerations in the remainder of this chapter. Since BE has received the most attention as an American dialect, it is referred to more frequently than other less familiar nonstandard dialects. The literature on BE, reflecting recent social history, is voluminous, and discussion tends to be heated. Questions that have intellectual potential are often discussed emotionally. That is why it is necessary to establish the various perspectives that a person discussing dialect might hold; then it is possible to discuss attitudes toward BE. Only then can the dimensions of the question of reading acquisition be outlined and evidence from research be presented. The final consideration is the significance of the effect of dialect on reading in the future.

DIALECT AND READING

Different Perspectives

Educators in the United States long held a prescriptive attitude toward American English, making the English spoken by educated Britons the standard to emulate.[2] In the past educators in the United States measured language forms against a normative concept of correctness. This fact, coupled with societal values that determined individual worth on the basis of a person's material success and upward mobility, set a clear goal for schools: children, in order to become educated, had to become facile in the form of language of the dominant group. The social changes of the 1960s forced educators to recognize the failure of schools to attain this language goal, and some people began to question the values underlying the goal.

It was as a result of questions raised over lack of success in teaching poor children, often from minority groups, that much attention has been focused on the language of those children during the last fifteen years. From July 1961 to June 1963, for example, there were only 5 entries under "Dialect" in the *Education Index*. In just one year, from July 1969 to June 1970, the number of entries rose to 26. Similarly, during the same time periods, a total of 22 entries under "Cultural Deprivation" expanded to 623 entries.[3] Although much of the writing tends to be polemic in nature, some of the studies constitute serious investigations of language functioning with relevance to instruction. Because the authors represented different disciplines, different perspectives have influenced the study of language.

One group of researchers, concerned with reading from the perspective of educational psychology, used standard measures of performance to measure verbal functioning and to demonstrate that poor, minority children appear to lag behind students who are in the middle class and are white. Martin Deutsch was one who examined the use of abstract language in first and fifth graders and found poor, black fifth graders farther behind their middle-class, white peers. He suggested that there was a cumulative deficiency.[4] Others found differences in the ability to categorize,[5] to make auditory discriminations,[6] and to solve problems.[7]

From a different point of view this body of literature was later referred to as representing the "deficit" position. Others who have studied language development from the same perspective have raised legitimate questions about the lags present in the development of poor, minority children.[9] These researchers found parallel levels of syntactic complexity but different forms in the language acquired by preschool children, whatever their dialect. Doris Entwhisle's study of word associations found the word associations of poor children, whether black or white, to be more flexible than those of middle-class white children at the beginning of their school experience. This apparent flexibility did not, however, persist.[10] Comparisons of social groups at different ages led Stephen and Joan Baratz to suggest that school has a negative effect on language development.[11]

Another group of researchers, working from the perspective of the sociolinguist, examined the language of black adults (and adolescents) who used the nonstandard dialect of northern cities. Trained to assume that no language form is inherently superior to another as a mechanism for communication, these researchers isolated patterns of speech to find specific features that varied from the standard dialect.[12] As a result of this work, sociolinguists posited that BE-speaking children use a different, not a deficient, language. They further suggested modifications in curriculum to align school programs with the children's language.

Both approaches taken by educational psychologists and by sociolinguists differ in their instructional implications. The studies of psychologists that show lags in language functioning were used by Siegfried Engelmann to demonstrate that the language of inner-city children was inadequate for learning to read.[13] Sociolinguists' studies of language difference, in turn, led them to propose that, while the language possessed by BE-speaking children was adequate, the mismatch between spoken BE and the language of reading texts would interfere with learning to read. Differences between the two groups gave rise to the polemic tone present in much of the literature. What is interesting is that, in spite of the differences, both positions suggest that the basis for problems encountered by children when they are learning to read lies in their language.

Yet a third perspective present in language study suggests that the problem can be found in the sociology of the classroom. For example, rural children attending elementary school in northern Florida who spoke BE produced complex, sophisticated syntactic structures when telling stories of family and friends contrasted with truncated utterances when discussing school-related topics.[14] And Labov noted that young adolescent boys were sensitive to the social aspects of a given situation.[15] In test situations, lower-class youngsters responded to urgings for more elaborated speech; middle-class youngsters needed no such urgings.[16] High school students who volunteered to take part in lessons on SE usage exhibited defensiveness and suspicion when asked to tape their speech,[17] which confirms Susan Ervin-Tripp's suggestion that lower-class young people are more sensitive to language situations than middle-class young people.[18] It may well be social characteristics of the classroom that place constraints on the verbosity of BE-speaking pupils, but it is important to note that these situational effects have been observed in language *production* rather than in language *comprehension*. They are, therefore, less critical if applied to learning to read. The problems of classroom language are complicated, however, by the attitudes people hold toward BE dialect.

Attitudes toward Nonstandard Dialect

If the language output of BE-speaking pupils is to increase, it may be necessary to encourage the use of nonschool speech style by providing nonthreatening situations in classrooms. Since the style of non-school speech is apt to contain more nonstandard features than school speech does, [19] the teacher's attitude toward nonstandard dialect is critical in determining whether it is realistic to expect teachers to sanction nonstandard speech in classes in order to promote language development. Research in attitude toward dialect has shown that teachers and others respond negatively to nonstandard dialect.

College students rated taped "network" English higher than variations of BE and the dialect of educated southern whites. Black students rated the taped speech of educated southern whites low. Southern white students rated the taped speech of black Mississippians low. These subjects were sensitive to different dialects and held biases specific to race and locale. [20] Teachers were also found to make judgments about language according to race and use of BE. [21] When pre-service teachers were asked to respond to a semantic differential test on viewing videotapes of black, Chicano, and Anglo children speaking in SE and in the expected nonstandard dialect, they made stereotypic responses. [22] Indeed, when race of teacher and pupil was the same, there was less stereotyping if socioeconomic status of the pupils was high than if it was low, testifying to the specificity of teacher bias. [23] Furthermore, teachers' expectations appear to be affected by dialect spoken, especially in language-related subjects. The more "ethnic and nonstandard" the perception of language, the lower the expectation of success. [24]

In contrast to this disheartening evidence of bias toward nonstandard dialect, two studies showed that children with increased experience change their attitudes toward people, though not necessarily toward dialect. In one study, after only four months of reading multi-ethnic books, white second graders showed a marked reduction in biased responses to pictures of black children. In the second study, first graders who read multiethnic texts and who participated in a multiethnic literature program showed a significant reduction in bias. [26] Whether children have a negative attitude toward dialect and whether that attitude can change need study. And, of course, further study of teachers' attitudes is also needed.

Research into attitudes toward nonstandard dialect shows that it is easily identified, negatively assessed by teachers and college students, and leads to low expectations for success in school. This biased negative attitude toward nonstandard dialect means that teachers will probably not allow nonschool speech in classrooms, and, given the tendency toward bias, it is not surprising that BE dialect, once specified, might result in the expectation that dialect itself was a cause of low achievement in reading.

Assumption of Dialect Interference

It was generally accepted by sociolinguists in the late 1960s that a mismatch between dialect and text existed for BE speakers.[27] This mismatch would not negate the possibility that BE speakers *could* learn to read, but it would account for lower achievement in reading. Many educators initially accepted this assumption, even though it rested on the idea that written language is the representation of oral language, but the idea was questioned later.[28]

A number of alternative solutions have emerged.[29] For example, Walt Wolfram identified two basic strategies: retention of conventional materials and adjustment in teaching, and revision of materials. If the first strategy were adopted, teachers would either be responsible for teaching SE dialect before teaching reading or they would allow dialect renderings of text. If the second were chosen, producers of reading materials would attempt to neutralize distinctions arising from use of dialect or rewrite texts with BE features. There were four possible alternatives.[30]

First, if SE dialect were to be added to the oral repertoire of BE-speaking preschoolers before they were taught to read, presumably there would be no mismatch when it was time for reading instruction. This idea is impractical. For one thing, the postponement of reading instruction for some children, the BE speakers, and not others is discriminatory. Besides, fairly common drill-type programs to change language have not proved successful.[31] And even more promising language programs that encourage active speech and rich literature in kindergarten[32] may not be enough exposure to allow for full acquisition of SE features. The supposed mismatch might still exist.

Second, to accept dialect "renderings" of text in oral reading is merely acceptance of a natural phenomenon. Kenneth Goodman's study of oral reading miscues (any reading behaviors not expected from text) illustrates that BE speakers often respond orally with common BE features.[33] In fact, as pupils increase their proficiency in reading, there are more, not fewer, BE features in their oral reading. This testifies to the natural use of dialect in oral reading.

A third alternative is to neutralize contrasting features. Since there is no need to change conventional spelling patterns, writers can avoid syntactic contrasts. The avoidance of grammatical contrasts, however, results in unnecessary circumlocutions in beginning texts. For example, a major point of contrast lies between SE use of the copula (He *is* singing.) and BE use of an uninflected *be* (He *be* singing.) or absence of the copula (He singing now.). Avoiding the use of the verb *to be* would severely restrict writers.

The fourth alternative, and the one most widely discussed, is to prepare written text with BE grammatical and lexical items—that is, to rewrite traditional beginning reading texts to BE. According to proponents of this alternative,[34] youngsters who start with material that has familiar language structure gain the same linguistic advantage that SE-speaking beginning readers already have. This alternative is testable, and two attempts have been made to test it. In one attempt, however, the parents of children reading from BE texts objected to their use as being unfair and biased.[35] The other attempt showed positive effects from the use of BE texts in just one classroom. No broader study has been reported.[36]

Beyond the lack of empirical support for the use of BE texts for beginning reading, there are social problems that could arise from the wide-scale use of dialect texts. Use of such books in desegregated classrooms would amount to resegregation. Even if BE texts for beginning readers were found to be salutary, it is doubtful that there would be concomitant development of texts written in the white Appalachian, Down East Maine, or some other dialect. To select one nonstandard dialect for development into texts could rightfully be called discriminatory. Finally, sensitive use of dialect texts would require that teachers understand more about dialect than it is probably realistic to expect.

A fifth alternative has been suggested—use of the language experience approach to beginning reading.[37] Study of the long-term effects of child-dictated discourse for reading material has shown positive results,[38] especially where pupils' language proficiency was low.[39] This alternative is not primarily based on the existence of a mismatch between dialect and text; it is appropriate for all children. It maintains a link between spoken and written language that minimizes possible discrepancies between oral language and text.

The four original alternatives for responding to the supposed mismatch between the oral language of young BE speakers and prose in traditional texts include: teaching young BE-speaking children SE before they learn to read, accepting dialect renderings in oral reading, neutralizing text language, and teaching reading with texts rewritten in BE. Although none of these alternatives has clear empirical support, the ideas persist. The use of language experience, on the other hand, does have empirical support, and it is not dependent on the underlying assumption that children's use of nonstandard BE dialect interferes with their learning to read because their oral language does not match the language of the text. Dialect interference in learning to read remains a critical consideration when determining instructional approaches for the teaching of reading.

Evidence of Interference

In Listening

If the use of BE dialect prevents children from understanding oral SE in the classroom, one might reasonably expect to find similar interference in reading since both involve the decoding of language. The findings of listening comprehension studies suggest, however, that young BE speakers exhibit an underlying competence in comprehending oral SE speech. Sentence repetition studies show that such speakers encode a long spoken sentence into their own dialect before reproducing it.[40] Joan Baratz has interpreted these findings as an indication that people are operating with separate language systems in these dialect reproductions.[41] One could also interpret the results as evidence that comprehension of sentences exists, whatever the dialect, and that sentences are repeated in comfortable speech patterns. Labov found that BE dialect features, even when deeply ingrained in some speakers, do not cause misinterpretation of sentence meaning.[42]

Some researchers measured the listening comprehension of extended discourse. According to Estelle Peisach's study of the listening comprehension of stories, the oral speech features of BE dialect do not inhibit understanding. Black first graders from poor homes used language redundancies in an oral cloze task (the supplying of deleted words) as well as white first graders. No differences were found in understanding material presented with teacher speech and material presented with peer speech.[43] Walter Gantt, Robert Wilson, and Mitchell Dayton found that in third graders, socioeconomic status was a greater factor than dialect in listening.[44] And, Imogene Ramsey found that BE-speaking first graders answered literal questions about stories equally well whether the stories had been presented in SE or BE.[45] Finally, while white, middle-class children did show reduced recall of material presented in BE dialect, Paul Weener found that black children from low socioeconomic backgrounds did not have differential recall according to dialect of presented materials.[46]

The evidence gleaned from listening studies is consistent and indicates that dialect is not a critical factor in listening comprehension. The Weener study suggests that SE speakers may be monodialectal in their listening ability but BE speakers are bidialectal. Perhaps it is through watching television that BE-speaking children acquire the ability to understand SE dialect. In spite of the evidence that no listening interference appears to exist, dialect may interfere with a student's ability to learn to read.

In Reading

There are conspicuously fewer research studies examining the question of whether BE dialect causes difficulties in reading than there are articles and books on the topic — testifying to the controversial aspect of the content. Some of the studies are correlational; some examine oral reading behavior; some compare reading comprehension of traditional prose and of prose written with BE features.

In three correlational studies relating success in beginning reading with dialect, there are conflicting results. Joan Baratz used a sentence repetition test to measure the dialect preference of young first and second graders and found that children who were monodialectal BE speakers did not read as well as bidialectal and monodialectal SE speakers. No mention was made of control of socioeconomic status or of IQ.[47] In another study there was positive correlation between achievement in kindergarten and scores on a sentence repetition test for children who were dominant SE speakers but a negative correlation between these factors for dominant BE speakers. These data suggest that facility in BE has no relation to school success.[48] In a third study, however, Estelle Fryburg found that general proficiency in language, again as measured in sentence repetition, and not preference for one dialect over another, correlated positively with reading success.[49] Further study is needed of the relationship between language development and prereading skills. It is likely that the general level of language development rather than the use of a specific dialect will be found to be critical in reading success, given the pattern of results found in other studies involving reading and dialect.

It is, as was mentioned above, natural for persons to render text in their dialect as they read orally. The extent of this phenomenon is actually widespread. Barbara Hunt found that 46 percent of the oral errors in strict application of the criteria for the Gray Oral Reading Test were the result of BE dialect usages. Hunt also concluded that, since girls were both better readers and more apt to make dialect errors, the rendering of dialect was indicative of good reading.[50] A study by Carl Rosen and Wilbur Ames also attests to the naturalness of responding with BE features in oral reading. They found that dialect responses were higher when reading connected discourse and grew more extensive as subjects continued reading.[51] Herbert Simons and Kenneth Johnson found that second and third graders who were BE speakers (as measured by a sentence repetition text) did not use context clues or sound-symbol clues in oral reading as efficiently for material written with BE features as they did for material written in the traditional manner.[52] And in oral reading of isloated words, Simons found that black children in grades two, three, and four who were proficient readers did no better on words that appeared in BE form than they did with corollary homophones. With poor readers there were differences. Since it was the "standard" set of words that were read better by poor readers at two grade levels, however, there was clearly no support for the idea of interference in this study.[53] This was true for each of the oral reading studies discussed above.

Studies of reading comprehension are most relevant to the question of interference. Simons and Johnson found no difference in comprehension where passages with BE features and traditional passages were being read orally.[54] And, although the test of significance was not reported, Carol Hochman stated that regular passages and those rewritten to include BE features from the California Reading Test were equally understood by middle-grade pupils speaking SE and BE who were reading the passages silently.[55] In Patricia Nolen's more careful study of how well second and fourth graders comprehended regular and rewritten passages from the Diagnostic Reading Scales, there appeared to be no significant difference related to dialect of passage or of speaker.[56] Angela Jaggar discovered, however, that her subjects (third- and fourth-grade BE-speaking children),when reading silently, read regular passages with greater comprehension than they read equivalent passages containing BE features.[57] An order of presentation effect for BE-speaking subjects suggests that they quickly became accustomed to prose that contained familiar structures. In another study of reading comprehension it was found that BE-speaking children could comprehend the copula bidialectally, whereas SE-speaking children could not.[58] BE-speaking youngsters, given more exposure to prose written with BE features, might become as bidialectal in reading as Weener's study indicated that they are in listening. More research is needed to confirm this suggestion. It appears that SE-speaking youngsters are monodialectal in listening and reading. What is more important to the question of interference, however, is that in none of the studies of reading comprehension did BE-speaking children exhibit greater difficulty when reading traditional passages than they did when reading rewritten ones.

Another important study confirms these findings on comprehension. Paul Melmed examined a variety of reading instruction tasks, with third-grade pupils as subjects. He used a set of word pairs that Labov had found were homonyms for BE speakers (seed = see, row = road, six = sick, and so on). The word pairs used contrasted on the following BE characteristics: r-lessness, l-lessness, final consonant cluster reduction *(desk* becomes *des),* and vowel variation. The word pairs were presented in tasks related to auditory discrimination, oral listening comprehension, isolated word reading, and silent paragraph reading comprehension. BE-speaking children showed confusion in both isolated word tasks, particularly in the auditory discrimination ones. There was no confusion of the words while listening or reading silently when they were set in context, however.[59]

There are two additional considerations to be made about interference in reading as a result of dialect. The first is a question raised by Joan Baratz about the subjects used in Melmed's study that is also relevant to the other studies reviewed here. She claimed that, since the children tested were already reading, they had not experienced interference and, therefore, none could be found. Hence, little has been discovered about how dialect might interfere with learning to read in many other children.[60] To counter her argument in light of the literature, it is difficult to imagine that BE dialect causes interference in some children and not in others. In many instances distinguishing fac-

tors have not been found. Observational study of children just beginning reading would address Baratz's concern.

As for the second consideration, Melmed's study pointed out an important issue for teachers. The data suggest possible confusion that
may arise in phonics instruction by requiring auditory discrimination
of features not distinguished in BE dialect. This possible source of instructional confusion was also suggested by Labov.[61] When teachers
attempt to help children develop working generalizations about
sound-symbol correspondences, they expect pupils to make distinctions in sounds that BE speakers may not hear. Should such instruction become incomprehensible to pupils, they may stop expecting to
find reliable patterns of sounds to help in pronouncing words. Two
reports of specific difficulties in phonics lessons showed that teachers'
ignorance of BE features caused pupils to interpret critical words differently from their teachers, thereby causing the pupils to fail to grasp
the point of the lesson.[62] This confusion is evidence of indirect interference, which is correctable through teacher training and improved
instruction; it is not evidence of direct interference.

The available literature provides no direct causative link between
BE dialect and poor oral reading or poor reading comprehension. In
fact, seldom in educational research is such a clear, consistent pattern
to be found. Thus, the assumption that there is inteference appears to
be invalid, and the search for alternative instruction to modify a mismatch between oral dialect and written prose does not appear to be
necessary. Researchers and others must look beyond dialect interference to explain why poor, black youngsters often do not read as well as
their middle-class, white peers.

Beyond Interference

A number of factors might draw attention away from the question
of interference and turn it toward other relevant issues in reading.
First, there is the possibility that others might realize how little empirical support there is for the idea of interference. Second, data from the
National Reading Assessment demonstrate that there has been a wel-
come, but slight, improvement between 1971 and 1975 in the reading
comprehension performance of nine-year-olds. The comprehension
performance of black children is now not quite as far below that of
middle-class, white children. But there has been no corresponding
improvement in the reading of thirteen- and nineteen-year olds

generally, and the gap in performance according to racial group at that level is still great.[63] Attention may gradually be drawn toward older pupils. Third, the social aspects of language use may attract study and ultimately result in improved functioning in classrooms. Fourth, it is hoped that there will be increased research on teacher attitude and attempts to change it, and that these efforts will improve teacher training.

At the start of this chapter, three questions were raised. The first question concerned the instructional adjustments needed because of language interference. Research on listening and reading comprehension does not show interference, although the presumed existence of such an interference has resulted in the development of alternative major adjustments in instruction. I would conclude that there is no direct interference and that no major change is needed in beginning reading instruction.

The second question was related to the attitudes of school personnel toward nonstandard dialect and whether those attitudes were detrimental to learning. Work in the area does show that teachers are biased against nonstandard dialect, a bias that lowers their expectation that a student will succeed in language-related schoolwork. The literature on expectation, however, is not conclusive. Any firm conclusion that a language-specific negative attitude inhibits language learning would be unwarranted at this time. One thing, however, is clear. The area needs further study.

The third question centers around methods appropriate for teaching reading and writing to nonstandard speakers. Research is not directed at specific teaching areas. There are, nevertheless, instructional directions present in the research literature. For the most part instruction for nonstandard speakers should resemble that for standard speakers. There is one special teaching direction for BE-speaking pupils that is implied in the research literature, however. During the early stages of reading, when phonics is taught to help youngsters achieve independence in word attack, teachers must take great care that instruction is suitable. That is, when developing understanding of some final single consonants, final consonant clusters, and some vowel features, teachers must understand that many BE-speaking pupils do not differentiate critical sounds. Either these children ought to be trained in auditory discrimination prior to phonics, or such items should be eliminated from the phonics program. In the first case, time is needed to practice hearing and producing the relevant sounds in words before phonics is taught. In the second case, there would be elimination of study of final consonants, single and in cluster, and avoidance of the study of short vowels. In either case, a number of productive phonic principles would still apply.

It would appear that, while special materials are not required for black English-speaking youngsters to learn to read, research is needed to determine social aspects of language use in classrooms in an effort to improve classroom learning environments. Research into teacher attitude and its change may also contribute to improving learning environments. That, it seems, is the ultimate goal.

NOTES

1. William Labov, *Language in the Inner City: Studies in the Black English Vernacular* (Philadelphia, Pa.: University of Pennsylvania Press, 1972), 3-35.

2. Albert H. Marckwardt, "Issues in the Teaching of Standard English," *The Florida FL Reporter* 12 (Spring-Fall 1974): 21-24, 94.

3. *Education Index, July 1961-June 1963*, Volume 13, ed. Minnie A. Seng (New York: H. W. Wilson Co., 1963); *Education Index, July 1969-June 1970*, Volume 20, ed. Julia W. Ehrenreich (New York: H. W. Wilson Co., 1970).

4. Martin Deutsch, "The Role of Social Class in Language Development and Cognition," *American Journal of Orthopsychiatry* 25 (January 1965): 78-88.

5. Vera P. John and Leo S. Goldstein, "The Social Context of Language Acquisition," *Merrill-Palmer Quarterly* 10 (July 1964): 265-275.

6. Vera John, "The Intellectual Development of Slum Children: Some Preliminary Findings," *American Journal of Orthopsychiatry* 33 (October 1963): 813-822.

7. Robert D. Hess and Virginia C. Shipman, "Early Experience and the Socialization of Cognitive Modes in Children," *Child Development* 36 (December 1965): 869-886.

8. Stephen S. Baratz and Joan C. Baratz, "Early Childhood Intervention: The Social Science Base of Institutional Racism," *Harvard Educational Review* 40 (Winter 1970): 29-50.

9. Alice F. LaCivita, John M. Kean, and Kaoru Yamamoto, "Socio-economic Status of Children and Acquisition of Grammar," *Journal of Educational Research* 60 (October 1966): 71-74; Thomas H. Shriner and Lynn Miner, "Morphological Structures in the Language of Disadvantaged Children," *Journal of Speech and Hearing Research* 11 (1968): 604-610; Courtney B. Cazden, "Subcultural Differences in Child Language," *Merrill-Palmer Quarterly* 12 (July 1966): 185-219.

10. Doris P. Entwhisle, "Semantic Systems of Children: Some Assessments of Social Class and Ethnic Differences," in *Language and Poverty: Perspectives on a Theme*, ed. Frederick Williams (Chicago: Markham Publishing Co., 1970), 123-139.

11. Baratz and Baratz, "Early Childhood Intervention," 29-50.

12. William Labov *et al.*, *A Study of the Nonstandard English of Negro and Puer-*

to Rican Speakers in New York City, 2 vols. Report on Cooperative Research Project 3288 (New York: Columbia University, 1968); Labov, *Language in the Inner City,* 3-196; Roger W. Shuy, *Discovering American Dialects* (Champaign, Ill.: National Council of Teachers of English, 1967).

13. Siegfried Engelmann, "How to Construct Effective Language Programs for the Poverty Child," in *Language and Poverty,* ed. Williams, 102.

14. Susan H. Houston, "A Reexamination of Some Assumptions about the Language of the Disadvantaged Child," *Child Development* 41 (December 1970): 947-963.

15. Labov, *Language in the Inner City,* 206-211.

16. Reported in Courtney Cazden, "The Situation: A Neglected Source of Social Class Differences in Language Use," *Journal of Social Issues* 26 (Spring 1970): 35-60.

17. Claudia Mitchell-Kernan, "On the Status of Black English for Native Speakers: An Assessment of Attitudes and Values," in *Functions of Language in the Classroom,* ed. Courtney B. Cazden, Vera P. John, and Dell Hymes (New York: Teachers College Press, 1972), 208.

18. Susan Ervin-Tripp, "Children's Sociolinguistic Competence and Dialect Diversity," in *Early Childhood Education,* Seventy-first Yearbook of the National Society for the Study of Education, Part II, ed. Ira J. Gordon (Chicago: University of Chicago Press, 1972), 123-155.

19. Houston, "A Reexamination of Some Assumptions about the Language of the Disadvantaged Child," 947-963.

20. G. Richard Tucker and Wallace E. Lambert, "White and Negro Listeners' Reactions to Various American-English Dialects," *Social Forces* 47 (June 1969): 463-468.

21. Frederick Williams, "Psychological Correlates of Speech Characteristics — On Sounding 'Disadvantaged,' " *Journal of Speech and Hearing Research* 13 (September 1970): 472-488.

22. *Id.,* Jack L. Whitehead, and Leslie M. Miller, "Ethnic Stereotyping and Judgments of Children's Speech," *Speech Monographs* 38 (August 1971): 166-170.

23. Tom D. Freijo and Richard M. Jaegar, "Social Class and Race as Concomitants of Composite Halo in Teachers' Evaluative Rating of Pupils," *American Educational Research Journal* 13 (Winter 1976): 1-14.

24. Frederick Williams, Jack L. Whitehead, and Leslie M. Miller, "Relations between Language Attitudes and Teacher Expectancy," *ibid.,* 9 (Spring 1972): 263-275.

25. John H. Litcher and David W. Johnson, "Changes in Attitudes toward Negroes of White Elementary School Students after Use of Multiethnic Readers," *Journal of Educational Psychology* 60 (April 1969): 148-152.

26. Anna V. Yancy and Jane M. Singh, "A Study of Racial Attitudes of White First Graders," *Elementary English* 42 (May 1975): 734-736.

27. *Teaching Black Children to Read,* ed. Joan C. Baratz and Roger W. Shuy (Washington, D.C.: Center for Applied Linguistics, 1969).

28. Kenneth S. Goodman and Carolyn Burke, "Dialect Barriers to Reading Comprehension Revisited," *Reading Teacher* 27 (October 1973): 6-12.

29. Jean R. Harber and Diane N. Bryen, "Black English and the Task of Reading," *Review of Educational Research* 46 (Summer 1976): 387-405; Mary Ann Somervill, "Dialect and Reading: A Review of Alternatives," *ibid.,* 45 (Spring 1975):

247-262; Robert L. Venezky, "Nonstandard Dialect and Reading," *Elementary English* 47 (March 1970): 334-345.

30. Walt Wolfram, "Sociolinguistic Alternatives in Teaching Reading to Nonstandard Speakers," *Reading Research Quarterly* 6 (Fall 1970): 9-33.

31. Richard Rystrom, "Dialect Training and Reading: A Further Look," *ibid.*, 5 (Summer 1970): 581-589.

32. Bernice E. Cullinan, Angela Jaggar, and Dorothy Strickland, "Language Expansion for Black Children in the Primary Grades: A Research Report," *Young Children* 29 (January 1974): 98-112.

33. Goodman and Burke, "Dialect Barriers to Reading Comprehension Revisited," 6-12.

34. Joan C. Baratz, "Teaching Reading in an Urban Negro School System," in *Teaching Black Children to Read,* ed. Baratz and Shuy, 92-115; William A. Stewart, "On the Use of Negro Dialect in the Teaching of Reading," *ibid.*, 156-219.

35. Joan C. Baratz, "The Relationship of Black English to Reading: A Review of Research," in *Language Differences: Do They Interfere?* ed. James L. Laffey and Roger Shuy (Newark, Del.: International Reading Association, 1973), 109.

36. Lloyd Leaverton, "Dialectal Readers: Rationale, Use, and Value," *ibid.*, 114-126.

37. Somervill, "Dialect and Reading," 258-259.

38. Bernice L. Serwer, "Linguistic Support for a Method of Teaching Beginning Reading to Black Children," *Reading Research Quarterly* 5 (Summer 1969): 449-467.

39. Estelle Fryburg, "The Relations among English Syntax, Methods of Instruction, and Reading Achievement of First Grade Disadvantaged Black Children," unpublished dissertation, New York University, 1972.

40. Baratz, "Teaching Reading in an Urban Negro School System," 92-115; Thomas S. Frentz, "Comprehension of Standard and Negro Nonstandard English Sentences," *Speech Monographs* 38 (March 1971): 1016; Catherine Garvey and Paul McFarlane, "A Measure of Standard English Proficiency of Inner-City Children," *American Educational Research Journal* 7 (January 1970): 29-40; Labov *et al.*, *Study of the Nonstandard English of Negro and Puerto Rican Speakers in New York City,* I, 31-334.

41. Baratz, "Teaching Reading in an Urban Negro School System," 111.

42. Labov *et al., Study of the Nonstandard English of Negro and Puerto Rican Speakers in New York City,* I, 312.

43. Estelle Cherry Peisach, "Children's Comprehension of Teacher and Peer Speech," *Child Development* 36 (June 1965): 146-180.

44. Walter N. Gantt, Robert M. Wilson, and C. Mitchell Dayton, "An Initial Investigation of the Relationship between Syntactical Divergency and the Listening Comprehension of Black Children," *Reading Research Quarterly* 10 (Winter 1974-75): 193-211.

45. Imogene Ramsey, "A Comparison of First Grade Negro Dialect and Standard English," *Elementary English* 49 (May 1972): 688-696.

46. Paul D. Weener, "Social Dialect Differences and the Recall of Verbal Messages," *Journal of Educational Psychology* 60 (June 1969): 194-199.

47. Baratz, "The Relationship of Black English to Reading," 108.

48. Robert L. Politzer, Mary R. Hoover, and Dwight Brown, "A Test of Proficiency in Black Standard and Nonstandard Speech," *TESOL Quarterly* 8 (March 1974): 27-35.

49. Fryburg, "The Relations among English Syntax, Methods of Instruction, and Reading Achievement of First Grade Disadvantaged Black Children."

50. Barbara Carey Hunt, "Black Dialect and Third and Fourth Graders' Performance on the *Gray Oral Reading Test,*" *Reading Research Quarterly* 10 (Fall 1974-75): 103-123.

51. Carl L. Rosen and Wilbur S. Ames, "Influence of Nonstandard Dialect on Oral Reading Behavior of Fourth Grade Black Children under Two Stimuli Conditions," in *Better Reading in Urban Schools,* ed. J. Allen Figurel (Newark, Del.: International Reading Association, 1972), 45-55.

52. Herbert D. Simons and Kenneth R. Johnson, "Black English Syntax and Reading Interference," *Research in the Teaching of English* 8 (Winter 1974): 339-358.

53. Herbert D. Simons, "Black Dialect Phonology and Word Recognition," *Journal of Educational Research* 68 (October 1974): 67-70.

54. Simons and Johnson, "Black English Syntax and Reading Interference."

55. Carol H. Hochman, "Black Dialect Reading Tests in the Urban Elementary School," *Reading Teacher* 26 (March 1973): 581-583.

56. Patricia S. Nolen, "Reading Nonstandard Dialect Materials: A Study at Grades 2 and 4," *Child Development* 43 (September 1972): 1092-1097.

57. Angela M. Jaggar, "The Effect of Native Dialect and Written Language Structure on Reading Comprehension in Negro and White Elementary School Children," unpublished dissertation, New York University, 1973.

58. Susanna Pflaum, "The Impact of Dialect on Reading Comprehension of Selected Syntactic Structures," unpublished paper, University of Illinois at Chicago Circle, 1976.

59. Paul Jay Melmed, *Black English Phonology: The Question of Reading Interference,* Monographs of Language-Behavior Research Laboratory (Berkeley, Calif.: University of California, 1970).

60. Baratz, "The Relationship of Black English to Reading," 107.

61. Labov, *Language in the Inner City,* 3-35.

62. Herbert D. Simons, "Black Dialect and Learning to Read," in *Literacy for Diverse Learners,* ed. Jerry L. Johns (Newark, Del.: International Reading Association, 1974), 7-11; Gloria Channon, "Bulljive — Language Teaching in a Harlem School," *Urban Review* 2 (February 1968): 5-12.

63. " 'Johnny,' 'Mary' CAN Read: 9-Year-Olds Improve Reading Skills," *NAEP Newsletter* 9 (October 1976): 1-2.

8. Non-English-Speaking Children and Literacy

María Elena de Valdés

Few areas of educational theory remain as underdeveloped as that of reading instruction for the child whose first language is not the dominant one of society. There is an extensive bibliography on the theory and practice of reading instruction, but only recently has attention been given to the problems of teaching reading to children whose prereading experience is in a language other than the language of instruction.[1] Teaching reading to such children is basically different from teaching reading to English-speaking children in an English-speaking community. The difference lies in the key role of the prereading language experience on the development of reading skills.

In the United States there is currently an increased interest in bilingual-bicultural education,[2] but only a few of the publications in this field consider the many problems from a substantive viewpoint. The issue addressed by most writers on bilingualism is the effect of educational deprivation on the non-English-speaking child, and research has been concerned primarily with the preferred language for initial literacy. The social and educational problem of highest priority for educators is the growing number of functionally illiterate students in Spanish-speaking communities. Thus, in 1974 there were an estimated 10,795,000 Spanish-speaking people officially in the United States, with the majority concentrated in the Southwest, the ancestral Spanish-speaking area of the United States. The aggregate data show that for this group the median school year completed is the ninth grade.

But if the 689,000 recent Cuban immigrants — a middle-class group with economic and educational resources — were excluded, the median school year completed drops to the seventh grade. A good indicator of the real educational levels of these people comes from data about Mexican-Americans in Texas. The median school year completed for Mexican-American girls was 7.0 and for boys, 7.6. Illiteracy is, as a matter of fact, the major cause of the high dropout rate.[3] While moral pleas for social justice and cultural pluralism are a political reality, review of the issues with reference to social science research, not just education, provides a more practical background for classroom application. What, for example, has psycholinguistics done in more than twenty years of research on bilingual education?[4] What insights have been amassed by the considerable work in sociolinguistics in the past decade?[5] And how do these findings correlate with the recent inquiries of social anthropology?[6] Further, the process of reading itself must be examined from a theoretical perspective, utilizing the impressive work of linguistics and the applied linguistics of instruction in a second language.[7] Finally, our data must be assessed in view of the realities facing the non-English-speaking child. It is extremely difficult to generalize when one is concerned with complex social, economic, and psychological factors. What is clear is that in social groups most affected by social, economic, and psychological margination there is a high degree of functional illiteracy. If our framework of inquiry is viable, we shall be able to point out common recurring factors and thus provide educational planners a set of goals in this area.

Thus, this chapter attempts to use relevant research from linguistics, social sciences, and education in order to address the problems of reading for the non-English-speaking child in the United States. The discussion is more suggestive than conclusive. In spite of the difficulties involved, an analysis of social, linguistic, and learning factors and their influences on bilingual education is required for a substantive view of the problem.

DIMENSIONS OF BILINGUALISM

Bilingualism is not a problem unless society chooses to make it one. Joshua Fishman states:

. . . while competence in two languages can be a decided asset to those who have this command (indeed, most language learning in schools is based on just such an assumption), the bilingualism of hundreds of thousands of Americans is a liability in their lives, and this for no reason inherent in the nature of bilingualism per se. It is our treatment of bilinguals and of bilingualism that brings this sad state of affairs into being and, therefore, it is this treatment that must be altered.[8]

Bilingualism is the natural linguistic reality for millions of people. It is estimated that one-half of the world's population speaks more than one language, but it is only among select groups and in few countries that this natural human resource is developed. Fishman continues: "After two centuries of pretense to the contrary, it is time that the diversity of American linguistic and cultural existence be recognized and channeled more conscientiously into a creative force, rather than be left at worst as something shameful and to be denied, or at best something mysterious to be patronized."[9] The goal that bilingual children be biliterate is a valid educational objective and is achieved in many educational systems, for example, Canada, Nigeria, Sweden, and Switzerland.

There are, however, linguistic circumstances in the United States that must be considered in making a specific assessment of the varieties of bilingualism. Teachers not involved directly with non-English-speaking children erroneously assume that these children have attained the same level in their language as their peers have in English. For example, the assumption that Spanish-speaking children in the United States are the same as Spanish-speaking children anywhere in the Spanish-speaking world is a fundamental mistake, for it fails to recognize the linguistic environment of these children. (Because Spanish-speaking children constitute a majority of non-English-speaking students in this country, the principal focus in this chapter is on them.) The variables of the bilingual environment are the usage and variety of language in the home, the school, the community, and the nation. Two typical cases among Spanish-speaking children illustrate the dimensions of the linguistic factor:[10] a child from a Spanish-speaking home in a Spanish-speaking community may be either bilingual or monolingual in the home-community language; a child from a Spanish-speaking home in an English-speaking community will normally pass from incipient bilingualism in early childhood into monolingualism in English unless there is extraordinary reinforcement of the home language. While both cases might be labeled "bilingual" in school, such is not the case.

Although the problems in each case are different in many respects, the linguistic problem common to both is the nonuse of preschool linguistic experience in school literacy training. In both cases the critical aspects of the non-English-speaking child's linguistic experience — the home and community forms of the spoken language and the language of instruction in the school — come into conflict, and the conflict eventually leads to inadequate literacy development in both. This, in turn, causes frustration, failure, and eventually dropping out. Thus, in spite of the different levels of language attainment originally present, the only form of bilingualism acceptable for success in school is biliterate bilingualism.

But biliterate bilingualism is difficult to achieve because we are still victims of a fundamental pedagogical error of the early nineteenth century. The idea of literacy as an intellectual activity separate from oral language has been perpetuated by the study of classical languages wherein the student was trained to read and to translate a dead language but would never be able to speak that language. The student of a classical language had already become literate in a first language, however, and could transfer his understanding of literacy into the classics. Thus the student was fluent in all aspects of his first language before he attempted to study the classical language. A problem arises for the young child who has to be taught to relate oral fluency to the written language. Furthermore, if the child does not have oral fluency in the language of instruction, the attempt to relate oral to written patterns is even more difficult.

A written language is a symbolic code that conveys meaning between the writer and the reader, but only when a previously established common storehouse of mutual expressions and a shared language system are present. Communication via the written language can break down at two broadly defined levels: the first is the initial encounter and the failure to achieve basic recognition of a collection of graphemes as the symbol of a morpheme; the second is the failure to relate the morpheme to experience.[11] The non-English speaker lacks the mutual expressions and shared language system and often fails to recognize English graphemes as symbols of morphemes. Even on achieving this recognition, the child is often unable to relate the morpheme to experience.

RESEARCH PERSPECTIVES

All languages are effective systems of communication, and all children acquire the variations in the system used in their home and to some extent in their community. We assume that this ability is part of a child's innate endowment as a human being.[12] Beyond this starting point every aspect of language acquisition, language development, and the process of reading is fraught with questions that cannot be resolved at this stage of linguistic research.

Research in social or natural sciences generally has field application only after a consensus of contemporary inquiry is attained. But since educators cannot always await such consensus to initiate field application, they have to superimpose research on already existing field applications. Such imposition is, of course, difficult to achieve. But, in bilingual education, which is faced with governmentally imposed mandates, an inadequate supply of properly prepared teachers, uncertainty about future support, wide diversity in program organization, and even conflicting goals, some direction from research is required.

A first area of research to consider is the universal process of language development. David McNeill carefully assesses the role played by parental speech as "essentially directional; it provides a child with some basis for choosing among the options offered by the linguistic universals."[13] Consequently, the child's first language is as close or as far from the written standard language as is the linguistic orientation given by parental speech. But, as we have pointed out before, the acquisition of language prior to reading is a complex phenomenon that can best be understood as the interaction of language in the home, the community, and the school.[14] If parental speech provides direction, we need to know how that occurs.

A second area of research is the assessment of language usage in the community. It has been proposed that practice plays the major role in language acquisition. As a matter of fact, prior to the recent work in psycholinguistics it was assumed that the principal source of language was repetition of language patterns. But, as McNeill comments in his review of the literature, "it is conceivable that practice is important within the restricted portion of language acquisition that has to do with the discovery of the locally appropriate expression of the linguistic universals."[15] Other research has clearly discounted the possibility that practice alone can account for the acquisition of new forms.[16] It is reasonable to assume, however, that language patterns are strengthened by usage, not merely by imitation, as the child produces novel forms when applying new language structures in new contexts.

A third area of research relates to class.[17] The most marked factor affecting growth of the child's language ability comes from what linguists call "expansion of child speech."[18] This occurs when the parent repeats what the child has said but with the addition of missing grammatical indicators. For example, an extension involving verbal structure is indicated when the child says, "Tim name Tim," and the parent responds, "Tim's name is Tim"; in the case of word order, the child might say, "Table hit head," and the adult would respond, "No, the head hit the table." The assumption here is that the child can understand more than he can verbalize. This assumption has been tested informally by me and others in extended experimentation. It may be that social class membership may have its greatest importance in the extension of children's speech. The tendency to engage in speech expansion is greatest among parents who feel that a child has something to say and who are willing to devote time and effort to facilitate the growth in the child's capacity to speak clearly and fluently. Social class values and child-rearing practices can thus be a major factor in the development of language ability.[19]

A fourth area is the influence of the dominant language on the weaker language.[20] The long-debated issue of code interference has received much attention from psycholinguistic researchers, notably Wallace Lambert, G. Richard Tucker, and their colleagues.[21] Their findings indicate that it is not the phonetic or grammatical characteristics of the dominant language over the weaker language that interfere but rather that parental attitudes are decisive factors in determining language preference.

The same socioeconomic pressures that motivate non-English speakers in North America to learn English also create a prevailing attitude of margination among those who are not fluent in the dominant language.[22] Consequently, certain types of bilingualism are strongly affected by the context of language acquisition. Lambert reported that

Coordinate bilinguals in contrast to compound bilinguals appear to have more functionally independent language systems. . . . [For example] Bilinguals were classified as having learned their two languages in either separated or fused contexts. It was hypothesized that experience in separated as compared with fused language acquisition contexts comparatively enhances the effectively separated use of the bilingual's two languages.[23]

Thus, in application to bilingual education, separated contexts appear warranted.

In turning from psycholinguistics to social anthropology, we encounter another facet of the same reality. Why do Spanish-speaking people maintain their group identity?

We can recognize basic group identity as one of the fundamental traits of man.[24] An identity problem among Spanish-speaking persons in the United States often arises because of a pseudoparallel drawn by even highly educated critics of bilingual education between the Spanish-speaking population and the non-English European immigrants of the late nineteenth and the early twentieth centuries. There is in fact no parallel. When the European immigrant left his home country, he was determined to make a new life for himself and to acquire a new status in the dominant English-speaking society. The Spanish-speaking population settled in the territory of what is now the United States long before it was part of the national domain. As a result, subsequent groups of immigrants from the Spanish-speaking world arrive into an established cultural enclave — not the English-speaking group — and their group identity ties them into a marginal situation.

As with blacks in the United States, identification with the dominant group produced the classical psychological patterns of self-rejection and self-hate. When members of such groups no longer yield to this condition, group identities break down and produce new problems for both individuals and society. Spanish-speaking people are now in the midst of this conflict of identities. These people have distinctive physical characteristics and have created names for themselves (for example, Chicano and Latino), but, contrary to blacks, retain certain sociocultural traits, thus giving them linguistic ties to both standard Spanish and a local dialect.[25] While blacks must struggle with two linguistic codes — the standard of the dominant group and their own — Spanish-speaking Americans may have to contend with at least four — standard Spanish, the local dialect and the nonstandard English dialect, and standard English.[26] Two observations can be made from this assessment: the group identification of Spanish-speaking people is linked with their language at the deepest levels of personality; and the varieties of language are doubled, for the speaker must contend with two standard languages and at least two localized codes of group expression and identification.

Added to these difficulties is a traditional pedagogical attitude toward bilingualism. Joshua Whatmough is typical of researchers and other educators prior to the 1960s. "Rarely is either of two languages — to limit consideration to two only — learned as well, even in childhood, as either one would have been if the child had confined himself to only one of them."[27] The oversight of researchers like What-mough and those who preceded him was to consider language exclusive of its sociocultural context.

Wallace Lambert and Elizabeth Peal explored the effects of bilingualism on intellectual functioning. A group of monolingual and a group of bilingual ten-year-olds from six French schools in Montreal were administered verbal and nonverbal intelligence tests and measures of attitudes toward the English and French communities. Contrary to previous research, this study found that bilinguals performed significantly better than monolinguals on both verbal and nonverbal intelligence tests. Several explanations are suggested as to why bilinguals have this general intellectual advantage. "They have a language asset, are more facile at concept formation, and have a greater mental flexibility. The results of factor analysis applied to the data supported the hypothesis that the structure of intellect for the two groups differs. The bilinguals appear to have a more diversified set of mental abilities than the monolinguals."[28]

The evidence from cultural anthropology indicates that the Spanish-speaking communities in the United States are vigorous cultural entities whose main source of cohesion is their language and the linguistically related facets of culture. Harry Hoijer writes: "It has become clear that a culture is more than a fortuitous assemblage of traits; each culture possesses, in addition to its trait content, a unique organization in terms of which its distinct components are significantly related to one another."[29]

BASIC READING AND LITERACY

Reading is a highly complex neurological achievement, and yet we tend to take it for granted until we are confronted by failure. Reading acquisition can be developed, however, in an orderly manner if the conditions for it are right.

The examination of the progressive steps involved in the acquisition of literacy (Chapter 2), when applied to the nondominant language and the speaker, clarifies the issues of reading and language of initial literacy. English-speaking children have been taught to speak and read French in English-speaking Canada with some success; that is, they received initial instruction in a weaker language.[30] Spanish-speaking children in Philadelphia, on the other hand, have received their basic instruction in English, which was their weaker language.[31] It should be noted, however, that the sociolinguistic configurations of these situations were almost inverse. Whereas French was the weaker language to the Canadian children (and it was likely to continue so because they lived in an English-speaking community), the Spanish-speaking children in Philadelphia passed from a stage where Spanish was dominant through an unstable compound to a stage where English was dominant.

Many advocates of bilingual instruction in the United States propose that instruction begin in the dominant language (for example, Spanish) and not in the weaker (for example, English) in order to avoid retardation of the reading process. The issue concerning the language to be used in teaching pupils from non-English-speaking homes is highly controversial. As with most educational issues that have sociopolitical overtones, much heat has produced little light.[32]

Once the choice has been made regarding the language of instruction, the first task is to develop the oral fluency and vocabulary of the children to a high level of competence either in the dominant or in the weaker language. There is no choice as to whether oral competence or the introduction of print should come first. Graphemes are meaningless without reference to morphemes. A reading program in English for non-English-speaking children usually fails because these children are confronted with written language for which they have no oral equivalent with a meaningful referent. Eleanor Thonis insists on concepts that teachers in the field recognize, but that others, including some administrators, fail to grasp. She maintains that the ability to understand written English improves as the skills of oral language increase: "As pupils bring better comprehension of spoken English and larger speaking vocabularies to their reading, they grow in their understanding of the print of a second language."[33] Thonis goes on to point out that reading comprehension ultimately depends upon a knowledge of words, of groups of words, and of their order, according to the rules of the language. At times the written and oral forms of languages are not closely associated; French and English are such languages. In Spanish, on the contrary, there is a closer relationship between the spoken and written forms. Thonis makes a keen observation on this point:

For speakers of other languages, one of the biggest obstacles in reading English . . . may be found in the differences between the formality of language as written and the informality of English as spoken. People frequently use contractions, elliptical utterances, fragmented sentences and abbreviated forms which require the hearer to supply from his knowledge of spoken language, the necessary parts which have been omitted.[34]

It is a major cognitive achievement for an individual to acquire literacy in any language. Whatever methods are used, there is a basic dependence on the orderly and sequential development of skills. Other authorities concur with the assumption that reading instruction consists of the buildup of skills, with each new step resting solidly on the previous one. According to Thonis, "Two factors must be considered in the organization of the reading plan. The first is the consistent progression from the simple to the difficult and the second is its suitability for the pupils who will be expected to move steadily along the skills continuum."[35] Consequently, the Spanish-speaking child is given significant support when his preschool experience is utilized, and he is set back when he must "overcome" a resource that has become a handicap.

THE SITUATION IN THE UNITED STATES

Non-English-speaking children do not form a cohesive group, for their only common denominator is a lack of oral fluency in English. Any attempt to combine these children into the same category without recognizing their diversity of background and skills is not only foolish, but, in pedagogical terms, it is unethical and denies their rights as individuals.

The first step in teaching non-English-speaking children to read in English is to determine what stage of oral English competence the child has attained. If a child is attending school and is learning to read in the dominant language with a complementary program in English as a second language, an assessment of his English language capabilities can be made with some thoroughness.

The preliterate child who speaks a language other than English must be introduced to the written language in the same manner as children are taught to read in any language. The child can utilize his dominant oral code, but, if he is forced to exchange this code for another, he may be held back for a considerable period, especially when his dominant oral code is that of both home and community. Extensive delays of this nature are a major contributing cause of the low final limits of reading achieved among non-English-speaking children.

Once a careful assessment has determined that the child is literate in a dominant language other than English and that he has developed an oral command of English, the child is ready to learn how to read English. The child who can read and write in Spanish (or any Indo-European language) has a wealth of background skills, not the least of which is the confidence gained in reading the home language. For example, skill in word recognition can be transferred from one language to another. English, Spanish, French, Italian, and Portuguese share thousands of words with common roots in Latin (for example, *educación*-education). It may take slightly longer to acquire recognition skills when there are greater spelling differences (as in the case of *filosofía*-philosophy). Skills related to word order, false cognates, and grammatical items such as verbal inflection or the lack of it have to be stressed and practiced before skill develops in the second language.

The greatest challenge for the schools is to improve the literacy of non-English-speaking children whose home language is poorly developed. If these children have experienced failure in their attempts to read the first language, they are likely to experience further failure in attempts to read the second. They are not and will probably never go beyond functional illiteracy. In order to alter this situation, it is first necessary to change attitudes. These children must be convinced that they can participate in the classroom, that they can learn to read, and that they are important to the school and not marginal students waiting only for the legal age to drop out. If older children have no real literacy in the first language, teaching them exclusively in that language may result in renewed purpose and growth. Remedial reading programs are a necessity for these failing students.

Three problems are relevant to a discussion of reading instruction for minority children in the United States. First, the problem of code interference is acute when pupils have limited oral command of English. The root of the problem is not the first language, but, rather, an insufficient command of oral English. The oral language is the essential prereading experience that is lacking. Second, school staffs, especially in areas of immigrant population, have traditionally been ethnocentric and, therefore, hostile in their attitude toward ethnicity. But ethnicity is the only context in which the non-English language can survive. There is today, however, some indication of an incipient pluralism. Third, I concur with many commentators that the best methods are insufficient when teaching is poor and insensitive, while the best teaching can be successful with most methods.

What lies ahead? Although all parties concerned with education agree on the value of literacy in English, not all agree on who is to be the recipient, at what public cost, and by what means. Let us take up these issues in turn. Literacy for everyone is an effective slogan in the sociopolitical arena of a democracy, but there is also an economic side to literacy. The more homogeneous the social group, the more standardized and more economical the school system can be. In a heterogeneous society with a wide diversity of ethnic groups and languages, specialized education becomes an expensive necessity. The courts have decided the basic issue — there is to be literacy for all — but the practical task of realizing this goal has not been met throughout the nation. There are those who would delay the introduction of specialized bilingual-biliterate educational programs. One of the usual subjective reasons is expressed in the question, "If we did not have it, why should they?" And there are others who do not support the special teacher-training programs — which are the only way specialized bilingual education can meet the challenge — because they do not understand the complexity of the task the schools are asking the teacher to undertake. The detailed discussion of which methods are most effective can be left open until we have gained more experience in the field.[36] The highest priority today is a rigorous retraining program for teachers and new programs for future teachers. In the area of curriculum design and teaching methodology there is a need to develop programs that pay as much attention to the content as to the form of the language. Educational research must not lose sight of the fact that the basic function of language is to communicate. The vehicle can be attractive but it is the passenger who counts in the end.

NOTES

1. See *Reading for the Disadvantaged: Problems of Linguistically Different Readers,* ed. Thomas E. Horn (New York: Harcourt, Brace and World, 1970); Joyce Morris, "Barriers to Successful Reading for Second-Language Students at the Secondary Level," *TESOL Quarterly* 2 (September 1968): 158-163; Eleanor Wall Thonis, *Teaching Reading to Non-English Speakers* (New York: Collier Macmillan,

1970); *id., Literacy for America's Spanish Speaking Children* (Newark, Del.: International Reading Association, 1976). Good in-service booklets include Vicki Gunther and Dionioes Montoya Sampson, *Teaching Reading to Children Whose First Language Is Not English* (Chicago: Chicago School Board, 1974); Maria Moylan, Irma Joseph O'Neill, and Perry Zirkel, "Reading for the Spanish-Speaking Child: An Overview," ERIC: ED 106 238, 1974.

2. Theodore Anderson and Mildred Boyer, *Bilingual Schooling in the United States* (Austin, Texas: Southwest Educational Development Laboratory, 1970); Kathleen A. Buto *et al., A Better Chance to Learn: Bilingual-Bicultural Education* (Washington, D.C.: United States Commission on Civil Rights, 1975); Josúe M. González, "Coming of Age in Bilingual-Bicultural Education," in *Inequality in Education* (Cambridge, Mass.: Center for Law and Education, Harvard University, 1975), 5-17.

3. *The Minority Report: An Introduction to Racial, Ethnic, and Gender Relations*, ed. Anthony C. Dworkin and Rosiland J. Dworkin (New York: Praeger, 1976).

4. A good collection of early psycholinguistic studies of language development is in *The Genesis of Language: A Psycholinguistic Approach*, ed. Frank Smith and George A. Miller (Cambridge, Mass.: M.I.T. Press, 1966). A direct application of psycholinguistics to bilingual education is by Wallace E. Lambert *et al.,* in *Language, Psychology, and Culture*, ed. Anwar S. Dil (Stanford: Stanford University Press, 1972).

5. *Readings in the Sociology of Language*, ed. Joshua A. Fishman (The Hague: Mouton, 1968); *Advances in the Sociology of Language I and II*, ed. *id.* (The Hague: Mouton, 1972); Jane Macnab Christian and Chester C. Christian, "Spanish Language and Culture in the Southwest," in *Language Loyalty in the United States*, ed. Joshua A. Fishman (The Hague: Mouton, 1966), 280-317; *Language in Social Groups: Essays by John J. Gumperz*, ed. Anwar S. Dil (Stanford: Stanford University Press, 1971); *Language in Sociocultural Change: Essays by Joshua A. Fishman*, ed. *id.* (Stanford: Stanford University Press, 1972).

6. *Selected Writings of Edward Sapir in Language, Culture, and Personality*, ed. David G. Mandelbaum (Berkeley: University of California Press, 1958); *Ethnicity: Theory and Experience*, ed. Nathan Glazer and Daniel P. Moynihan (Cambridge, Mass.: Harvard University Press, 1975).

7. This area is especially rich, and, therefore, only the basic sources for bilingual studies are cited here. The following are books on second-language study that point up the problem areas of language learning in two languages: Nelson Brooks, *Language and Language Learning, Theory and Practice* (New York: Harcourt, Brace and World, 1964); Robert Lado, *Language Teaching: A Scientific Approach* (New York: McGraw-Hill, 1964); and Robert L. Politzer, *Foreign Language Learning: A Linguistic Introduction* (Englewood Cliffs, N.J.: Prentice-Hall, 1965). Of more direct application to the area of Spanish-English bilingual study are William E. Bull, *Spanish for Teachers: Applied Linguistics* (New York: Ronald Press, 1965); and Robert P. Stockwell, Donald J. Bowen, and John W. Martin, *The Grammatical Structures of English and Spanish* (Chicago: University of Chicago Press, 1965).

8. See Joshua A. Fishman, "Language Maintenance in the United States," in *Language in Sociocultural Change*, ed. Dil, 18.

9. *Ibid.*, 40.

10. Christian and Christian, "Spanish Language and Culture in the Southwest," 299-313.

11. See Thonis, *Teaching Reading to Non-English Speakers*, 67-85.

12. See Dwight Bolinger, "Some Traits of Language and Language Acquisition," in *Teaching the Bilingual*, ed. Frank Pialorsi (Tucson: University of Arizona Press, 1974), 69-83. For a discussion and review of research of a language acquisition device as the innate inheritance of all children, see David McNeill, "Developmental Psycholinguistics," in *The Genesis of Language*, ed. Smith and Miller, 15-83.

13. McNeill, "Developmental Psycholinguistics," 65.

14. See Hans Hörmann, *Psycholinguistics*, tr. H. H. Stern (New York: Springer-Verlag, 1971), 266-296.

15. McNeill, "Developmental Psycholinguistics," 67-68.

16. See George A. Miller, "Some Preliminaries to Psycholinguistics," *American Psychologist* 20 (January 1965): 15-20.

17. McNeill, "Developmental Psycholinguistics," 75.

18. See Jerry A. Fodor, "How to Learn to Talk: Some Simple Ways," in *The Genesis of Language*, ed. Smith and Miller, 105-122.

19. Dan I. Slobin, "Imitation and the Acquisition of Syntax," paper presented at the Second Research Planning Conference of Project Literacy, 1964, and cited by McNeill, "Developmental Psycholinguistics," 73.

20. The general question of code interaction could not be studied with more than passing interest on very limited data because of the lack of basic linguistic-demographic study. This situation has changed rapidly owing to the work in the last half decade. In the case of Spanish-English speakers in the United States, the hard data have been provided in *Bilingualism in the Barrio*, ed. Joshua A. Fishman, Robert L. Cooper, and Roxana Ma. (Bloomington: Research Center for the Language Sciences, Indiana University, 1971).

21. See Wallace E. Lambert, "Psychological Studies of the Interdependence of the Bilingual's Two Languages," in *Language, Psychology, and Culture*, ed. Dil, 300-330. For the studies related to attitude, see Wallace E. Lambert *et al.*, "A Study of the Roles of Attitudes and Motivation in Second Language Learning," in *Reading in the Sociology of Language*, ed. Fishman, 473-491; Wallace E. Lambert and G. Richard Tucker, *Bilingual Education of Children* (Rowles, Mass.: Newbury House, 1972); and Wallace E. Lambert and Elizabeth Peal, "The Relation of Bilingualism to Intelligence," in *Language, Psychology, and Culture*, ed. Dil, 111-159, especially 148-152.

22. For a study of language shift, see Joshua A. Fishman, "Language Maintenance and Language Shift as a Field of Inquiry: Revisited," in *Language in Sociocultural Change*, ed. Dil, 76-134; and for commentary on the sociocultural factors, see Joshua A. Fishman, "Planned Reinforcement of Language Maintenance in the United States," *ibid.*, 20 ff.

23. Wallace E. Lambert, J. Havelka, and C. Crosby, "The Influence of Language Acquisition Contexts on Bilingualism," in *Language, Psychology, and Culture*, ed. Dil, 20.

24. Harold R. Isaacs, "Basic Group Identity: The Idols of the Tribe," in *Ethnicity*, ed. Glazer and Moynihan, 29-52.

25. See Christian and Christian, "Spanish Language and Culture in the

Southwest," 280-317, and especially 299 ff. The major study demonstrating the diversity of the minority language community is *Bilingualism in the Barrio,* ed. Fishman, Cooper, and Ma.

26. For a discussion of teaching strategies to cope with this situation, see Thonis, *Teaching Reading to Non-English Speakers,* 103-135.

27. Joshua Whatmough, *Language: A Modern Synthesis* (New York: Mentor Books, 1957), 55-56.

28. Lambert and Peal, "The Relation of Bilingualism to Intelligence," 155.

29. Harry Hoijer, "Linguistic and Cultural Change," in *Language in Culture and Society,* ed. Dell Hymes (New York: Harper and Row, 1964), 455-468, quotation on 457.

30. One of the most notable successes has been the Toronto French School where English-speaking children are immersed in a French program in kindergarten through first grade and are taught to read in French (their second language). French and English are used on a fifty-fifty basis from the second grade to the end of high school. The students are primarily from the upper middle class in Toronto. See also Lambert and Tucker, *Bilingual Education of Children,* for the experience in Montreal.

31. See Buto *et al., A Better Chance to Learn,* 119.

32. One of the first modern studies on the question was Nancy Modiano's often cited article, "The Most Effective Language of Instruction for Beginning Reading: A Field Study," in *Teaching the Bilingual,* ed. Pialorsi, 159-166. Modiano concluded that: first, children who do not speak the national language learn to read it with comprehension more efficiently if they first learn to read in their mother tongue; second, ability to communicate with one's students appears to outweigh language (content) or instructional methodology for successful teaching; third, the more comfortable and less pressured people feel about learning a second language the faster they learn it (p. 165). See also Patricia Lee Engle, "Language Medium in Early School Years for Minority Language Groups," *Review of Educational Research* 45 (Spring 1975): 283-325. This article aptly summarizes the arguments for and against the use of the vernacular as the first language of instruction. Engle correctly points out that the two approaches are not a clear either-or situation. For, while instruction in the vernacular will subsequently become bilingual education, the inverse is not true. Further and even of greater consequence than linguistic questions are sociocultural factors. These include the sociolinguistic makeup of the community; the sociocultural factors of attitude and identity; the advantages and disadvantages of the vernacular as a working language. There is, consequently, no global generalization for all, since what may be acceptable for Mexican-American communities in Los Angeles may not be appropriate for Puerto Rican communities in New York. There are, however, two universal statements on which there appears to be a consensus: children must first speak the language in which they are to be taught to read; minority languages are a human national resource that should be maintained.

33. Thonis, *Teaching Reading to Non-English Speakers,* 164.

34. *Ibid.*

35. *Ibid.,* 167.

36. In this assessment I concur with Modiano that communication with one's pupils is more important than one specific method or another.

9. Learning Disabilities and Remedial Reading

Margaret Ann Richek

The goal of American education is to provide those skills which enable each individual to function autonomously, to contribute to society, and to appreciate the moral and aesthetic values of his culture. In order that this goal may be achieved, special help has traditionally been provided for those individuals who would otherwise be unable to realize their true potential. Reading skills form the cornerstone of education, and yet it is estimated that a substantial number of American children are not acquiring the ability to read at a rate commensurate with their intellectual capacities. The field of remedial reading was established to assist these children. In contrast to developmental reading, which develops skills in the general reader, remedial reading aids those not progressing satisfactorily. Remedial reading has been provided in elementary and high schools and in university clinics since the 1920s.[1] Certification for remedial reading specialists and graduate programs to train them are also long established.

Although its roots go back to the early nineteenth century, the field of learning disabilities is relatively new in education. The term "learning disabilities" was coined as recently as 1963.[2] Researchers and practitioners in this field have had a major impact upon the principles and practices of remedial reading. The purpose of this chapter is to document and assess these influences. To accomplish this, the principles and practices of remedial reading will be outlined, and the influence of learning disabilities will be assessed at each major point. At the present time, the original concepts of learning disabilities are undergoing intensive scrutiny: some practitioners are abandoning them; others assert their validity. Since the original concepts of learning disabilities have profoundly affected remedial reading, they receive first consideration here. Newer trends in the field of learning disabilities also have promising implications for remedial reading, and these "new directions" will be considered.

In the following sections, current principles and practices of remedial reading will be outlined in five areas: the scope of remedial reading, the history of the two fields, the causes and correlates of reading disabilities, the diagnosis of the disabled reader, and the remediation of reading difficulties. The traditional and modern contributions of the field of learning disabilities will be evaluated in each area.

THE SCOPE OF REMEDIAL READING

Remedial reading programs are intended for those children whose ability to read is not commensurate with their intellectual potential for reading.[3] Such children are generally referred to as exhibiting a "reading disability." Estimates of the percentage of American elementary school-age children who need special reading assistance range from about 10 to 15 percent.[4]

Children whose progress is slow in acquiring reading skills do not constitute a homogeneous group. Roy Kress describes two types of programs for children displaying different degrees of reading disability.[5] "Corrective" reading programs are provided for children who have a limited degree of reading disability and who respond fairly readily to the traditional reading procedures used in classrooms, when those procedures are carefully sequenced and paced. Corrective instruction usually occurs within the classroom or in small groups outside the classroom on a weekly or semiweekly basis. "Remedial" programs are for children whose reading disability is more severe and who require treatment in a clinical setting with sophisticated techniques and regular treatment.

Even within the remedial classification, there are differences in children's progress. Often remedial readers show rapid improvement when they are treated individually. Many researchers and clinicians feel, however, that a small number of cases seem peculiarly resistant to improvement, even with the most refined and sophisticated of remedial techniques. Authorities view this phenomenon in different ways. MacDonald Critchley, for example, sees it from a medical point of view. He states: "Neurologists believe that within the community of poor readers there exists a hard core of cases where the origins of the learning defect are inborn and independent of any intellectual short-comings which may happen to coexist."[6] M. D. Vernon, studying reading disability from an educational viewpoint, asks, "Is there, in addition to the normal variations in reading ability we have just discussed, an independent dyslexic syndrome or syndromes lying outside the normal range of variation? Are these innate disabilities aggravated perhaps but not caused by environmental circumstances? . . . The evidence adduced in the preceding chapter would seem adequate to establish the existence of a basic disability in at least some backward readers."[7] In such cases, underlying perceptual or neurological causes may be suspected.

Professionals in remedial reading, learning disabilities, and medicine have long recognized the existence of a hard core of backward readers. However, the attempts of these authorities to apply labels has resulted in a confusing plethora of terms. "Dyslexia" originally referred to this type of difficulty, but the term is now often used to refer to less severe reading disabilities, and abolition of its use has been urged.[8]

THE HISTORY OF THE TWO FIELDS

A brief survey of the history of remedial reading reveals how diverse the influences upon it have been.[9] The first report of an otherwise normal individual experiencing difficulty learning to read was written in the field of medicine in 1896.[10] Beginning in the second decade of the twentieth century, the phenomenon of reading disability began to attract attention within the field of education. Several important developments occurred in the 1920s and early 1930s. The first widely influential books appeared in the early 1920s, and, during the same years, the first remedial reading clinic was established at the University of California, Los Angeles. William Gray reported in 1922 the existence of diagnostic and remedial facilities in "several cities."[11] Batteries of tests for remedial readers were first published in the late 1920s. Grace Fernald and Helen Keller developed an influential method of teaching remedial reading—the kinesthetic or tactile method.[12] Samuel Torrey Orton postulated in the 1930s that severe reading difficulties might be due to incompletely established lateral dominance in the brain, resulting in "strephosymbolia."[13]

While many new developments came from outside the field of education, reading specialists also made substantial contributions. Two specialists in education, Marian Monroe and Helen Robinson,[14] investigating cases being treated for remedial reading, stressed the multiplicity of possible causes. The educational viewpoint within remedial reading tended to be intensely practical. It has been traditionally skeptical of the usefulness of the contributions of more theoretical fields to the actual remedial situation. Thus, educators in remedial reading often questioned the use of such terms as "congenital word blindness," arguing that it is difficult to rule out other psychological and instructional factors that might be causing a reading disability.

From roughly 1935 to 1955, two new trends were noted. First, numerous investigations on the emotional causes of reading disabilities were undertaken, and several researchers found emotional liability to be a correlate of poor reading and a factor in the success of treatment. Second, a publication by a layman at the end of this period had a profound influence on the total concept of teaching reading, as well as on remedial reading. Rudolph Flesch's *Why Johnny Can't Read* postulated that failure to teach phonics resulted in reading disability.[15]

From 1955 to approximately 1970, new developments in remedial reading occurred as a result of growth in population, increased federal funding, and renewed attention to reading as a basic skill. Ophthalmology and optometry made theoretical contributions. Practitioners in these fields had long stressed the importance of physical visual defects in reading disability. However, emphasis was now placed upon defects of visual attention and faulty visual habits.[16] Developments within education and psychology also had profound effects upon remedial reading. Although the analysis of skills had long been a traditional concern of remedial reading, it was refined by the work of Robert Gagné[17] and other educators. Within psychology, research on operant conditioning led to new formulations by Israel Goldiamond and Jarl Dyrud,[18] as well as others, on the application of behavior modification techniques to theory and practice in remedial reading.

The History of Learning Disabilities

The history of the field of learning disabilities goes back to research on brain functioning and trauma in the late 1800s and early 1900s.

Investigators included John Hughlings Jackson and Sir Henry Head, who studies the biological correlates of aphasia (lack of ability to communicate), and Kurt Goldstein, who examined the behavior of veterans injured in World War I.[19] A. A. Strauss and others applied their discoveries to institutionalized children, seeking to distinguish between brain-injured children and those exhibiting familial retardation. They postulated that children suffering from the specific perceptual impairments and behavioral symptoms typical of Goldstein's patients might be brain injured although their injury might be too subtle to diagnose.[20] The existence of "minimal brain damage" as a possible cause of poor functioning in children was the subject of an influential book by A. A. Strauss and Laura Lehtinen.[21] In time, this concept came to be used to explain learning difficulties in the general population. Newell Kephart helped to initiate this trend with his influential book, *The Slow Learner and the Classroom*.[22] Thus, the field of learning disabilities came into existence within the realm of education.

While no longer confined to the sphere of medicine, the field of learning disabilities remains strongly influenced by medical formulations. Researchers and practitioners have traditionally concentrated on the neurological, perceptual, and communicative deficiencies of children exhibiting learning difficulties. These concepts have had profound influences upon principles and practices in remedial reading. As will be explained in the following sections, however, many specialists in learning disabilities now reject these traditional formulations. For these researchers, the field of learning disabilities has offered an opportunity to take a broad view of the child who is experiencing difficulties in a range of areas, including those of an academic and nonacademic nature. This has given valuable new insights into reading difficulties.

THE CAUSES AND CORRELATES OF READING DISABILITIES

The Concept of Many Factors

Investigators of remedial reading have continuously searched for causes of reading disability. This search is fraught with methodological pitfalls. First, a possible causal factor (such as faulty eye movements) may be correlated with reading disability and yet not cause the disability. Another cause (for example, visual difficulties) may lead to both. Or, when a symptom such as emotional instability is present, it is difficult to know whether the emotional state is the cause or the effect of the reading difficulty. An underlying abnormality may weaken other abilities so that many immaturities or abnormalities may result. Several investigators have found that poor readers have a number of weak underlying abilities.[23]

A second problem in establishing causes is the fact that even the most serious debilities do not always result in a reading disability. For example, a brain disturbance such as cerebral palsy, which in general is associated with decreased learning ability, does not prevent some from earning advanced degress.

In Robinson's pioneering study, thirty failing readers were examined by a multidisciplinary team who established probable causes for their reading disability. Twenty-two of the thirty cases were subsequently treated. The results of this treatment enabled the investigators to clarify further probable causes. A wide variety of causes appeared to be responsible for the disabilities, and the more acute the reading disability, the greater the number of probable causes. The two most prevalent factors were visual difficulty (cited in 50 percent of the cases) and social problems (cited in 54.5 percent of the cases). In spite of the large number of probable causes, no clusters of correlated factors could be discerned for the characterization of subgroups.[24]

Studies before and after Robinson's work have associated many factors with reading disabilities. Theodore Harris summarizes the prevailing viewpoint in the field of remedial reading: "the basic principle of the multiple causation of reading disability in the causal diagnosis of reading disability is supported by a substantial body of research evidence which indicates that there is no single known cause to which severe disability may be attributed."[25] Thus, both traditional and modern research leads to the conclusion that a variety of factors may result in low reading achievement, but that none necessarily causes reading disability.[26]

The Perspective of Learning Disabilities

The field of learning disabilities has made two major contributions in the search for causes and correlates. First, professionals in the field have traditionally associated the learning-disabled child, who customarily has reading difficulties, with organic or perceptual processing liabilities and have, therefore, investigated the possibility of a learning disability syndrome. Second, and more recently, researchers have,

through a new multidisciplinary approach, investigated several correlates of reading disabilities.

As the preceding section indicates, no one pattern can generally
characterize the remedial reader. And yet, as was stated in the first
section of this chapter, many practitioners within remedial reading
feel that there is a hard core of cases who are severely disabled and respond little, if at all, to remedial treatment. One of the tenets upon
which the field of learning disabilities was founded is that there exist
children whose problems are based on subtle neurological or perceptual deficiencies. Hard-core cases of reading disability would be likely
candidates for such neurological or perceptual impairment.

The traditional organic model of learning disabilities implies a subtle physical cause, of which difficulty in school is a resulting symptom.
In its strongest formulation, a medical model implies that a group of
individuals who exhibit certain symptoms will also exhibit, with considerable regularity, a common underlying cause and that the allevia-
tion of these symptoms will result from determining and removing this
cause. The historical antecedents of the field of learning disabilities
among institutionalized children suffering brain injury and trauma
and the traditional concerns of educational research with psychological processing make this model attractive. The external search by
science for simple but inobvious causes for complex phenomena
would, moreover, make the validation of such a disease model an in-
valuable contribution to educational theory and practice. Evidence
for this claim is summarized below.

The strongest verification of the claim would be the discovery of a
virus, the existence of a common brain lesion, or some phenomenon of
equal demonstrability. In the absence of such a discovery, one might
ask for tentative verification of the medical model in the form of evidence that a group of children who shared the diagnosis of "learning
disabled" also shared some noneducational symptoms. Perhaps the
strongest case that could be made is the independent confirmation of
brain dysfunction in the learning disabled. Unfortunately, this has
been difficult to establish. Indeed, several attempts to find such evidence have been made. For example, Freda Weaver Owen and her
colleagues conducted a thorough neurological examination of
seventy-six underachieving students that revealed that only three students in this group showed signs of abnormal neurological functioning. An electroencephalogram (EEG) was administered to a subsam-

ple of the children in their study. The abnormality of the EEG tracings did not appear to be associated with learning problems.[27] John Meier, investigating the prevalence of various signs traditionally associated with learning disabilities in 101 second-grade learning-disabled children and 19 controls, found that "considerable numbers of EEG abnormalities were reported in both the disabled and the control group."[28]

A less rigorous test of the medical hypothesis would be the systematic association of a constellation of behavioral features with difficulty in learning. Indeed, certain behavioral characteristics are thought to occur frequently in learning-disabled children and have come to be referred to as "soft signs." These include poor performance on tests of perception, difficulties in communicating, motor problems, hyperactivity, and distractibility. Several studies have attempted to verify the existence of these signs, in learning-disabled children, but the results have not been encouraging. For example, Donald Routh and Robert Roberts located eighty-nine children who had been referred to a university clinic because of poor performance in school and examined each to determine the presence or absence of supposed symptoms of minimal brain damage.[29] These measures were correlated to determine whether a cluster of symptoms would define a syndrome. Not only did the syndrome fail to materialize, but the symptoms failed to correlate significantly with any tests of reading, writing, or spelling.

In another study, five tests of perceptual functioning that are commonly used to identify learning-disabled children were administered to fifty-nine children who had been so labeled and to thirty controls. The performance of the two groups differed at a significantly reliable level on only one of the five tests.[30] Finally, Meier, investigating both learning-disabled children and controls, found an incidence of soft signs in 90 percent of the former, but also in 75 percent of the latter.[31]

These findings seem to indicate that a distribution of symptoms usually associated with a disease, in which a large percentage of those with the disease are found to have that symptom and a large percentage of those not having that disease are found to lack that symptom, has failed to materialize. Moreover, reliable clusters of symptoms have not appeared. Thus, at the present time, there seems to be no identifiable syndrome of learning disabilities stemming from common experience or trauma.

In view of these findings, the increasing rejection of the organic model is understandable. Despite the inability to demonstrate a stable symptomatology characteristic of a disease syndrome, the fact remains that there are many schoolchildren achieving below their potential level. In response to the needs of these children, the field of learning disabilities has taken on an increasingly multidisciplinary tone. This has resulted in the exploration of many factors associated with reading disabilities. Two such factors are the social and language behaviors of learning-disabled children. Problems in the social sphere have long been recognized as a factor in learning disabilities. Recently, Mary Cowgill, Seymour Friedland, and Rose Shapiro have found teachers' reports of social problems in kindergarten to be effective predictors of learning disabilities.[32] Tanis Bryan and her associates have studied the social behavior of learning-disabled children in depth.[33] Delayed and deviant language development has also been investigated as a factor in learning disabilities. For example, the studies of Eleanor Semel and Elizabeth Wiig have shown that learning-disabled children exhibit delayed development of skill in comprehending logical and grammatical structures.[34] Learning-disabled children are also deficient in productive language.[35]

THE DIAGNOSIS OF THE DISABLED READER

The Remedial Reading Tradition

Over the fifty-year history of remedial reading, relatively standard diagnostic procedures have been established. The traditional diagnosis has concentrated on an analysis of reading skills, in an effort to determine which skills require remediation. The investigation of correlates and possible causes of reading disability, however, is also a part of diagnosis. In general, the more severe the disability, the more thorough the investigation.

Several writers in the field of remedial reading have given principles of diagnosis. George Spache, for example, states several.[36] First, he notes that diagnosis is a continuous process of verifying hypotheses. Second, he states that diagnosis should be pragmatic; that is, any diagnostic procedure should be done with a direct instructional consequence in mind. Theodore Harris, however, criticizes remedial practices on just this point: "There is no direct evidence from the reading literature that those involved in remedial-reading theory or practice have shown the same concern as those in the medical profession for the importance of prognosis, to which . . . diagnosis must be related for effective action."[37] Other authorities in remedial reading object to the administration of tests from the field of learning disabilities on just this basis. Third, Spache feels that the diagnosis must be thorough. Fourth, he states that the diagnosis must avoid overfractionating the act of reading, which is integrated into many presumably component subskills. This last principle is a direct challenge to the basic approach underlying most diagnostic procedures in reading—the "skills approach."

Remedial reading is widely identified with the skills approach by specialists both within and outside the field.[38] This approach presumes that reading can be subdivided into component skills, that these skills can be inventoried, and that provisions can be made to develop these skills through training. Diagnosis is linked to subsequent remediation, for skills that are discovered to be lacking will be subsequently taught. Using the skills approach, the diagnostician usually proceeds from the general to the specific. Thus, it may first be decided whether the problem is in the area of comprehension or word recognition. After this decision, more specific skills within the child's broad area of deficiency will be tested. Eldon Ekwall presents a representative analysis of reading skills in greater detail.[39] The skills approach has the advantage of specificity to the ultimate task of reading. Thus, in order to improve reading, the professional diagnoses and teaches reading subskills.

Nevertheless, the assumptions that the components of reading—word recognition and comprehension—can be divided into distinct subskills and that these subskills can be reliably learned through training have been repeatedly challenged. Investigations into the independence of various subskills have yielded disappointing results, and, while some maintain that reading is composed of several subskills, others find no evidence for such division. Reviews of the literature have been written by Fredrick Davis and by Roger Farr.[40]

Although there is evidence that analyzing reading in terms of component skills may not be entirely theoretically motivated, it is the algorithm used by most reading diagnosticians, particularly for word recognition skills. Paul Berg summarizes the predominant attitude: "Obviously, teachers do not teach 'pure' skills in isolation any more than tests can measure them. Therefore, it is possible that the teacher who gives the tests gets from the data the kind of information needed to improve instruction, even though neither the test results nor his teaching deal with precisely defined or measured skills."[41]

Diagnostic instruments commonly used by reading specialists can be

divided into several categories. First, there are standardized measures
of achievement and potential that are used to identify the existence of
a reading disability. Second, the analysis of reading behaviors is made
through the use of informal reading inventories. Third, reading may
be further analyzed by tests specifically designed to measure subskills
and by the administration of sample lessons. Finally, sophisticated
diagnoses include the investigation of noneducational factors and psychological processing. Of course, not all diagnosticians use each type
of instrument. In 1963 an extensive survey indicated that the informal
reading inventory, the group intelligence test, and standardized
measure of reading achievement were most generally used.[42]

To identify the disabled reader, a test of reading achievement is
compared with a measure of intellectual potential. Although this is a
relatively standard procedure, the variety of instruments used to assess
both achievement and potential and the different formulas used to
compare them cause variation in actual results.[43] Measures of achievement may be based on an informal reading test or a standardized test.
Often, these two types of instruments do not yield consistent grade
placements.[44] The measure of intellectual potential may also vary,
depending upon the test used. Group measures are generally considered less reliable and contain a greater possibility of error than individual intelligence tests.

Several types of instruments are used to analyze reading behaviors.
A basic test employed by reading diagnosticians is the informal
reading inventory (IRI), which, in its most basic form, is a set of sequentially graded selections from which the child reads orally. Most
informal reading inventories follow the selections with comprehension
questions, and some also add silent selections. The IRI enables the
diagnostician to observe and analyze reading behavior firsthand. It
has been criticized, however, on many grounds, including possible
bias in selecting samples, the unreliability of generalizing from oral
reading behavior to silent reading behavior, and the unreliability of
the short selections.[45] Another source of error—the reliability of the
examiner in coding errors—is not reported in the literature, but has
been extensively reported to me.[46] An informal inventory can be used
to establish current functional reading levels. However, the criteria
that should be used to establish these levels are subjects of dispute. In
sum, the IRI seems to be most useful as a tool that enables the
diagnostician to observe rather than to quantify reading behavior.
William Powell eloquently summarized this viewpoint: "The value of

the IRI lies not in its identification of what has been called the instructional level (and the other levels by interpolation) because there are probably more effective and efficient methods of accomplishing such tasks . . . . The real value of the IRI is that it affords the possibility of evaluating reading behavior in depth."[47]

Several published batteries (for example, the *Diagnostic Reading Scales*[48] and the *Gates-McKillop Reading Tests*[49]) containing informal reading inventories coupled with several diagnostic tests are often used. These tests are designed to yield a complete analysis of reading behavior, but, in practice, are often used in conjunction with other reading tests. The diagnostic tests generally cover the areas of sight words and phonics. Reviews of these tests often criticize them for inadequate or incompletely described standardization. At least one study reveals that they often yield varying grade placement scores.[50] And, yet, in general, they offer an excellent way to assess reading skills directly. Other individual tests measure only selected reading subskills. Skills considered to be prerequisite to reading, such as knowledge of letter sounds and the ability to distinguish the visual form of letters, are also measured on various tests.

With increased interest in criterion testing (that is, the use of nonnormed tests that are valid because they are samples of actual behaviors to be mastered), informal tests have gained new respectability. Gathering diagnostic information by the use of actual examples of potential lessons has been recommended by many experts.[51] These tests enable the diagnostician to see how the child will cope with remedial efforts and thus to integrate the diagnostic and remedial efforts.

A thorough diagnosis includes information that extends beyond the measurement of reading behavior. A physical, educational, and social history is generally obtained through interviews, and, if certain indicators are present, the child may be referred to a medical specialist or counselor. Many reading clinics have facilities for screening visual and auditory acuity. Pure tone hearing is tested, and vision is checked for anomalies of refraction and binocular difficulties. In recent years, visual and auditory perception and basic psycholinguistic processing skills have been added to the thorough diagnostic procedure. These are contributions from the field of learning disabilities.

Contributions of Learning Disabilities

The field of learning disabilities has traditionally maintained that subtle brain dysfunction, perceptual dysfunction, or communicative dysfunction may underlie disability in academic achievement. It becomes imperative, therefore, to obtain measurements that may index organic involvement and that measure perceptual or communicative dysfunction. It is particularly important that these measures be diagnostic, that is, that they pinpoint specific areas of deficit that may be remedied later through perceptual or communication training. Thus, the field of learning disabilities is traditionally associated with a "process approach" — as distinct from the skills approach of remedial reading.[52] Tests measuring reading skills are generally used for reading diagnosis because they sample the child's actual reading behavior. In contrast, tests of perceptual and language skills must demonstrate their usefulness through an association between perceptual functioning and reading. Several theoreticians have postulated the relationship between visual-motor, auditory, and language processes and academic deficiencies.[53]

Tests developed within the tradition of learning disabilities have unquestionably had a profound practical effect on remedial reading. Many tests, including the *Illinois Test of Psycholinguistic Abilities,*[54] the Wepman *Auditory Discrimination Test,*[55] and the *Frostig Developmental Tests of Visual Perception*[56] are now standard in well-equipped clinics. It is often difficult in practice to separate the conceptually distinct tests of readiness skills, which seem to belong to a skills approach to diagnosis, and the tests of perception, which belong to a process approach.

Like the skills approach of remedial reading, the process approach contains certain inherent assumptions that validate the use of perceptual tests.[57] Stephen Larsen identifies four that, he believes, derive from a medical model of learning disabilities: first, children who have learning problems are disabled in basic psychological processes; second, current diagnostic instruments enable the diagnostician to identify the "underlying disorder"; third, the disorder is amenable to remediation; and, fourth, if the underlying disorder is ameliorated, performance in academic areas (reading, spelling, arithmetic) will be improved.

Empirical support of Larsen's first point — that children with learning problems are perceptually disabled — has not been consistently demonstrated. For example, Larsen, Dorothy Rogers, and Virginia Sowell found that four out of five perceptual tests did not discriminate between groups of normal and underachieving children.[58] Two extensive reviews of the literature have been reported by the same research group.[59] One investigated the relationship of the auditory perceptual skills of auditory discrimination, memory, blending, and auditory visual integration through the use of correlation coefficients cited in previous studies. The authors concluded that demonstrated relationships were not large enough (a correlation of .35 was used as a criterion) to warrant inclusion as an educationally useful relationship. The second study investigated the visual perceptual skills of visual discrimination, spatial relationships, visual memory, and discrimination, and the same conclusions were drawn. Both reviews cite many studies in which differences were found between good and poor readers. In many of these studies, however, the investigators had not controlled for intelligence, which led the authors of the review to comment that general intellectual ability may have accounted for observed differences: "When children are separated into groups on the basis of reading achievement, they are inadvertently separated on intellectual ability as well, unless this contaminating variable is taken into account by the investigator. Since mental ability was not controlled for in half of these studies, the resultant differences are not too surprising."[60]

It thus appears that, among the subjects of these studies, the correlation of perceptual skills and reading ability is not high. This does not, however, preclude the fact that, in the relatively small percentage of those who are hard-core remedial reading cases, perceptual functioning may be an important inhibiting factor. In general, tests of perceptual functioning are only administered to children with a severe reading disability. In general, the usefulness of the link between perception and reading has not yet been adequately tested.

Larsen's second claim for the process approach — that current diagnostic instruments allow identification of an underlying disorder — means that tests measure what they purport to measure and that they are reasonably independent of each other. As with tests of reading subskills, factor analyses cast doubt upon this assumption. For example, the *Frostig Developmental Tests of Visual Perception*[61] is divided into five subskills, but factor analytic studies have found only one or two statistically independent factors.[62] The *Illinois Test of Psycholinguistic Abilities*[63] was developed from a theoretical model of considerable complexity. Various investigators have attempted factor analyses and, in general, have not found all of the theoretical distinctions upheld by empirical study.[64] It appears, in sum, that the measurement of separate abilities in at least some tests of processing is open to serious doubt.

Since the assumptions underlying tests of processing may be called into question, one may doubt the wisdom of using such tests as a diagnosis for remedial reading. Two factors, however, should be borne in mind. First, some of the "perceptual" elements, such as visual discrimination and blending, are generally considered readiness skills by reading specialists trained in the skills tradition. Thus, low correlations between these subtests and reading performance also involve implications for the skills approach. Second, many studies include children who are either reading up to grade level or who are only moderately disabled. Too few studies have involved the very disabled readers for whom perceptual tests have their most extensive clinical application. Meanwhile, reading clinicians will undoubtedly continue to use tests of perception and underlying language functioning for the diagnostic information they yield in cases of severe reading disability.

Larsen's third and fourth assumptions — that the "underlying disorder" is amenable to remediation and that, if the disorder is ameliorated, performance in academic areas will be improved — are discussed in the section "Remediation in Remedial Reading," below.

THE REMEDIATION OF READING DIFFICULTIES

Remediation in Remedial Reading

The skills approach is traditionally applied in remediation of reading difficulties as well as in their diagnosis. If the function of diagnosis is to identify reading skills that must be taught, the function of remediation is to teach them. Albert Harris and Edward Sipay identify four principles of remedial instruction: basing remedial instruction on diagnosis; starting from what the pupil knows; selecting appropriate material; and securing motivation.[65] In accordance with these principles, the student is given a program that is individualized to his specific needs in both reading skills and in the level of the instructional materials to be used in remediation. After the student's skills are evaluated, he is taught the next highest skill, in a conceptually ordered hierarchy of skills, which is necessary to improve his reading. Thus, for example, if word recognition skills have not been mastered, his teacher is unlikely to design his program to concentrate on comprehension skills.

Tailoring remedial reading instruction to the child's individual needs is generally considered the most critical part of effective remediation:

In considering the writings of those who have worked with dyslexics, the most frequently encountered verdict is that there is no *one* method and that any method requires to be used flexibly . . . . Even those who have very definite and different methods to offer, agree that there is no "panacea." They respectively hedge their claims with such statements as "this does not mean that these methods are the only ones that will produce results," "no remedial method has universal application" and "I am not suggesting that dyslexic children should be taught by one method and one method only."[66]

Many remedial reading programs are similar to developmental reading programs, except that they are conducted at a lower level and at a slower pace and generally contain more systematic development of reading subskills. In other programs, however, more unorthodox methods are used. A survey published in 1963 confirms this: "A variety of instructional methods and materials was employed in most of the special reading programs. As one reading coordinator declared, 'The methods and materials used depend upon the degree of retardation, the extent and type of problem, and the child's emotional status.' In other situations, however, the methods and materials did not vary greatly from those in regular classroom reading programs."[67] Arthur Traxler's listing of popular techniques, which was based on a 1952 survey, offers a glimpse into remediation using a skills approach; it also presents the variety of problems included under the term "remedial reading": "Among the teaching procedures listed in the questionnaire, those checked most frequently included 'instruction in finding main ideas and supporting details,' 'drill on enlarging the sight vocabulary,' 'instruction in reading directions,' 'instruction in oral reading,' 'instruction in skimming,' and 'study of affixes and roots.' The most popular teaching procedure seemed to be the common, everyday one of drilling on enlarging the sight vocabulary."[68]

Several types of materials are designed especially for the remedial reading situation. Reading series designed to be "high interest-low vocabulary" are published by several companies and are often the backbone of the remedial program. These materials are written to appeal to older children in subject matter and format, but they use a reading vocabulary that is several years less mature. Other publications concentrate on the development of specific subskills. The upsurge of interest in remedial reading that began in the early 1960s has resulted in an increased variety of materials, including comic books, love stories, and sports adventures. In addition, many books, word cards, and games designed for use in the developmental setting are also being used in the remedial situation. Finally, mechanical devices such as tape recorders, filmstrips, low-level computers, tachistoscopes, and pacers are also employed in some settings.

A 1963 survey of reading instruction in elementary schools revealed that teacher-devised materials and trade books, particularly the high interest-low vocabulary type, were the most widely used materials. It was also customary to employ reading games, skills workbooks, and practice exercises. Basal readers, that is, graded series of books designed to foster reading in the developmental classroom, were also utilized in a variety of ways; other supplementary books were also used.[69]

In the remedial situation various materials are used in a variety of ways for many different aims. It is this eclecticism, this individualization, that is the heart of the remedial program and enables it to serve readers as diverse as the third grader reading at the first-grade level and the twelfth grader whose lack of skills needed for studying literature and social studies is impeding his progress.

In general, however, children who are at the beginning stages of reading (regardless of their age level) need a systematic introduction to reading skills. Any of the approaches to beginning reading employed in the developmental program may be used here. If the teacher selects a developmental program, he must first choose between a whole-word approach (such as that used in the famous Scott, Foresman "Dick and Jane" basal readers) and a sound-symbol approach, which emphasizes the regularity of letter-sound correspondences in English. Extensive variations are available within these approaches. Harris and Sipay suggest that selection of the initial method of reading instruction should be based primarily on the pupil's preference. The instructor is thus teaching to the student's strengths. As early as possible, symbols of sight and sound should be combined to provide flexible word recognition. This advice is based on the assumption that:

The majority of cases of reading disability do not have special types of mental or neurological deficits, but result from such causes as lack of reading readiness when first exposed to reading instruction, uncorrected sensory defects, discouragement, emotional disturbance, and poor teaching which is sometimes aggravated by linguistic and cultural mismatches between teachers and pupils. If that is so, the remedial work with those cases should not have to be radically different from the general methods used by primary grade children.[70]

There remains, however, that hard core of cases that do not respond to this type of remedial instruction. For these children, specialized methods are needed. Several such methods have been developed, both within remedial reading and in learning disabilities. These methods will be discussed in the next section on the contributions of learning disabilities to remediation.

There are several organizational aspects to remedial performance, including the optimum duration of the tutoring program, the frequency of remedial reading, the organization of remedial reading instruction, and the type of tutor to be used.

It seems that, in general, the gains from remedial programs are proportional to the length of tutoring. Spache, comparing thirteen studies of remedial reading programs, finds the rate of gain approximately equal for programs that lasted less than six months and programs that lasted more than six months. Of seven studies that investigated remedial gains and duration of programs, Spache reports that six found no differences in rate of gains when instructional time was varied.[71]

Another potentially important factor is the frequency of tutoring. Spache postulates that, since gains are proportional to time spent in a program, it seems reasonable that the more frequent the meetings, the more progress will result.[72] On the other hand, several researchers have found that greater frequency of instruction does not result in a commensurate rise in achievement.[73] There should be further investigations on this point.

A decision that has considerable implications for the resources of the school is whether the child is to be tutored individually or in a group. Little evidence suggests the superiority of individual instruction.[74] Groups should not, however, include more than six or seven students.[75]

The use of peers and semiprofessionals as tutors enables a school system to extend services to a considerable number of pupils who could not be covered by a reading specialist. Recently, there have been several encouraging reports of tutoring by nonprofessional personnel. Linda Devin-Sheenan, Robert Feldman, and Vernon Allen have reviewed the literature on this subject.[76]

There is little doubt that remedial reading programs effectively increase the level of reading at the conclusion of the program. Spache,
in a review of eighteen studies, finds that the average gain in grade
equivalent scores is 1.8 months for one month of instruction.[77] Thus,
remedial readers in special programs almost double the progress expected in normal development when measured at the termination of
the program.

In spite of the short-term results of remedial reading programs,
long-term effects appear to be doubtful. After reading instruction is
discontinued, remedial readers usually tend to revert to their former
rate of reading growth, falling further and further behind their class-
mates. In a review of twelve studies of long-term effects Spache notes
only two that indicate that readers are functioning at grade placement
levels.[78] H. C. M. Carroll found the same trends in studies done in
England.[79] Several factors may contribute to this situation. First,
when children are returned to the same conditions that initially caused
the failure, it can often be expected to recur. Or, teachers may not
provide for readers who, while they have improved, are still functioning only marginally on the class level. Third, the initially positive effects may be due to the psychological benefits of remedial instruction
rather than to the actual benefits of instruction. Some evidence suggests, in fact, that psychological counseling produces the same results
as remedial reading programs.[80] There is, however, a bright note.
When some contact with students continues after a remedial program
has ended, greater gains are made than if the connection is broken.[81]
In addition, there is some evidence that highly intelligent children
whose remediation continues for several years eventually show considerable achievement despite their early problems.[82] Spache suggests,
nevertheless, that the remedial program be considered only a treatment to relieve the student's symptoms temporarily and that he may
have to return for additional help at various times in his educational
career.[83]

Contributions of Learning Disabilities

The field of learning disabilities has made three distinct types of
contributions in three areas: perceptual training for fostering reading
improvement, visual and auditory modalities as related to the method
of reading instruction, and approaches to tutoring hard-core remedial
readers.

As stated in the section on diagnosis, learning disabilities have traditionally been identified with the process approach, which contrasts directly with the skills approach of remedial reading. The process approach assumes that underlying perceptual deficits impede reading progress and that training in these deficit skills will thus improve reading. Training can be divided into three process areas: visual-motor, auditory, and psycholinguistic. Several researchers and practitioners have developed specific materials to remediate processing difficulties.[84] Larsen's third and fourth basic assumptions concerning process training—that the perceptual disorder is amenable to instruction and that, if the underlying disorder is ameliorated, performance in academic areas will improve—are relevant to remediation.

Perhaps the most extensively reviewed of the three process areas is visual-motor processes.[85] In general, reviews have found, at best, mixed results for programs of this type. Donald Hammill, Libby Goodman, and J. Lee Wiederholt discovered that, as they examined several specific programs, the majority show that visual-motor processes cannot be trained. For example, in six of eight "well-controlled" studies in which the Frostig-Horne program was used no improvement was reported in perceptual processes. In reviewing eleven well-designed studies using techniques recommended by Newell Kephart, the authors found that only four of twenty-five total posttest results showed significant improvement in perceptual skills.[86] Results of the transfer of such training were even less encouraging. Of fourteen studies that employed the Frostig-Horne program in the hope of increasing reading abilities, thirteen had no effect. Of ten studies employing the Getman-Kephart techniques, only three showed increased performance on any reading measures.[87] In view of the lack of evidence for the assumption that deficit areas can be trained, the authors seriously doubt that visual-motor activities should be recommended for reading improvement. These authors conclude by stating that:

the results of attempts to implement the Frostig-Horne materials and Kephart-Getman techniques in the schools have for the most part been unrewarding. The readiness skills of children were improved in only a few instances. The effect of training on intelligence and academic achievement was not clearly demonstrated. Particularly disappointing were the findings which pertained to the effects of such training on perceptual-motor performance itself. For if the training is not successful in this area, can the positive benefits of such instruction reported by a few authors be anything other than spurious?[88]

In another review of the literature, Spache finds more cause for optimism concerning visual-motor training.[89] Reviewing specific programs, Spache, like Hammill, Goodman, and Wiederholt, finds that the Frostig-Horne perceptual materials have little effect on perceptual skills or reading. Citing reviews of Carl Delacato's program, which focuses on gross motor exercises such as crawling, Spache, like many others, finds little value in this method.[90] He finds, however, that in fifteen of twenty-three other studies, visual-motor processes could be successfully trained. In addition, he reviews several studies that analyze the transfer of visual-motor training to reading readiness and reading measures. He cites twenty studies where no such transfer was noted and twelve where it was. He observes that, in general, primary students, students of lower socioeconomic status, and students with low IQs are most likely to gain from visual-motor perceptual training.

Although there have been well over one hundred studies on the subject, it is difficult to draw conclusions on the efficacy of visual-motor training for remedial readers. Three factors exacerbate the problem. First, at least some of the studies are poorly conceived. Hammill, Goodman, and Wiederholt cite the lack of control groups, the short duration of treatment, and the possible operation of a novelty effect, among other limitations. They eliminated over half the studies in their review because of methodological flaws.[91] Second, many of the reviews that evaluate the efficacy of such training do not distinguish among studies concerning the mentally retarded, the learning disabled, primary-aged children, and the reading deficient, thereby making interpretation for severely disabled populations difficult. Third, perceptual training experiments that produce no significant gains are more likely to be published than unsuccessful reading programs. Thus, a relatively large number of unsuccessful perceptual training programs are gaining scholarly attention. In view of these factors, the effects of visual-perceptual training can neither be assumed nor totally dismissed, but should be subject to further investigation.

The two remaining areas of perceptual training — auditory skills and psycholinguistic training — have not been as extensively investigated as have visual-motor skills. On the basis of their review of over fifty studies correlating selected auditory skills and reading ability, Hammill and Larsen find little reason for training in auditory skills.[92] Robinson sees the issue of the effects of auditory skills on reading as remaining unresolved.[93] Regarding the importance of psycholinguistic training, Hammill and Larsen[94] detect few beneficial effects of training based on the diagnosis of the *Illinois Test of Psycholinguistic Abilities.*[95]

The process approach to remediation of reading difficulties has gradually fallen into theoretical disrepute with many leaders in both remedial reading and learning disabilities. In an extensive review of practices in twenty-one states, Samuel Kirk and John Elkins find that the process approach is not widely used for remediation, even within the field of learning disabilities.[96] A review of studies in visual-motor skills reveals, nevertheless, that this approach may have some merit for ameliorating severe reading difficulties. Perhaps, with careful investigation, some benefit may also be found for auditory and psycholinguistic training.

A second contribution of the learning disabilities approach is the concept of modality. Doris Johnson and Helmer Myklebust, for example, postulate that significant differences may exist between visual and auditory modes in an individual. They identify both visual and auditory dyslexics. It is thought that, in general, individuals with stronger visual abilities should be taught by a sight word method, and those with stronger auditory abilities should be taught by a phonics method.[97] John Paul Jones reviews the literature on modal preference.[98] Most studies have failed to produce the expected "aptitude-treatment" interaction for initial reading instruction. In view of these findings, the concept of modality preference for learning initial reading skills is not promising. Like the process approach, however, it has not been extensively tested with remedial readers.

As the traditional concepts of perceptual training and modality preference have assumed less importance in the field of learning disabilities, researchers have turned their attention to other aspects of treatment. Two fields of potentially great importance are the use of behavior modification techniques and the use of drugs for remediating learning difficulties.[99]

The field of learning disabilities has made a third contribution to remedial reading: the identification of methods to be used with the hard core of remedial readers who do not improve when standard reading techniques are employed. Professionals identified with both reading and learning disabilities have contributed methods that have extended the repertoire from which the remedial reading teacher may choose. These methods will be briefly described here; more extensive discussions of them may be found elsewhere.[100] It should be noted that each of these methods teaches reading directly, rather than concentrating on perceptual or prerequisite skills.

Perhaps the best known of the specialized methods is the kinesthetic approach developed by Fernald and Keller, which was first published in 1921.[101] In this approach, the child learns words first by tracing them, then by writing them without tracing, and finally by recognizing them in print. Only after the child uses likenesses in words to identify new words is any analysis of phonics attempted.

Successors to Orton, an early leader in the field of learning disabilities, have developed a phonics method that is found most prominently in the writings of Anna Gillingham and Bessie Stillman.[102] The method they advocate is essentially that of systematically learning letter sounds and blending them into short words. It includes a kinesthetic component for learning letter sounds.

Another method also emphasizing phonics clues is the *Writing Road to Reading* by Romalda Bishop Spalding and Walter T. Spalding, which combines writing and spelling with the learning of sound-symbol correspondences.[103] Finally, a new approach, labeled the "neurological impress remedial technique,"[104] uses a read-along procedure to produce a neurological memory trace for words.

As unique as these methods may seem, the remedial reading teacher often modifies them or combines them with other less demanding methods in actual remedial practice. This, of course, is in accord with the remedial principle of individualizing the method to the child's needs. These methods should, nevertheless, receive further empirical validation with hard-core remedial cases. Perhaps this validation will come in the form of case studies, a format that has already been extensively used in the Fernald-Keller approach.

CONCLUSIONS

Researchers and practitioners in the field of learning disabilities have made substantial contributions to remedial reading in the form of research into correlates and causes of reading disabilities, and into their diagnosis and remediation. In the area of causes and correlates, these investigators have thoroughly researched the evidence for a syndrome of "minimal brain dysfunction." Though the evidence for such a syndrome is not strong, its investigation is, nevertheless, a contribution to science. Experts in learning disabilities have recently expanded the realm of correlated factors into several realms, including social behaviors and attentional behaviors. In the sphere of diagnosis, researchers have contributed a variety of perceptual tests that are widely used clinically, while in remediation they have provided the concepts of perceptual training and of teaching to preferred modality. While these contributions have been increasingly criticized, there is at least some evidence to indicate that visual-motor activities may help some children acquire reading skills. Professionals in learning disabilities have also contributed some of the specialized techniques of teaching reading that are used with hard-core cases. In recent years, as experts in learning disabilities have assumed a more eclectic view of their field, they have investigated such topics as use of drugs and behavior modification.

The concept of minimal brain dysfunction as a cause of learning difficulties and the process approach have come into increasing disfavor within and outside the field of learning disabilities. Both represent, nevertheless, additional options for diagnosis and treatment, particularly for the hard-core nonreader. Remediation based on perceptual training should be further investigated with such readers, perhaps by using case studies.

The skills approach to remedial reading has become more respected and more widely used. Programs based on this approach have normally resulted in at least temporary gains in reading achievement. Further research is needed, however, to determine the specific treatments to improve reading. Finally, since long-term benefits are difficult to demonstrate in remedial programs, factors that encourage lasting effects should be further investigated.

NOTES

1. Nila Banton Smith, *American Reading Instruction* (Newark, Del.: International Reading Association, 1965), 192-193.

2. Samuel A. Kirk, "Behavioral Diagnosis and Remediation of Learning Disabilities," in *Conference on Exploration into the Problems of Perceptually Handicapped Children* (Evanston, Ill.: Fund for Perceptually Handicapped Children, 1963), 1-7.

3. In this chapter the literature considered is that concerned with school-age children. Thus, the word "children" is used in several places.

4. Albert J. Harris and Edward R. Sipay, *How to Increase Reading Ability*, 6th ed. (New York: David McKay, 1975), 14-15.

5. Roy A. Kress, "When Is Remedial Reading Remedial?" *Education* 80 (May 1960): 540-544.

6. MacDonald Critchley, *The Dyslexic Child* (Springfield, Ill.: Charles C Thomas, 1970), 101-102.

7. M. D. Vernon, *Reading and Its Difficulties* (New York: Cambridge University Press, 1971), 176.

8. For discussion of this issue, see Richard B. Adams, "Dyslexia: A Discussion of Its Definition," *Journal of Learning Disabilities* 2 (December 1969): 616-633.

9. Information on the history of remedial reading has been drawn from Smith, *American Reading Instruction;* Albert J. Harris, "Five Decades of Remedial Reading," in *Remedial Reading: Classroom and Clinic,* 2d ed., ed. Leo M. Schell and Paul C. Burns (Boston: Allyn and Bacon, 1972), 18-35.

10. W. Pringle Morgan, "A Case of Congenital Word Blindness," *British Medical Journal* 2 (November 1896): 1387, cited in Harris, "Five Decades of Remedial Reading."

11. William S. Gray, *Remedial Cases in Reading: Their Diagnosis and Treatment* (Chicago: University of Chicago Press, 1922), 3.

12. Grace M. Fernald and Helen Keller, "Effects of Kinesthetic Factor in Development of Word Recognition," *Journal of Educational Research* 4 (December 1921): 355-377.

13. Samuel Torrey Orton, *Reading, Writing and Speech Problems in Children* (New York: W. W. Norton, 1937).

14. Marion Monroe, *Children Who Cannot Read* (Chicago: University of Chicago Press, 1932); Helen M. Robinson, *Why Pupils Fail in Reading* (Chicago: University of Chicago Press, 1947).

15. Rudolph Flesch, *Why Johnny Can't Read* (New York: Harper and Brothers, 1955).

16. Summaries of optometric and ophthalmological influences on reading disabilities may be found in George D. Spache, *Investigating the Issues of Reading Disabilities* (Boston: Allyn and Bacon, 1976), 365-432.

17. Robert M. Gagné, *The Conditions of Learning,* 2d ed. (New York: Holt, Rinehart and Winston, 1970).

18. Israel Goldiamond and Jarl E. Dyrud, "Reading as Operant Behavior," in *The Disabled Reader: Education of the Dyslexic Child,* ed. John Money (Baltimore: Johns Hopkins Press, 1966), 93-115.

19. Tanis Bryan and James Bryan, *Understanding Learning Disabilities* (Port Washington, N.Y.: Alfred Publishing Co., 1975), 16-20.

20. *Ibid.,* 21-22; Alan O. Ross, *Psychological Aspects of Learning Disabilities and Reading Disorders* (New York: McGraw-Hill, 1976), 12.

21. A. A. Strauss and Laura E. Lehtinen, *Psychopathology and Education of the Brain-injured Child* (New York: Grune and Stratton, 1947).

22. Newell C. Kephart, *The Slow Learner in the Classroom* (Columbus, Ohio: Charles C. Merrill, 1971).

23. Anne E. Bell and M. S. Aftanas, "Some Correlates of Reading Retardation," *Perceptual and Motor Skills* 35 (October 1972): 659-667; Robinson, *Why Pupils Fail in Reading.*

24. Robinson, *Why Pupils Fail in Reading,* 210-218.

25. Theodore K. Harris, "Reading," in *Encyclopedia of Educational Research,* 4th ed., ed. R. L. Ebel (New York: Macmillan, 1969), 1094-1095.

26. Summaries of the literature on causal and correlated factors may be found in

Robinson, *Why Pupils Fail in Reading,* 7-102, and in Harris and Sipay, *How to Increase Reading Ability,* 238-312.

27. Freda Weaver Owen *et al.,* "Learning Disorders in Children: Sibling Studies," *Monographs of the Society for Research in Child Development* 36, Serial No. 144 (No. 4, 1971): 27, 32-36, 64-65.

28. John H. Meier, "Prevalence and Characteristics of Learning Disabilities Found in Second Grade Children,"*Journal of Learning Disabilities* 4 (January 1971): 14.

29. Donald K. Routh and Robert D. Roberts, "Minimal Brain Dysfunction in Children: Failure to Find Evidence for a Behavioral Syndrome," *Psychological Reports* 31 (August 1972): 307-314.

30. Stephen C. Larsen, Dorothy Rogers, and Virginia Sowell, "The Use of Selected Perceptual Tests in Differentiating between Normal and Learning Disabled Children,"*Journal of Learning Disabilities* 9 (February 1976): 85-90.

31. Meier, "Prevalence and Characteristics of Learning Disabilities," 15.

32. Mary L. Cowgill, Seymour Friedland, and Rose Shapiro, "Predicting Learning Disabilities from Kindergarten Reports," *Journal of Learning Disabilities* 6 (November 1973): 577-582.

33. Tanis Bryan, "An Observational Analysis of Classroom Behaviors of Children with Learning Disabilities," *ibid.,* 7 (January 1974): 35-43; *id. et al.,* "Come On, Dummy: An Observational Study of Children's Communications," *ibid.,* 9 (December 1976): 661-669.

34. Eleanor M. Semel and Elizabeth H. Wiig, "Comprehension of Syntactic Structures and Critical Verbal Elements by Children with Learning Disabilities," *ibid.,* 8 (January 1975): 53-58; *id.,* "Comprehension of Linguistic Concepts Requiring Logical Operations by Learning Disabled Children," *Journal of Speech and Hearing Research* 16 (December 1973): 627-636.

35. Susan A. Vogel, "Syntactic Abilities in Normal and Dyslexic Children,"*Journal of Learning Disabilities* 7 (February 1974): 103-109; Joseph A. Rosenthal, "A Preliminary Psycholinguistic Study of Children with Learning Disabilities," *ibid.,* 3 (August 1970): 391-395; Wilbur A. Haas and Joseph M. Wepman, "Dimensions of Individual Difference in the Spoken Syntax of School Children," *Journal of Speech and Hearing Research* 17 (September 1974): 455-469.

36. George D. Spache, *Diagnosing and Correcting Reading Disabilities* (Boston: Allyn and Bacon, 1976), 8-12.

37. Harris, "Reading," 1094.

38. Spache, *Diagnosing and Correcting Reading Disabilities,* 292-294; Stephen D. Larsen, "The Learning Disabilities Specialist: Role and Responsibilities," *Journal of Learning Disabilities* 8 (October 1976): 502-503; Janet W. Lerner, "Remedial Reading and Learning Disabilities: Are They the Same or Different?" *Journal of Special Education* 9 (Summer 1975): 120-121.

39. Eldon E. Ekwall, *Diagnosis and Remediation of the Disabled Reader* (Boston: Allyn and Bacon, 1976), 50-63.

40. Fredrick B. Davis, "Research in Comprehension in Reading," *Reading Research Quarterly* 3 (Summer 1968): 499-545; Roger Farr, *Reading: What Can Be Measured?* (Newark, Del.: International Reading Association Research Fund, 1969), 33-79.

41. Paul C. Berg, "Evaluating Reading Abilities," in *Assessment Problems in Reading,* ed. Walter M. MacGinitie (Newark, Del.: International Reading Association, 1973), 30.

42. Mary C. Austin and Coleman Morrison, *The First R: The Harvard Report on Reading in Elementary Schools* (New York: Macmillan, 1963), 123.

43. Emery P. Bleismer, "A Comparison of Tests Used with Retarded Readers," *Elementary School Journal* 56 (May 1956): 400-402; James C. Reed, "The Deficits of Retarded Readers—Fact or Artifact?" *Reading Teacher* 23 (January 1970): 347-352; Robert H. Bruininks, Gertrude M. Galman, and Charlotte R. Clark, "Issues in Determining Prevalence of Reading Retardation," *ibid.,* 27 (November 1973): 177-186.

44. Farr, *Reading,* 99-109.

45. Spache, *Investigating the Issues of Reading Disabilities,* 302-314.

46. Personal communications from Susanna W. Pflaum-Connor (March 1977) and William D. Page.

47. William R. Powell, "The Validity of the Instructional Reading Level," in *Readings for Diagnostic and Remedial Reading,* ed. Robert M. Wilson and James Geyer (Indianapolis, Ind.: Bobbs-Merrill, 1972), 100.

48. George D. Spache, *Diagnostic Reading Scales* (Monterey: California Test Bureau, 1963).

49. Arthur I. Gates and Anna S. McKillop, *Gates-McKillop Reading Diagnostic Tests* (New York: Bureau of Publications, Teachers College, Columbia University, 1962).

50. Rozanne A. McCall and Robert B. McCall, "Comparative Validity of Five Reading Diagnostic Tests," *Journal of Educational Research* 7 (March 1969): 329-333.

51. See, for example, Ekwall, *Diagnosis and Remediation of the Disabled Reader,* 27-28; Harris and Sipay, *How to Increase Reading Ability,* 166-167, 228-233.

52. Larsen, "The Learning Disabilities Specialist," 501-502; Lerner, "Remedial Reading and Learning Disabilities," 120-121.

53. Doris J. Johnson and Helmer R. Myklebust, *Learning Disabilities: Educational Principles and Practices* (New York: Grune and Stratton, 1967); Marianne Frostig, "Visual Perception, Integrative Functions, and Academic Learning," *Journal of Learning Disabilities* 5 (January 1972): 1-15; Joseph M. Wepman, "Auditory Discrimination, Speech, and Reading," *Elementary School Journal* 60 (March 1960): 325-333; Samuel A. Kirk and Winifred D. Kirk, *Psycholinguistic Learning Disabilities: Diagnosis and Remediation* (Urbana: University of Illinois Press, 1971).

54. Samuel A. Kirk, James J. McCarthy, and Winifred D. Kirk, *Illinois Test of Psycholinguistic Abilities,* rev. ed. (Urbana: University of Illinois Press, 1968).

55. Joseph M. Wepman, *Auditory Discrimination Test* (Chicago: Language Research Associates, 1972).

56. Marianne Frostig, *Frostig Developmental Tests of Visual Perception* (Palo Alto, Calif.: Consulting Psychologists Press, 1964).

57. Larsen, "The Learning Disabilities Specialists."

58. Larsen, Rogers, and Sowell, "The Use of Selected Perceptual Tests in Differentiating between Normal and Learning Disabled Children."

59. Donald D. Hammill and Stephen C. Larsen, "The Relationship of Selected

Auditory Perceptual Skills and Reading Ability," *Journal of Learning Disabilities* 7 (August-September 1974): 429-434; *id.*, "The Relationship of Selected Visual-Perceptual Abilities to School Learning," *Journal of Special Education* 9 (Fall 1975): 281-291.

60. Hammill and Larsen, "The Relationship of Selected Auditory Perceptual Skills and Reading Ability," 433.

61. Frostig, *Frostig Developmental Tests of Visual Perception.*

62. Norman L. Corah and Barbara J. Powell, "A Factor Analytic Study of the *Frostig Developmental Tests of Visual Perception,*" *Perceptual and Motor Skills* 16 (January 1963): 59-63; F. S. Ohnmacht and Arthur Olson, "Canonical Analysis of Reading Readiness Measures and the Frostig *DTVP,*" paper presented at the meeting of the American Educational Research Association, Chicago, 1968.

63. Kirk, McCarthy, and Kirk, *Illinois Test of Psycholinguistic Abilities.*

64. John McLeod, "Dyslexia in Young Children: A Factorial Study with Special Reference to the *ITPA,*" University of Illinois, IREC papers in education, 1966, cited in Spache, *Investigating the Issues of Reading Disabilities,* 158; Phillip A. Smith and Ronald W. Marx, "The Factor Structure of the Revised Edition of the *Illinois Test of Psycholinguistic Abilities,*" *Psychology in the Schools* 8 (July 1971): 349-356; Phillip Newcomer *et al.,* "Construct Validity of the ITPA," *Exceptional Children* 40 (April 1974): 509-510.

65. Harris and Sipay, *How to Increase Reading Ability,* 314-315.

66. Olive C. Sampson, "Fifty Years of Dyslexia: A Review of the Literature 1925-1975, II Practice," *Research in Education* 15 (May 1976): 47.

67. Austin and Morrison, *The First R,* 123.

68. Arthur E. Traxler, "Current Organization and Procedures in Remedial Reading," *Journal of Experimental Education* 20 (March 1952): 309-310.

69. Austin and Morrison, *The First R,* 124.

70. Harris and Sipay, *How to Increase Reading Ability,* 400-401.

71. Spache, *Diagnosing and Correcting Reading Disabilities,* 329-331.

72. *Ibid.,* 333.

73. Asher Cashdan and P. D. Pumfrey, "Some Effects of the Remedial Teaching of Reading," in *Remedial Reading: Classroom and Clinic,* 2d ed., ed. Leo M. Schell and Paul C. Burns (Boston: Allyn and Bacon, 1972); Robert A. Hicks, "Reading Gains and Instructional Sessions," *Reading Teacher* 21 (May 1968): 738-739.

74. Edward A. Steirnagle, "A Five-Year Summary of a Remedial Reading Program," *ibid.,* 24 (March 1971): 537-543; Sister Rita Klosterman, "The Effectiveness of a Diagnostically Structured Reading Program," *ibid.* (November 1970): 159-162; Byrne K. Lovell and B. A. Richardson, "A Further Study of the Educational Progress of Children Who Had Received Remedial Instruction," *British Journal of Educational Psychology* 33 (February 1963): 3-9.

75. Steirnagle, "A Five-Year Summary of a Remedial Reading Program"; Asher Cashdan, Peter D. Pumfrey, and Elizabeth A. Lunzer, "Children Receiving Remedial Teaching in Reading," *Educational Research* 13 (February 1971): 98-105.

76. Linda Devin-Sheenan, Robert S. Feldman, and Vernon L. Allen, "Research on Children Tutoring Children: A Critical Review," *Review of Educational Research* 46 (Summer 1976): 355-385.

77. Spache, *Diagnosing and Correcting Reading Disabilities,* 329-331. In the developmental school situation, students are expected to gain approximately one month on a standardized test for each month of instruction. Remedial readers, however, do not normally show such gains. Thus, the gains reported by Spache are somewhat above those expected from average readers and well above those expected from remedial readers without treatment.

78. *Ibid.,* 336.

79. H. C. M. Carroll, "The Remedial Teaching of Reading: An Evaluation," *Remedial Education* 7 (January 1972): 10-15, cited in Harris and Sipay, *How to Increase Reading Ability,* 345.

80. For a review, see P. D. Pumfrey and C. D. Elliot, "Play Therapy, Social Adjustment, and Reading Attainment," *Educational Research* 12 (June 1970): 183-193.

81. Bruce Balow, "The Long-Term Effect of Remedial Reading Instruction," *Reading Teacher* 18 (April 1965): 581-586.

82. Margaret B. Rawson, *Developmental Language Disability: Adult Accomplishments of Dyslexic Boys* (Baltimore: Johns Hopkins Press, 1968); Helen M. Robinson and Helen K. Smith, "Reading Clinic Clients—Ten Years After," *Elementary School Journal* 63 (October 1962): 22-27.

83. Spache, *Diagnosing and Correcting Reading Disabilities,* 340-341.

84. Marianne Frostig and David Horne, *The Frostig Program for the Development of Visual Perception* (Chicago: Follett Educational Corp., 1964); Esther H. Minskoff, Douglas E. Wiseman, and J. Gerald Minskoff, *The MWM Program for Developing Language Abilities* (Ridgefield, N.J.: Educational Performance Associates, 1972); Charles H. Lindamood and Patricia C. Lindamood, *Auditory Discrimination in Depth* (Boston: Teaching Resources, 1969).

85. Bruce Balow, "Perceptual-Motor Activities in the Treatment of Severe Reading Disability," *Reading Teacher* 24 (March 1971): 518-520; Helen M. Robinson, "Perceptual Training: Does It Result in Reading Improvement?" in *Some Persistent Questions on Beginning Reading,* ed. Robert C. Aukerman (Newark, Del.: International Reading Association, 1972), 135-150, 137-141; Stephen E. Kleisus, "Perceptual-Motor Development and Reading: A Closer Look," *ibid.,* 151-159; Donald Hammill, Libby Goodman, and J. Lee Wiederholt, "Visual-Motor Processes: Can We Train Them?" *Reading Teacher* 27 (February 1974): 469-478; Spache, *Investigating the Issues of Reading Disabilities,* 401-432.

86. Hammill, Goodman, and Wiederholt, "Visual-Motor Processes," 471.

87. *Ibid.,* 474-475.

88. *Ibid.,* 476.

89. Spache, *Investigating the Issues of Reading Disabilities,* 420-423.

90. *Ibid.,* 404-409.

91. *Ibid.*

92. Hammill and Larsen, "The Relationship of Selected Auditory Perceptual Skills and Reading Ability."

93. Robinson, "Perceptual Training," 141-142.

94. Donald D. Hammill and Stephen C. Larsen, "The Effectiveness of Psycholinguistic Training," *Exceptional Children* 41 (September 1974): 401-411.

95. Kirk, McCarthy, and Kirk, *Illinois Test of Psycholinguistic Abilities.*

96. Samuel A. Kirk and John Elkins, *Characteristics of Children Enrolled in the Child Service Demonstration Centers,* Final Report, Grant OEG 0 714425, Bureau number BR-H-12-7145 B, Bureau of Educational Handicapped, DHEW/OE (Tucson: Department of Special Education, University of Arizona, 1974). ERIC: Ed 111 164.

97. Johnson and Myklebust, *Learning Disabilities.*

98. John Paul Jones, *Intersensory Transfer, Perceptual Shifting, Modal Preference, and Reading* (Newark, Del.: International Reading Association, 1972), 15-23.

99. For summaries, see James M. Kauffman, "Behavior Modification," in *Perceptual and Learning Disabilities in Children,* Volume 2, ed. William M. Cruickshank and Daniel P. Hallahan (Syracuse, N.Y.: Syracuse University Press, 1975); Ross, *Psychological Aspects of Learning Disabilities and Reading Disorders,* 28-61, 98-106.

100. Sampson, "Fifty Years of Dyslexia," 41-46.

101. Fernald and Keller, "Effects of Kinesthetic Factor in Development of Word Recognition."

102. Anna Gillingham and Bessie W. Stillman, *Remedial Training for Children with Specific Difficulty in Reading, Spelling, and Penmanship,* 7th ed. (Cambridge, Mass.: Educators Publishing Service, 1966).

103. Romalda Bishop Spalding with Walter T. Spalding *The Writing Road to Reading,* 2d rev. ed. (New York: William Morrow, 1969).

104. R. G. Heckleman, "Using the Neurological Impress Remedial Technique," *Academic Therapy Quarterly* 1 (Summer 1966): 235-239.